398

U. S. WEST

THE SAGA OF

WELLS FARGO

# U. S. WEST

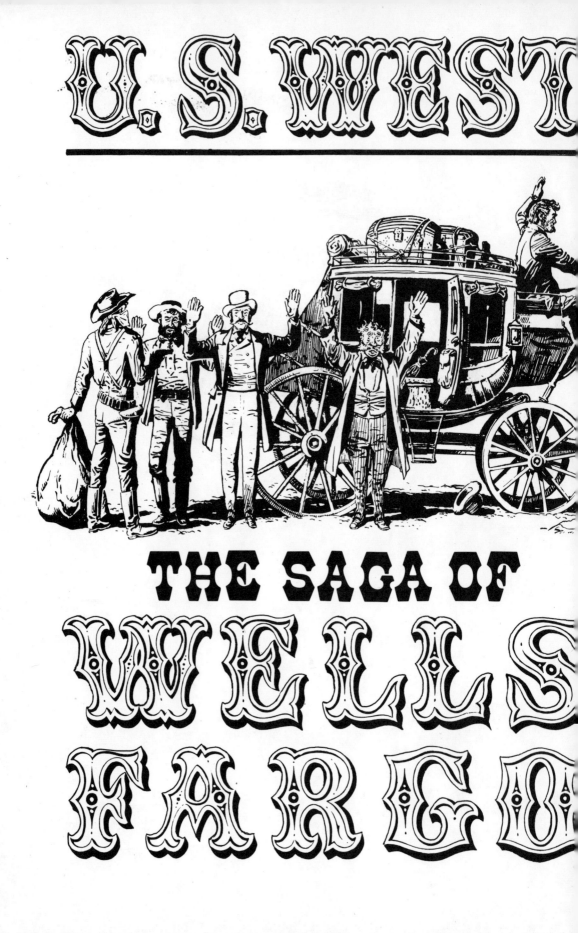

# THE SAGA OF
# WELLS FARGO

BY
# LUCIUS BEEBE
### AND
# CHARLES CLEGG

**BONANZA BOOKS • NEW YORK**

E. S. HAMMACK

*"Because the king's business required haste —"*
I SAMUEL XX: 8

*"I must walk toward Oregon and not toward Europe."*
HENRY THOREAU

# Contents

FOREWORD . . . . . . . . . . 9

THE BEAVER HAT . . . . . . . . 12

MONTGOMERY STREET . . . . . . . . 27

MOTHER LODE . . . . . . . . . . 46

RIDING PONY . . . . . . . . . 75

THE SAGA OF C STREET . . . . . . . 91

SILVER SUITE: . . . . . . . . . 130

    I.   THE BAD MAN FROM BODIE . . . . . 130

    II.   ALONG THE EASTERN MARCHES . . . . 144

    III.   PREDICAMENT AT PANAMINT . . . . 160

    IV.   CANDELARIA CHRONICLE . . . . . 169

VIGNETTES OF VIOLENCE . . . . . . . 176

AFFAIRS OF THE NABOBS . . . . . . . 199

SUCH AS A KING SHOULD BUILD . . . . . 225

THE LAST BONANZA: . . . . . . . . 238

    I.   TONOPAH . . . . . . . . . 238

    II.   GOLDFIELD . . . . . . . . 251

    III.   RHYOLITE . . . . . . . . 270

    IV.   RAWHIDE . . . . . . . . 282

THE LAST ROUNDUP . . . . . . . . 291

CHRONOLOGY . . . . . . . . . . 304

BIBLIOGRAPHY . . . . . . . . . 311

ACKNOWLEDGMENTS . . . . . . . . 314

INDEX . . . . . . . . . . 315

# Foreword

THERE are, in the heroic blazon of the American West, many names which clutch at the heart and lay hold of the imagining: Santa Fe, Union Pacific, the Oregon Trail, Dodge City, Pony Express, the Staked Plains, Virginia City, the Chisholm Trace, Tombstone, Gould and Curry, Sutter's Mill, Washoe, the Overland Trail. They are not mere places or institutions or even legends: they are hallmarks, part of the pattern of a manner of life at once vanished and deathless, the fabric of old times and the spacious way, of dreams and desires and destinies. They are names that beat upon the remembrance like the night wind against the storm lanterns of ghostly coaches, and they connote spacious images and cloudy trophies in the minds of many men.

One of the names is Wells Fargo.

For the story of the West is a saga of losers and finders. Mostly they were finders, and the names are the symbols of their finding; old Jesse Chisholm who fashioned an almost limitless empire of cattle and kingly hospitality along the lawless frontier of the Southwest; Union Pacific, itself the greatest empire of them all, spanning a continent with the ceaseless traffickings of the flanged wheel upon the steel rail; Deseret, another kind of empire, flowering and then withering, but leaving the impress of its going behind it forever from Salt Lake to the Cajon Pass.

Wells Fargo, too, was an empire, a vast domain of wealth and wealthy properties, of gold and coaches and horses, of banks and bullion vaults and stagehouses and, above all else, of the elimination, or at least of the abatement of time and distance. It was, in some times and places, an absolute monopoly of transportation, of law and of the facilities and functions of finance. The generally conceived limits of its empire were the Canadian border and the Pacific, the Mississippi River and the boundary of Old Mexico, but eventually it overflowed all but one of these. For literary purposes its province may be said to have been the Old West of the United States. Upon this vast and magnificent panoramic canvas it painted a legend of hell-and-high-water pioneering, of romance, adventure, achievement and glamor unsurpassed even by the most tremendous of all American epics, the railroad. Railroading, in fact, became a part of Wells Fargo.

If it were desirable for literary or historic reasons to reconstruct the cardiac chart of the Far West of the United States for the century between 1849 and 1949, one might search extensively before coming up with a parallel as accurate as may be found in the history of Wells Fargo. In some ways it would not be so much a parallel as an identical record, for Wells Fargo in fact *was* a great deal of the old Far West and is still a ponderable part of the California scene as this is being written.

Possibly the voice of purism may be heard raising itself to protest that there was no Wells Fargo in 1849, that it didn't come into existence until 1852, and that the authors of this book are straining for effect and to achieve the symmetry of round figures. By their own contemporary assertion, however, both of the entrepreneurs whose names are represented in the corporate title of Wells Fargo had been keeping a shrewd and calculating eye on express possibilities west of the Mississippi since the year 1849. It seems altogether probable that, at the first board meeting after the news of the discovery of gold reached New York, they looked at each other with what-did-I-tell-you expressions and sat right down to planning a California express. That it took them three years to commit themselves is but evidence of Yankee prudence.

In undertaking a book about Wells Fargo, or for that matter about almost any aspect of the old, romantic West of the United States, it must be understood that there is no such thing as any new or unexploited aspect of the subject and that anyone approaching the *matière* of the trans-Mississippi in the nineteenth century as an exploiter of new material is either deluded or an imposter.

There never was any period of a nation's history that is so completely documented, so thoroughly chronicled and so unqualifiedly a matter of record as the conquest or, perhaps, the colonization of the American West. For one thing the printing press and the daily or weekly newspaper followed the Henry rifle so closely as to be almost a coordinated part of its function. History was being made, and there wasn't a frontier editor or reporter who didn't know at the time that his files, within the passage of half a dozen decades, would be items of Americana. Then, too, the literary urge lay strongly, almost compulsively on every man jack and his brother who rolled a wagon out of Kansas or toted an Ames shovel up the Geiger Grade to the Washoe diggings. The diaries of the period are, simply, innumerable. Their contents is common currency in every community which boasts a historical society west of St. Joseph. One sometimes wonders if Hangtown, Gold Hill and San Francisco were not more authentic literary colonies than Concord.

In most libraries of consequence the bibliography of Western Americana in published form counts its titles in the thousands and in many the manuscript resources are of warehouse dimensions. The time was when the "discovery" and publication of the diary or personal record of a Forty-niner or Pony Express Rider was a major excitement in the field of letters, but it was soon discovered that there were not enough bookshelves in the world to hold them all.

When, therefore, such statistics as the weight and caliber of the slug fired into Mr. McCanles by Mr. Hickok is available to anyone who is curiously inclined, and when the decorative scheme of the Washoe Club in Virginia City is commonplace knowledge among all interested persons, what possible excuse is there for another book about the tumults and excitements of the Western frontier?

The answer is that there is just one legitimate historic and literary reason for such an essay, and that is the reorganization of the known and available material into a form which, for one reason or another, is an improvement on the organization and editorial economy of the other books that have gone before it.

Make no mistake, the antecedent literature, a very large portion of which treats Wells Fargo as an integral part of the pattern of staging and express rather than in its own individual right, is distinguished for many excellences. The formal, corporate chronicle of Wells Fargo is available in minute and painstaking detail. While skirmishing with the available Western Americana, it occurred to the authors of this book that, although no single writer within the period of Wells Fargo's flowering could produce a thousand words without a mention of the firm's name, little has been done to indicate how important Wells Fargo was as an institution. And almost no literature within our discovery concerns itself with the color and texture of the old Far West as a backdrop for the activities of the most celebrated of all banking and express services.

It is, for the record, not too much to remark that almost everything in California, Nevada and adjacent communities revolved about, depended upon, and believed in Wells Fargo. The Church of God figured very little in the existence and activities of the pioneers and prospectors. It was hardly formally represented at all. To the state in any form the frontier was profoundly, if a little self-consciously, indifferent, and its functions only became manifest upon severe provocation and then in a manner not usually to be described as parliamentary.

But beginning with the early fifties in San Francisco and continuing for a full half century it was almost impossible to exist throughout the Western States and Territories beyond the influence of the activities of Wells Fargo. In scores of communities the Wells Fargo agency was the foundation upon which rested shotgun law and arbitrary order, the punishment of crime, the protection of possessions, and also the sole instrument of communications, banking and business intercourse. In a very real sense, Wells Fargo was the state.

There might be no minister of the gospel and no accredited or generally recognized peace officer in a community, but there was pretty apt to be Wells Fargo. In the exercise of its ever-expanding and almost omnipresent variety of functions, it was the most important organization, at least until the coming of the Pacific Railroad, to be evolved by the westward course of empire. And long after that wet and windy morning at Promontory, Wells Fargo continued to dominate the business of transport and communication in the almost illimitable regions of the West not immediately served by the railroad and telegraph.

A note concerning the swift and informal departure from this world of a bandit apprehended in the northern California seventies gives a clue to the character of Wells Fargo and to its status in frontier communities. "Wells Fargo agents and Shasta folk caught the criminal," reported a newspaper paragraph, "and we are not disposed to trouble the courts about it."

The name Wells Fargo & Co. was the hallmark of the Old West for five full decades. Wherever there was treasure, trouble and transportation, throughout the most glamorous and effulgent half century in the history of the continent, its insigne was in evidence. It appeared above the doorways of strong rooms, embossed in flowered letters across the panels of stages, on postal franks and on the baggage and express cars of little gold and crimson trains as they rocked across the light iron of the first railroads.

Aboard the Butterfield Stages on the Ox-Bow Route to California the Wells Fargo strongboxes rode through the Joshua trees of the Arizona desert to El Paso and Fort Yuma. The six dancing ponies of Wells Fargo clattered into the Oregon wilderness and up the incredible grades of the Cascades to take bullion out of the Fraser River diggings within a few weeks of the first color to show in the prospecting pans. Wells Fargo was in Deadwood, in Santa Fe, in Carson City, in Victoria, in Fort Bridger, in the Boise Mines. Its shotgun messengers rolled through a sea of black powder smoke on the Central Overland trail; all the way across the trail from St. Joseph to the Washoe the *mochilas* of its mail riders were red with blood. The name of Wells Fargo and Overland bore weight of authority west of Salt Lake such as few corporate names have exerted at any time in the history of any land. Wells Fargo was blazoned on the express cars of the first varnish trains of the Central Pacific as they reeled down Truckee Canyon with smoking brakes even before Promontory. Through the counting rooms and into the vaults of Wells Fargo in Virginia City poured the bullion of the Comstock which paid for a civil war and raised palaces of incredible proportions and swaggering magnificence in Fifth Avenue, on Nob Hill and the Champs Elysées.

Wells Fargo was, from the very beginning, a participant in almost every frontier commotion of the Old West, so much so that when it by-passed or avoided a community as it did in the case of Panamint, it was a matter for universal remark. The pattern of California, Nevada, Oregon and Arizona, and to an only slightly lesser extent, New Mexico and Montana, from the coming of the first alkali-whitened prospector to the establishment of the frock-coated banker and long afterward, was the pattern of Wells Fargo. No longer ago than yesterday, there were places where for a time, Wells Fargo was in essence, in symbol and in fact the West of the United States.

Any extended perusal, such as has been necessary in undertaking this book, of the source material in its field and of the later use to which it was put by a variety of writers leads to one inevitable conclusion: that the Old West of the Wells Fargo years has been subject to more unabashed literary pillage than were ever the stagecoaches which were part of its economy, and that the trans-Missouri nineteenth century has probably been the most durable literary material since, say, the *Matière de Rome le Grant*.

The authors of this book hasten to go on record in acknowledging that they are indebted to existing literary sources for a very large portion of its content and that even some of what they believe to be tolerably fresh material gathered from a wide variety of sources may well, unknown to them, be a part of the published record. Their claim to consideration lies in the arrangement of the available material and the attempt to demonstrate that Wells Fargo did not operate in a vacuum but was a bold and dominant detail in the fabric of its own times.

Despite the fact that the activities of Wells Fargo as banker and carrier up to the time of the first World War were almost universal in the West, their greatest concentration in point of melodrama as well as of factual density was in California during the gold-rush times of the Mother Lode, and in Nevada from the discovery of the Comstock through the Goldfield bonanza, which was practically over by 1910. The authors' choice of locales and backgrounds for this informal chronicle has been highly selective and makes no claim of being definitive. The authors also have been inevitably influenced in considering the different aspects of Wells Fargo in direct reverse ratio to the attention previously accorded them by other chroniclers. The literature of California in the fifties is inexhaustible and all the interested world knows the story of Placerville, Columbia and Tuolumne; but how many people know even the whereabouts of Panamint, Rawhide or Rhyolite? It might be cynical to suggest that California is a vastly populous commonwealth possessed of a well-recognized capacity for reading and even buying books about itself and that it has therefore been favored with the attentions of historians quite beyond anything achieved by Nevada, a community which has always preferred the business of living to reading and has never been described as precisely the Big Rock Candy Mountain of book salesmen.

Aside from the comparative novelty of any mention of Nevada, there is in the ensuing pages a great deal of happy commotion which, to the temperate-minded, might appear unseemly in a corporate biography conceived even by the most robust imagination. Wells Fargo's business was with gunmen, adventurers, gamblers, highbinders and the suddenly wealthy. Much of its business was transacted in an atmosphere pleasantly perfumed with strong waters. In scores of communities, Wells Fargo, like the stages, the telegraph company and the officers of the law, maintained its business offices in saloons.

Somebody once slightingly remarked to Wyatt Earp, the most famous of all peace officers ever to appear on the Wells Fargo pay roll, that most of his life seemed to have been spent in dance halls, fandango houses and saloons. "There were no Y.M.C.A.s in my time," said Earp.

Had there been Y.M.C.A.s it would not have been to Wells Fargo's profit to have frequented them.

Wells Fargo flourished and waxed wealthy in an atmosphere of unabashed hooray. In many cases its management was less notable for its sagacity than for its frontier spaciousness of gesture and its gambler's impassiveness in the face of adversity. Wells Fargo didn't admire stage robbery or embezzlement, but these were inevitable in the course of the business it pursued. Its losses over the years were staggering, but its revenues were more so. Of all the hell-and-high-water outfits of the Old West, Wells Fargo was the most indifferent to hell in its various manifestations and the most contemptuous of flooded streams and washed-out bridges. The symphony of its progress was orchestrated to popping wine corks, the bright clatter of steel-shod hooves and other glad, Fourth of July overtones.

Because its beginnings were in the nineteenth century, Wells Fargo was, primarily, a company of men who dominated and towered immeasurably above the machines which served them, just as the East India Company, the Hudson's Bay Company or the men of the first thirteen United States of America had dominated the machines which, in an only slightly cruder mechanical age, had served them.

The age of the triumphant machine and the retreat of men was at hand, but Wells Fargo was the last great company of individuals acting in reasonable concert to escape its implications and infamies. Until the very end of the nineteenth century, the most complicated and effective machinery at the disposal of the American West was the rifled gun, the magnetic telegraph, and the simple internal expansion locomotive and stationary steam engine. The West was independent of the monstrous and obscene manufactories of the East. Until the end of the century it was common practice for men to make their own cartridges, and ball ammunition from Hartford and Bridgeport was still suspect by men to whom precision in any artifact was represented by human handiwork. The Virginia and Truckee Railroad never needed to send out of Carson for the working part of a locomotive, a car truck or a hoist engine if it were not so minded. Everything useful to its purpose could be manufactured on its own premises.

In the age of Wells Fargo the machine had yet to dominate the imagination or inhibit the personal achievements of the individual. As a result the personnel of the company was not composed of thin-blooded technicians in pestilential laboratories, or of chemists in horn spectacles, or even of the shabby and mannerless traders in sack suits who are now the diplomats and statesmen. Lloyd Tevis, Leland Stanford and John Valentine would have never been favorably impressed by atomic science, and Hank Monk and Jim Miller would have spat heartily at the notion of housing commissions, social security and old-age pensions for mendicants.

The machine properties of Wells Fargo were so simple in design and so limited in their application as to be almost elemental: the horse-drawn vehicle, black, slow-burning gunpowder, the strap-iron-bound strongbox and the eight-wheel, American-type railroad locomotive capable of rolling a dozen wooden cars on a level and but little more than its own weight on a grade of two per cent. Often the coach had to be helped up a hill by the passengers, the effective range of the black powder was a hundred yards and the box was pervious to a strong man with a common hatchet.

The implications of such an economic pattern are, obviously, limitless. The dangers that surrounded men, where they existed at all, were simple dangers: the gun-toting criminal, the axle broken at the gallop on the high pass above King's Canyon, the January blizzard in the Cascades. None of them existed in the minds of men, and men were more considerable for it. Vitamin deficiency was a negligible consideration in an age when bear meat was universal and on every menu. It is doubtful if Black Bart the stage robber realized that he was a product of uncompensated paranoia and suffered from an antisocial fixation induced by a consciousness of inferiority.

As a result of these admirable simplicities of life, the story of Wells Fargo is a story of men and places. It has no commerce with the realm of abstract ideas, the economics of a frustrated society, the fatuous ideologies or any of the other diseases which, like high blood pressure and trench mouth, arrived with the age of machines and science and geopolitics.

In the year 1949, after nearly a century of useful and wealthy existence, The Wells Fargo Bank still flourishes, green bay tree like, only a few blocks down Montgomery Street from the red-brick offices opposite Adams & Co., where on the morning of its first California day, the staff lined up for the first official picture of Wells Fargo's stovepipe hats. Across the way from it is the Palace, scene of so many chapters in the secret landfarings of its detectives and agents, messengers and trusty functionaries. Further down Market Street are the offices of the mighty Southern Pacific Company, partner in so much high enterprise and daring venture in the days of the old kings of the Pacific coast. And around them all surge, perpetual and ceaseless, the tides of life and vitality so much more lively and vital than these things are anywhere else on the American continent.

In the Boot Hills of Deadwood and Tombstone are the headstones of the gunmen with the inscription: "Wells Fargo Never Forgets." In the graying recollections of old men everywhere from the Missouri to the Embarcadero are memories of the steel shutters and treasure chests, the express cars, special agents and beautiful wood-burning locomotives that were part of the panoramic whole of the Wells Fargo picture. In the museums are the waybills and Winchesters, the micrometric scales and the golden Concord coaches that were the riding properties of the most breath-taking pageant of human venturing since the dawn of the continent.

And over the counters and through the vaults of Wells Fargo still flows the flooding torrent of wealth which made the American dream a tangible reality and which makes the name of Wells Fargo a legend of continuity above the changes of time and despite the mutations of many decades.

It is a tale, it seems to us, that is worth the telling.

L. B.

C. C.

*Carson City*

# CHAPTER I

## The Beaver Hat

THE late New England spring lay over the countryside like a
benison. Near the Massachusetts-Providence Plantations line, it
flowed over the split-rail fences, sown acres and stands of
trees with benevolent impartiality and engulfed with pervasive
warmth the southern slope of Sharon Hill. There, under a gentle canopy
of soot, was to be seen rolling down the right of way, on which were precariously laid two parallel rails of hand-wrought strap iron, the afternoon
train of the Boston and Providence RR. And to be seen was to be admired,
as it smoked serenely upon its lawful occasions. It avoided the inconveniently
heavy grade through Mr. Shanley's meadows by passing up the ravine near
the Reverend Mr. Hontoon's church, while occasionally following the base
of a hillslope to roll splendidly across a brief wooden trestle spanning a
brook or creek.

At the head end of the train brigade was a new locomotive engine from the
Philadelphia erecting shops of William Norris. Its uncommonly tall stack was
crowned with a sleeve of crenelated iron and its four drive wheels were joined
to the cylinders internally instead of by the conventional outside motion of
today. The engine driver, as he was then known by the English term, controlled his locomotive from an open platform and the fireboy stoked his boiler
with lengths of fuel wood.

Behind this triumph of the locomotive builder's genius trailed eight or ten
brightly lacquered stagecoaches fitted with flanged wheels and loosely connected by insecure couplings. Each held a dozen persons with no comfort at
all and offered only a minimum of protection against the elements or the rain
of fiery particles being impartially distributed over the landscape from the
engine stack. The little train, with its brave yellow coaches and seemingly
monstrous engine, paused at frequent intervals to wood up from convenient
fuel piles beside the track and when it did so the coaches crashed together
with dismaying violence and gentlemen inside pulled their beaver hats down
firmly over their ears and hoped for the best.

Under one of these beaver hats, a white one with austere rather than fashionable lines, were a number of letters addressed to individuals and firms in
New York. The hat was the property of L. B. Earle and his entire business was
carried literally under his hat. It was a business which, within the next three
decades, was to span the American continent and provide a romantic interlude

in continental transportation whose only rival for glamorous adventure was to be the Mississippi river packet. For the year was 1835 and Earle was the first expressman.

Earle had dined betimes in Boston that day at the Tremont House, where Dwight Boyden, the host, had himself carved the joint at the head of the long table. His guests wore carpet slippers provided by the management while servants cleaned their jack boots. This was an all-time high in hotel luxury and even Daniel Webster had commented favorably on Boyden's enterprise at the state banquet which had attended the opening seven years previous. The Tremont with its wealth of Turkey carpets, live potted palms and French ormolu clocks was the natural resort at mealtimes of Boston's leading merchants and bankers who found it increasingly convenient to dine there at midday and have their boots cleaned rather than go home to their fine houses in Louisberg Square or fashionable Winter Street. So it was natural that here Earle should pick up most of the business which was his bread and butter.

The business of the express messenger had its beginnings in Earle and the Boston and Providence RR in the middle thirties, and his various commissions to carry letters and occasional merchandise between Boston and New York were largely solicited by word of mouth. Later express companies were to advertise through the stately medium of the *Boston Transcript,* but Earle's fame was largely oral. At the same time, on the eastbound boat out of New York for Providence, and similarly attired in a capacious beaver hat, was traveling B. D. Earle, a brother, bound on a number of precisely similar commissions to deliver private mail. There was no train brigade as yet south from Providence and that leg of the journey was accomplished by steamer on Long Island Sound. About eighteen hours sufficed for the journey and it was thought tremendously up and coming to have the New York market quotations or the Boston ship arrivals known at the other end of the line in less than a day and night.*

Within a year or two the resources of even the most capacious beaver hats became too straitened for the brothers Earle, who had meantime taken to carrying parcels as well as letters and had become associated in a partnership with Henry Prew, a deliveryman of their modest staff. It was then that there appeared the identifying trade-mark of the Yankee express messenger — the picturesque carpetbag, which in turn gave way to a small trunk which the express messenger carried on the seat beside him, paying the railroad an extra

---

* An interesting sidelight on the Boston-New York train and steamboat connections in the thirties is furnished by Alvin Harlow who records that as railroads were extended to Bristol, Rhode Island, Stonington, Connecticut, and other points on Long Island, the competition for passengers by steamer captains became intense. Rate wars were followed by special inducements. The Bristol steamer provided a band concert on the pier at sailing time every afternoon, but the Providence boat topped them all with a concert at which free tea and cakes, always an inducement to Yankee patronage, were served to prospective passengers. These daily social functions were presided over by the general manager of the steamship company who acted as host, barker and master of ceremonies splendidly attired in a skirted frock coat, beaver hat and white kid gloves. The starting signal for the ship's engine was when he removed his kid gloves and, with an elegant gesture, tossed them over the pierside into the water. A new pair every day!

## EXPRESS BEGINNINGS

Above is the Boston-Providence train upon which the brothers B. D. and L. B. Earle were accustomed to ride, with their business under their beaver hats, to make connection at Providence with the steamer for New York. The train brigade is shown in this old line drawing crossing Roxbury Flats southwest of Boston with the gilded dome of Thomas Bulfinch's State House in the distance and the spires of Boston's historic churches on the sky line. The citizen with the carpetbag is a modern characterization of an early express messenger and may be taken as a composite of the Earles and Harnden. Below is the burning of the steamer Lexington in Long Island Sound in which, in January 1840, Adolphus Harnden lost his life and $40,000 he was carrying.

consideration for the space. The trunk, of course, was the direct lineal antecedent of the classic Wells Fargo treasure chest which will reappear so frequently throughout this narrative and which is as valid and romantic a property in any tally of American artifacts as the self-cocking revolver perfected by Samuel Colt, the great antler-crowned storm lanterns of the wood-burning locomotives, or the Concord coach itself.

It is pleasant to record that, a full century after the first commissions were executed by the brothers Earle between New York at one end of their run and Boston at the other, the New Haven RR, running in part over the original right of way of the Boston and Providence, still served Bostonians, and frequently in the capacity of personal messenger and courier service.

In the late forties of the twentieth century the conductors and trainmen of such famous Shore Line expresses as the *Merchants' Limited* or the *Yankee Clipper* were often entrusted by conservative Bostonians with the delivery of messages and small properties at the other end of the run. Forgotten galoshes, mislaid brief cases or documents in urgent requisition are still delivered in this informal manner, as is doubtless true of other friendly railroad men with personal traditions elsewhere in the land.

In nominating the brothers Earle as the first expressmen it is necessary to take advantage of a certain generally recognized historic tolerance. Even before the coming of the first railroads to New England the drivers of stages had been known to function in a more or less similar capacity, soliciting commissions at the taverns which served as staging terminals and executing them with an informal dependability which is a pleasant commentary on the integrities of the age. Indeed, almost any business or professional man known to be about to embark upon a journey, in a time when journeys were uncommon and no small adventure, was apt to be asked to deliver letters or sums of money to firms or individuals at his destination. But it was the regularity and precision of travel achieved with the advent of the railroads that first suggested the possibilities of commercial courier service on advertised schedules. Later in the same year in which our narrative opens, one Silas Tyler engaged with the management of the Boston and Lowell RR to run a daily express car in their trains, and the era of the expresses may fairly be said to have begun.

Actually the express messenger made his appearance during this period in such a variety of locales as to encourage the belief that the technique of his calling originated quite independently in the minds of a number of alert entrepreneurs. Because he was the first to evolve an extensive express service covering a considerable territory and to maintain extensive offices and an impressive list of employees, many historians incline to choose William F. Harnden as the father of the express, and no very great fault can be found with their choice. By 1839 Harnden, a north of Boston Yankee, was advertising a through railway express car between Boston and New York and maintaining a forwarding service all along this route with connections for Philadelphia and the South.

When Harnden went into business in the aforementioned year 1839 he made his first beginnings as "the father of the express business" and was, two years later, to employ as his Albany agent an ambitious New Englander with a broad brown beard named Henry Wells. Thirty-nine saw the first operations of the pioneer who was to elevate expressing to the rank of authentically big business. Forty-nine was to be the epochal year when the face of half the world would turn toward California with the inevitable consequence that Wells Fargo too would set its corporate face toward the golden and ineffable West. Fifty-nine was to be the year when Old Pancake would unearth the fabled Comstock Lode, inaugurating the saga of Virginia City and Wells Fargo's greatness in Nevada. Sixty-nine was to be the year of destiny at Promontory which would mark the end of overland staging for Wells Fargo and see it embarked on a new technique of express and treasure traffic and banking. And 1879 was to be the year of splendid climax of the highest gold production in the Nevada mines and of Wells Fargo's greatest empire.

Nor were the wealthy workings of the Mother Lode, source and fountainhead of Wells Fargo's beginnings, yet worked out. In September of that supreme year a miner shipped via Wells Fargo a consignment of no less than 900 pounds of gold valued at $190,000 which had been mined within the city limits of Sonora. Although the owners had arranged that this impressive treasure should be shipped in secret, to protect it from molestation, the secret came out when, a few miles out of Copperopolis, the coach hit a pothole in the road and the weight of gold broke its frame in the middle so that the bullion cascaded into the dusty highway. It was reported to be the biggest single shipment ever handled by Wells Fargo on a Mother Lode run.

Here the metronome of history begins to falter in its beat and the years of decision will appear in less symmetrical pattern, but for half a century the ninth year of each recurrent decade will be engrossed in red letters in the annals of Wells Fargo. Mark them well!

In the spring of 1839 the august *Boston Transcript* had evidently been favored by some post-free dispatch carried by William Harnden, for it remarked editorially that "Mr. Harnden may be confided in for honesty and fidelity in the discharge of his engagements, and it affords us much pleasure to recommend his 'Express' to the notice of our readers." Such endorsement and approbation from the court circular of Boston's commercial and mercantile aristocracy was of inestimable value.

William F. Harnden, who was born in 1813 in the sleepy hilltop town of Reading, Massachusetts, then on the Andover turnpike and later on the Western Division of the Boston and Maine RR, began his career of transportation as a conductor on the Boston and Worcester RR, actually punching tickets on the first passenger train out of Boston. In a few years we see him drifting into the same express service which occupied the pioneers Earle, namely between Boston and New York. Shortly thereafter he evolved the idea of a triangular service between Boston, New York and Albany, the latter leg of the triangle to be completed aboard Uncle Dan'l Drew's Hudson River steamers.

WELLS FARGO BANK

## HERE THE GOLDEN WEST CAME INTO BEING

X GOLD MINE FOUND.—In the newly made raceway of the Saw Mill recently erected by Captain Sutter, on the American Fork, gold has been found in considerable quantities. One person brought thirty dollars worth to New Helvetia, gathered there in a short time. California, no doubt, is rich in mineral wealth, great chances here for scientific capitalists. Gold has been found in almost every part of the country.

Five years before this photograph was taken and on this spot the gold was discovered that changed the entire history of the American West, that brought Wells Fargo into being and made California a synonym for wealthy resources. It shows Sutter's Mill in 1853 and it is generally believed that that bearded man in the white duster is James Marshall, immortal and unhappy discoverer of gold. To left is a dispatch to the San Francisco *Californian* for March 15, 1848 which was probably the most important single news item in the annals of the West.

22

Harnden's introduction to Uncle Dan'l had been engineered by Henry Wells who was, in 1836, engaged as a freight and passenger forwarder over the Erie Canal. Thus began a brief but significant friendship, or rather professional association, between the Father of Express and its most celebrated practitioner. In 1841, when Wells went to work briefly as Harnden's agent at Albany, his ideas were far more grandiose and expansive than those of his employer. Wells believed in the westering progress of empire and urged Harnden to extend his express out of Albany to Buffalo and in this enthusiasm he found a kindred spirit in another messenger on the upper New York State express routes named George Pomeroy. Soon Wells terminated his association with Harnden, and the same year, 1841, found Harnden and Pomeroy together with a third associate, Crawford Livingston, in business for themselves over the Albany-Buffalo express routes under the style of Pomeroy & Co.

Henry Wells was born in Thetford, Vermont, in 1805, the son of a Congregationalist clergyman who had moved to upper New York State when his son was eight. When he was twenty-two Wells had opened at Rochester a school for the cure of speech defects which was probably a by-product of a bad stammer in his own diction. Somewhere along the line he had contracted a marriage with an upstate woman named Sarah Daggett, and that is the extent of the formal record up to the time he went to work for Harnden. In the light of the voluminous biography which was to attend his later life, the deficiency may be excused.

It was during the existence of Pomeroy & Co., however, that the first really colorful achievement of the express industry set upstate New York by the ears and served as the handsomest sort of promotion for the crescent industry in general and Henry Wells in particular. As may be recalled by those who witnessed the film *Wells Fargo* a number of years ago, the opening sequences in this celluloid epic concerned themselves with the arrival at Batavia depot of an early train brigade, and the transshipment there from the baggage car to a waiting wagon of a quantity of fresh oysters, the first ever seen at such a remote distance from the Atlantic, en route to an enterprising restaurateur in Buffalo. In the film the beardless hero, whose career is a sort of synthesis of the achievements of the as yet unborn firm of Wells Fargo, arrived with his perishable freight just in time to have them served up for a luncheon in honor of a local banker who is thus favorably impressed with the potentialities of the express and invests heavily in it.

Actually the scenes of the film cleave with remarkable fidelity to the first really spectacular gesture in the professional repertory of Henry Wells. Pomeroy & Co. did bring fresh oysters to Buffalo to the delight and amazement of its citizens, and did it in very much the manner portrayed in the film, except for the detail that the bivalves had been opened at Albany to save on weight and space instead of on the kitchen tables of Laidley's Buffalo restaurant. Wells Fargo was destined in later years to bring oysters and other highly perishable sea food in jig time across the Western deserts to be served in scores of remote mining camps. The record of this rush grocery business will be encountered repeatedly and in due course, but the first

## THE FOUNDING FATHERS OF WELLS FARGO

Henry Wells (left) and William G. Fargo were both Easterners, but their names and the symbolism they evoked were to become synonymous with all that was most characteristic of the pioneer West.

oysters for Buffalo are, somehow, an episode at once naïve, touching and splendid, and set a pattern for the future. The fame of Laidley, whom Wells described as the George Rector of Buffalo, and of Wells the oyster express-man seemed assured from that day on.

A practice common to almost all the early expresses and express messengers, and to which the habit of the Earles, Harnden and Henry Wells was no exception, was the carrying gratis and without charge of newspaper dispatches and sometimes actual newspapers themselves destined for the exchange desks of editors in distant cities. These courtesies were in no way offensive to newspapermen and publishers and the messengers were frequently rewarded by little puffs or "reading notices" commending their reliability, industry, gentlemanly character and public services. Even as late as the Great Fire of Boston in 1872, when news was commonly transmitted by telegraph, but long before the age of wire photographs, artists' draw-ings of the holocaust were rushed to New York by the express companies then operating over the New York and New Haven RR. When they appeared the second morning after the conflagration in James Gordon Bennett's *Herald* the paper's dispatch and enterprise were widely mentioned.

In 1842, while he was still associated with Pomeroy, Henry Wells made the acquaintance of a fellow employee whose name, too, was to loom large in the annals of expressing and the American West. This was William Fargo. And so, for the first time, these two were in association in the business which was, eventually, to become almost synonymous with their joint names. William G. Fargo, a native of Onondaga County, New York, had been the first Auburn agent for the newly formed Auburn and Syracuse RR, and when he came to Pomeroy & Co. he was already wise in the ways of the express business as it was being evolved on a basis of cutthroat competition in the early forties.

Wells and Fargo saw eye to eye in many matters and repeatedly assured each other, perhaps at Laidley's buffet over oysters of their own importation and a mug of ale, that wherever express services were established, there would inevitably follow trade, industry, agriculture and the ever-changing frontier. Thus mutually encouraged, in 1845, they evolved Wells & Co's Western Express for the establishment of service west of Buffalo to Cincinnati, St. Louis and Chicago, and although Wells shortly sold his interest (the firm became Livingston, Fargo & Co) and took up residence in New York City to become associated with a new firm, Livingston, Wells & Co., he by no means ended his friendship and association with Fargo.

The death in 1847 of Crawford Livingston put an end to Livingston, Wells & Co., and for a time Henry Wells continued in business simply as Wells & Co. His most dangerous competition was to appear in 1849 from the rival stages and railroad connections of the firm of Butterfield, Wasson & Co., whose president was the immensely energetic and ambitious John Butterfield, and whose name like those of Wells and Fargo was in a few years to loom mightily throughout the American West. Everyone concerned in this rivalry was a shrewd and hard-bitten realist and in 1850, when it became universally apparent that they would soon contrive to effect each other's ruin, the three competing firms of Livingston & Fargo, Wells & Co. and Butterfield, Wasson & Co. were merged in a great combine capitalized for $150,000 in the name of the American Express Co. with Henry Wells as its first president. Its secretary was William G. Fargo and the line superintendent the redoubtable John Butterfield. Thus in the year 1850 the stage was set, the players rehearsed in their parts and businesses and the musicians of destiny attuned for the emergence of the mighty drama of Wells Fargo & Co.

Wells Fargo was not among the Forty-niners, however much it may lay claim to being among the pioneers. It was not until four years after the first discovery of gold by James Marshall at Sutter's millrace in Sonora that the directors of the American Express Co. in New York began to think seriously of California. Henry Wells and William G. Fargo had always had their eyes on the Far West but they were not yet willing to commit themselves to expansion on such a continental scale as was implied by setting up shop in California. This gold business might or might not be the McCoy.

When, in 1852, the executives of the American Express Co. set about the incorporation of a subsidiary to take over the banking and express businesses west of the Missouri River, they were unquestionably influenced in their decision by the California success of their deadliest rival, the firm of Adams & Co. Alvin Adams, still another north of Boston Yankee, had watched the rise of Harnden and the pioneer expressmen and, from modest beginnings along the route between Boston and Worcester, had in fourteen years evolved a business which was capitalized at the then astounding figure of a cool million dollars. Throughout the forties, while the American Express was getting small pickings in New York State and the Middle West, Adams was flourishing mightily all the way down the Atlantic seaboard and was king-pin in the Deep South where its headquarters were amidst the fabulously rich traffickings of New Orleans.

Consumed with jealousy at every new intelligence of Adams' success three thousand miles to the west the directors of the American Express Co. individually and collectively, were biting their nails and tapping their congress gaiter-enclosed feet. There had been gold in those hills after all and Alvin Adams' agent, D. H. Haskell, was passing most of it through his vaults in San Francisco en route to New York via the Isthmus of Panama. Something had to be devised. But quickly!

This something proved to be Wells Fargo & Co. And like Santa Fe, Union Pacific and the Overland Trail, its name was to take its place imperishably in the lexicon of the wonderful, American West.

# CHAPTER II

## *Montgomery Street*

WELLS FARGO was going to have to stir its stumps, and once the directors of the American back in Wall Street were convinced that, while Adams might have had the cream of the pickings until now, there was still a chance to get in on what seemed like a good thing, stir its stumps it did. Wells Fargo & Co. was organized in New York, in March, 1852, with Wells, Fargo and Johnston Livingston as its promoters and Edwin B. Morgan, a New York financier of impressive resources, as president, James McKay secretary, and a board of directors made up of cautious, conservative men of affairs who had some familiarity with the express business. Just sixty days later, a period of time which would indicate considerable enterprise today and which in the slower moving and more formal fifties was breath-taking, Wells Fargo's first announcement appeared in the *New York Times* to the effect that, as of that date, it was prepared to purchase and sell bullion and specie and to forward it and packages, parcels and freight of all descriptions between New York and San Francisco for reforwarding there to the other principal cities of California.

When, in 1849, the ever-expanding pattern of gold camps, settlements and towns began spreading fanwise to the north and east of San Francisco Bay, the greater part of its traffic passing through the booming township of Sacramento, the technique of the California express rider had reverted to the primal simplicities of the first express messengers back in the East who had carried their business under their beaver hats. Expressing was once again a private, personal undertaking maintained, for the most part, by single individuals who built up a following in a given diggings. They carried the mail and newspapers from the post office at San Francisco as far inland as was practicable by steamer or sailing packet and finished their journey into the Sierra foothills by horseback or afoot. The return trip with gold dust and other commissions from the picturesquely named vicinages of Dead Man's Gulch, Volcano, Whisky Hill, Git Up and Git, Slapjack Bar and even more wildly imagined communities, was made in the same manner with a fee to the rider which averaged two bits per letter and in the neighborhood of ten per cent of its value for gold dust.

By 1852, however, when the boom was three years old and Wells Fargo arrived on the scene, the express business was conducted approximately in the manner of operations of transport which had been maintained in the Eastern States before the coming of the railroads. Couriers, coaches and freight wagons clattered in the Sierra as far east as Nevada County and north as far as Portland by way of Tehama, Shasta and Yreka. The Southern Diggings at Jackson, Mokelumne Hill and Sonora were serviced by still other expresses out of Sacramento and Stockton, and the vaults and heavy iron doors of Adams and Company were fast becoming universal.

Wells Fargo came to San Francisco in July 1852, in the persons of Reuben W. Washburn, in charge of the banking department, and Samuel P. Carter, the express agent, and set about getting established in its own offices with commendable promptitude. Although, during the first year, the banking and express departments were to occupy the same premises, they were from the first separately conducted, and within another two years were separately housed.

The firm's advertisement in the *Alta California* of July 1, 1852, four days after Carter had arrived in California, read: "Offices in S. Brannan's new fireproof block, Montgomery Street between California and Sacramento." It was from this location that Wells Fargo was to divide the expressing business of North America with the parent American Express Co. along the Mississippi and Missouri Rivers with the understanding that neither would trespass upon the other's designated territory but would work as coagent in its half of the continent.

After the establishment of offices, the first move of the new branch obviously was the devising of a fast, secure ocean express service by way of Panama, with the home office of the American in New York. As a bid for business that hitherto had been going to Adams, the rate was immediately cut from sixty to forty cents a pound, an entirely successful bit of promotion made possible by a low freight rate across the Isthmus secured through agreement with the Panamanian freight-forwarding firm of Hurtado & Bros.. Even if Wells Fargo had seen no profit in the new rate it probably would still have inaugurated it as a gage of battle with Adams' who until then had a monopoly in the field.

Another gesture of defiance which, in years to come was to provide Wells Fargo with countless millions of dollars' worth of revenue freight, was the erection at Columbia in Tuolumne County a few years later of an agency to match the impressive reputation the new company was contriving for itself. The firm's equivalent of its public relations department of today proudly let it be known that the iron shutters for the windows of the Columbia branch office had cost $125 apiece in freightage alone, with the cost of all other furnishings in proportion. The wrought-iron balcony was manufactured in Troy, New York, and may be seen, graceful, ageless and secure, above Columbia's tranquil main street to this day. Down the street a way shortly afterward there appeared a branch of another California institution destined for immortality, the bank of Darius Ogden Mills. More than $55,000,000 worth of gold dust and nuggets were eventually to be weighed in the finely balanced scales of Wells Fargo's Columbia office and the scales themselves may be seen today in the Wells Fargo Bank's offices in San Francisco.

## HERE IT ALL BEGAN

The advertisement in the *Alta California* read: "Offices in Sam Brannan's new fireproof block, Montgomery Street between California and Sacramento." This was on July 1, 1852, four days after Samuel Carter, Wells Fargo & Co.'s first agent in California, had arrived in San Francisco. These are the premises and this the office staff in the first golden and prophetic year. Handily adjacent next door was the almost legendary saloon of Barry and Patten. From these two establishments the only a few years later all-powerful Banker to Bonanza and Expressman to El Dorado transacted "a general banking, exchange and collection business" in the early years of the old American West.

It was a wonderful, almost unbelievable San Francisco in which Wells Fargo found itself set down in 1852. Not a single item of architecture or even of water-front contour, at least on the San Francisco side of the Bay, would today be recognized by an observer from the Top of the Mark. It was then as now a city of incredible vitality and gusto for the business of living, but the tranquil, easygoing civilization of the Spanish ranchers still made its impress felt against the ever-changing backdrop of the city's life. Mexicans and Chilenos in native costumes were a commonplace on the street and Spanish tunes were played by wandering bands of street musicians who went from gambling house to gambling house where they were sure to find somebody in generous mood. Spanish still found a place in everyday language and Mexican dollars passed as currency. The Mission Dolores was something more than a ward in a great city.

Fires were commonplace, constant and catastrophic and the façade of the town was entirely changed every decade just as the human body is popularly supposed to renew itself, throughout, every seven years. Merchants, in those generous times, when burned out and with no place to store their merchandise often gave it away to passers by. Barry and Patten record that this practice was so common that a San Franciscan of the fifties encountering an acquaintance in a new suit or pair of boots would salute him with "Well, where was the fire?"

Traffic across the Isthmus was, of course, restricted to passengers, the mails and express shipments of such value that the saving on interest charges justified the expensive and difficult overland transportation, while heavy freight was routed, as it was destined to be for almost two decades longer, on the far longer trip around the Horn. The ice, which chilled the beverages of Wells Fargo and Adams & Co. with gelid impartiality in their noggins, at Barry and Pattens, all came from New England as witness a news item of February 1853:

> The fine ship *George Raynes*, Captain Penhallow, which arrived in our harbor on Friday evening after a quick passage, we learn belongs to the Boston & California Ice Company, of which Messrs. Flint, Peabody & Co., of this city, are agents. She left Boston with 902 tons of fresh pond ice, the largest cargo of its kind ever exported from that city, which annually furnishes large supplies for every part of the world. . . . The half-clipper ship, *Queen of the Pacific*, was also by last accounts receiving an equal amount of ice for this city. Several of the leading merchants of Boston and Salem, with Messrs. Flint & Peabody of this city, form their own company and having abundance of capital, owning their own vessels, with their arrangements now fully perfected, there is no doubt they will hereafter furnish a full and constant supply of this article, so necessary to comfort in warm weather.

An excitement of vertiginous proportions, and one which never diminished in intensity until the coming of the Pacific Railroad, was the arrival of mails from "the States," when all industry ceased, all commerce closed its

## BEFORE WELLS FARGO CAME

In 1850, while Wells Fargo was still unborn and Adams & Co. were flourishing in California, San Francisco Bay was crowded with abandoned ships whose crews and officers alike had deserted to seek their fortunes in the inland mines. Ordinary seamen were making $1,000 a day in the diggings and ships were left without even watchmen aboard. Later, many of these hulks, rendered unseaworthy from neglect, were beached on San Francisco's water front and became hotels, stores and saloons. Saloons with façades like ships' prows jutting over the sidewalk are a California institution to this day, reminders of an age of improvision.

# WELLS, FARGO & CO'S
# EXPRESS.

## A Joint Stock Company, Capital $300,000.

### DIRECTORS:

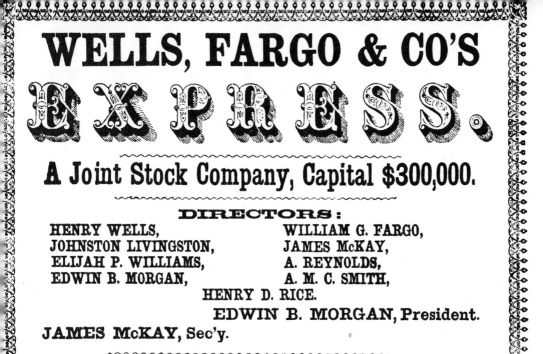

HENRY WELLS,     WILLIAM G. FARGO,
JOHNSTON LIVINGSTON,     JAMES McKAY,
ELIJAH P. WILLIAMS,     A. REYNOLDS,
EDWIN B. MORGAN,     A. M. C. SMITH,
HENRY D. RICE.

EDWIN B. MORGAN, President.

JAMES McKAY, Sec'y.

---

Having made advantageous arrangements with the United States and Pacific Mail Steamship Companies, for transportation, we are now prepared to forward

### GOLD DUST, BULLION, SPECIE, PACKAGES, PARCELS & FREIGHT,

Of all kinds, to and from NEW YORK and SAN FRANCISCO; thence to Sacramento, Marysville, Nevada, Stockton, Sonora, Columbia, Mokelumne Hill, Portland, Oregon City, and all the principal towns of California and Oregon.

☞ OUR REGULAR SEMI-MONTHLY EXPRESS, is despatched from San Francisco, on the 1st and 16th, and from New York on the 5th and 20th, of each month, *by the Mail Steamers*, in charge of OUR OWN MESSENGER through to destination.

### TREASURE & SMALL PARCELS,

Received for Shipment up to the latest moment before the departure of the Steamers.

### TREASURE INSURED

Under open Policies in some of the best New York Companies, or at Lloyds, in London, at the option of Shippers.

*Our Regular Semi-Monthly Express for Oregon*, is despatched by the Steamers of the Pacific Mail Steamship Company.

## INLAND ROUTES.

An EXPRESS for Sacramento and Marysville is despatched DAILY, (Sundays excepted) at 4 o'clock, P. M., in charge of careful and trusty Messengers, connecting at Sacramento with RHODES AND LUSK'S DAILY EXPRESS, to Shasta and Yureka, and with HUNTER & Co.'s DAILY EXPRESS to Placerville and all parts of El Dorado County.

*A Daily Express* is sent from our office in Sacramento, to Rough and Ready, Grass Valley, and Nevada. Also, a daily express to Auburn, Ophir, Yankee Jim's, and all parts of Placer County.

TODD'S EXPRESS for Stockton, Sonora, Mokelumne Hill, Mariposa, and all the principal Camps in the Southern Mines, is despatched daily from our office in San Francisco. Our Messengers are supplied with IRON SAFES for the security of treasure entrusted to their are. Our connections on the Atlantic side are equal if not superior to those of any other California Express. We connect at New York, with the following well known lines, viz :— *The American Express Company*, running via Buffalo and Dunkirk, to Cleveland, Sandusky, Toledo, Cincinnati, St. Louis, Detroit, Chicago, Galena, &c. *The Harnden Express* to Boston, Philadelphia, Baltimore, Washington, &c. *Pullen, Virgil & Co.'s* Vermont and Canada Express. *Davenport, Mason & Co.'s* New Bedford Express, and *Livingston, Wells & Co.'s* European Express.

## WELLS, FARGO & CO.,

OFFICES, { No. 16 Wall Street, New York.
{ No. 114 Montgomery Street, San Francisco.

October, 1852.         (see next page.)

doors, and the town, to a man, besieged the offices of the express companies to claim mail from home. The long arms of the semaphore atop Telegraph Hill which signaled the sighting of inbound vessels were clearly visible to most of the town and the news of an impending arrival called the entire Wells Fargo staff together from any part of the city against the impending crush at its counters.

Both arms of the semaphore extended on either side of the mast were the symbol indicating a side-wheel steamer, and since all the vessels of the Pacific Mail Steamship Co. were side-wheelers the implication was mails from Panama. One evening in a local music hall an actor, obedient to the directions of his script in some forgotten melodrama, rushed on stage with his arms thrown wide in amazement at a scene which greeted his gaze and spoke the author's line: "What does this mean?" From stage box to the farthermost gallery the audience roared in a single delighted shout: "Side-wheel steamer."

Money was easy, times were flush; and if anyone lacked in immediate resources he was sure that prosperity was just around the corner and it generally was. Change in denominations smaller than four bits was seldom required for the most trifling purchase or service, and Wells Fargo's mail clerks reported that recipients of mail from home frequently walked off the premises in such a coma of delight that they neglected to take change from double eagles and even from the fifty-dollar slugs of Moffatt & Co. for a single letter!

Adventure was in the air and San Francisco was awash with politely bred and well-educated youths whose degrees from Cambridge or New Haven and whose family antecedents on Beacon Hill or in Washington Square in no way deterred them from seeking occupation as swampers in saloons, as draymen or carpenters. Later, in the prophetic fifties, John Mackay is credited by legend with looking down into the seething El Dorado of Virginia City and, with a fine gesture, of tossing away his last silver dollar from the Divide above Gold Hill. "Let's enter like gentlemen," he said. But many a silk-hatted and velvet-cuffed gentleman arrived in the fifties in San Francisco from Salem or Philadelphia without even two bits in his pocket for such a splendid inaugural gesture.

Across the street from Wells Fargo's modest but convenient premises in Sam Brannan's fireproof block, the firm of Adams & Co. was becoming outrageous with pride and splendor and had gone into conference with a local contractor, John Parrott, for an office suitable to its status in the community. The stone blocks for Adams' new building, each one numbered in proper architectural sequence, were imported from China, and when the Chinese workmen employed in sorting and laying them struck for more pay Mr. Parrott was at a distinct disadvantage. Nobody else could read the Chinese characters which were a clue to each stone's place and purpose, and the Chinese won their argument hands down. Quarter-inch iron shutters brought around the Horn in the holds of clippers were fitted over the windows; safes, letter presses, ledgers and clerkly furniture of the most

## DOCKSIDE TRANSFER IN PANAMA

The Isthmus transfer at Panama, from Panama City to Aspinwall, was accomplished by Wells Fargo after the completion of the railway in 1855 in the freight and baggage cars of the Panama RR through the factors of their agents, Hurtado & Bros. Here in a midnight setting at the Aspinwall docks, the Pacific Mail Steamship Co.'s side-wheeler *Arizona* is being loaded with express matter by native porters while a messenger keeps tally of his shipment in the doorway of a freight car.

## "SIDE-WHEEL STEAMER"

Up till the building of the Pacific Railroad, as the Central Pacific-Union combine was generally known, Wells Fargo was vitally interested in the marine signals shown on Telegraph Hill. Most important in Wells Fargo's scheme of things was the signal which heralded the arrival of a side-wheel steamer, these being the property of the Pacific Mail carrying the mails from Panama.

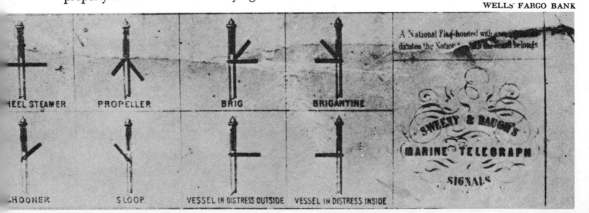

## HAPPY DAYS IN MONTGOMERY STREET

This scene of animation and pleasure may or may not depict the interior of Barry and Patten's premises next door to Wells Fargo in Brannan's "new fireproof block" in Montgomery Street, but it records faithfully the happy spirit of San Francisco in those distant and wonderful days. The clientele enjoying the music of the colored orchestra includes Spanish ranchers in serapes, "honest miners" from the diggings at Hangtown or Bedbug and Celestials in the pigtails that have since been outmoded. One of the less inhibited customers is demonstrating that, although he may not be able to absorb more whisky by conventional channels, he is still hopeful of gaining its benefits by the process of osmosis.

## THE WICKEDEST PLACE IN THE WEST

In the early fifties, when Wells Fargo was still a newcomer to San Francisco, the wickedest resort in town was the Bella Union, music hall, gambling den and vice parlors generally, in Portsmouth Square. Its Babylonish attractions were a byword from Boston to Valparaiso and Argonauts were almost as determined to savor its enchantments as they were to strike it rich in the diggings. At the extreme right in this fine collodion-plate picture is the City Hall, formerly the Jenny Lind Theater, and beside it the El Dorado Saloon. Below is an artist's conception of high life in the Bella Union a few years later.

elegant sort were also imported, and Adams & Co. was installed in breath-taking style with Page, Bacon & Co., Bankers, as cotenants of the building.

The staff at Wells Fargo contained their envy of such Babylonish doings and buried their noses in tall mugs at Barry and Patten's bar, little knowing that in the near future fate was preparing for them a lodgement in the very counting rooms which now so irked their pride. Bad times were in the offing and the first of San Francisco's recurrent cycles of boom and bust was just around the corner of Montgomery Street.

In the meantime events in San Francisco were shaping up for what was in later years to be known as "the great express panic." David Hale Haskell, Adams' manager, who had come from far-off Boston to see his firm, as he believed, impregnably intrenched and with limitless vistas of wealth stretching into the future, was not a careful businessman. Adams & Co. was as indifferent to losses running into thousands of dollars "as is a modern motion picture company," according to Harlow, who cites as an example the occasion when $25,000 was stolen from the Sonora to Stockton stage by the simple expedient of slitting open the rear boot into which it had carelessly been tossed while the shipment was in night transit. Upon another occasion a depositor at Adams was given, by a careless cashier, twelve fifty-dollar slugs instead of the eight called for by the terms of a draft, and when the payee returned to the bank to turn in the extra $200 he was grandly told that "no adjustments were made after the customer leaves the office."

In their remarkable book of reminiscences of San Francisco in those first golden years, Barry and Patten, the gracious and literate taverners who were Wells Fargo's first neighbors and whose memoirs of the old days were set down for the delight of a later generation which knows few saloon proprietors of such accomplishments and charm, record the progress of Adams & Co. toward its eventual downfall.

The chief and founder of the firm, Alvin Adams, they depose, came to San Francisco to ascertain the condition of his business. Such obsequious attentions were afforded the old gentleman on his westward passage as might have attended the progress of the President of the United States. At the pier a barouche with four matched steeds and the entire executive staff of his enterprises awaited him and he was escorted to hotel apartments such as might have been reserved for royalty. A banquet of magnificent proportions was tendered the unassuming and industrious businessman and throughout his stay in California the hospitality which was offered him by his associates was of such a bewildering variety that at no time did he have an opportunity to discuss the company's affairs, let alone cast up its accounts. "New excursions, wonderful sights, great natural curiosities must be visited; it would never do to return without having looked upon these world-wide wonders; expressed desires, remonstrances, expostulations, all were smiled away; they hurried him from place to place in one continual whirl, received here and passed on there with honors and attention never ending."

Bewildered with such flattery and attentions and just a might piqued at being allowed no part in his own business affairs, Adams retired to New York

## SEEING THE ELEPHANT WITH ALVIN ADAMS

When Alvin Adams was being shown the sights of San Francisco in the early fifties had he expressed an interest in the more Bohemian aspects of life he might have been taken, strictly on a sight-seeing basis of course, to such a hurdy-gurdy house as this. The street scene below he might have encountered several times a day as the enlightened electorate debated matters of public policy with occasional reference to muskets, sword canes, dirks, life preservers and self-cocking revolvers.

a few weeks later and immediately sent out a trusted and confidential elderly clerk for whose reception such a round of honors and jollifications could under no circumstances be excused. But to persuade this supposedly canny ambassador proved even easier than it had been in the case of the head of the firm. It was discovered almost immediately upon his arrival that he had a weakness for ardent spirits, and one after another the department heads of Adams' San Francisco branch took the by now mellowed proconsul on a round of the town's countless saloons. The old man forgot that double-entry ledgers or the daybook ever existed.

"He laughed so incessantly," wrote Barry and Patten, "that he could not give his mind to business details. He laughingly proposed to leave for home, rode to the steamer, laughing, and laughed more than ever when he found his stateroom lined with cases of his favorite schnapps, and sailed away, still laughing. . . . But soon the inevitable crash came and the insiders, heads of the house and clerks, laughed in their sleeves immoderately, but the poor outsiders, except for the bench and bar, felt like doing anything but laughing."

Perhaps the managers of Wells Fargo & Co., who also drank in Barry and Patten's and could scarcely have avoided witnessing this comedy of frustration, sensed what was toward and took steps accordingly. Certainly, although he was by no means ungracious or averse to reasonable pleasures, no such nonsense revolved about Henry Wells when he came out on a tour of inspection. The agency was handy to Barry and Patten, but its books were incontestably in order for the chief and the gold reserve in the vaults was very much available had he chosen to count it over to the last minted eagle. There was no jiggery-pokery afoot in the house of Wells Fargo.

Events in the California fifties marched with dramatic velocity. Wells Fargo, the Johnny-come-lately of the expresses, had appeared in San Francisco in 1852. By 1853 it was securely established under conservative but aggressive management so that by 1854 it had twenty-four offices located in every profitable region of the California countryside and was ready for the even then nourishing crisis which was, in the following year, to raise it to a position where no competition of any considerable dimensions even existed in its field.

Despite all and any extravagances which may have characterized the conduct of its affairs, Adams & Co. was very much in the Western saddle when Wells Fargo arrived on the scene. That the volume of mail business between San Francisco and the camps of Oregon and California which found its way to the Adams door was at first considerably great is attested by the vast preponderance of Adams hand-stamped franks now in the possession of collectors and historians. A more precise index, of course, are the records of gold shipments out of California for the East which were invariably available to the daily press and which are now, as they were then, regarded as the official record for those years. In 1852, Wells Fargo's first shipment to its New York correspondents was a mere $21,000 in dust and nuggets compared to Adams' whacking $600,000 and Page, Bacon's $682,000. The gulf between these figures steadily diminished with the more secure establishment of Wells

Fargo's affairs and the expansion of its facilities, but as late as November 1854, on the very eve of the great panic, Wells Fargo was only sending in a single shipment of $102,000 as against Adams' $200,000 and Page, Bacon's $404,000. The disparity in these sums serves to show how great the odds were against Wells Fargo at a time when affairs were shaping up for a show-down and to measure the opportunities for expansion should something remove these well-heeled competitors from the field.

Indeed, when the end came, it was the very volume of Adams' and Page, Bacon's exports and their consequent inability to stand a prolonged run on their resources which led to their failure, while Wells Fargo, which evidently made a practice of keeping a far larger cash balance on hand, was better prepared against such an emergency. At this stage of the game, Wells Fargo was a very prudent concern indeed.

Throughout the year of 1854 storm warnings appeared which no prudent banker could afford to ignore and which Wells Fargo's management both on the coast and in New York understood and heeded. A financial depression on a nation-wide scale was looming. Everywhere expansion had been carried on recklessly and in no field of enterprise with less regard to eventual realities than in that of the railroads. The United States was possessed by what amounted to a railroad mania and roads were chartered and under-written with a happy abandon in the belief that, regardless of agriculture, industry or population, to say nothing of duplication of routes, the flanged wheel must roll over the spiked rail to inevitable fortune. No railroad in the Middle West was in more unhappy case than the Ohio and Mississippi, then in process of construction between St. Louis and Cincinnati, and when its finances failed it carried down with it the bank of Page & Bacon of St. Louis, whose subsidiary, Page, Bacon & Co. of California, suffered a run on its resources as soon as the steamer *Oregon* arrived on February 18th with the bad news.

The desperate straits of Page & Bacon were known in New York nearly a week before the intelligence was available on the Pacific coast. Its drafts on a New York correspondent had been dishonored and a special meeting of the directors of Wells Fargo had been called to take advantage of this forewarning, but long before a messenger could arrive in California the crisis which has ever since been known as Black Friday had been precipitated and Wells Fargo in California had been forced to act on its own initiative without any communications from its New York office.

Page, Bacon of California held out as long as it could. It had recently made substantial shipments of bullion to the East and was in no condition to stand a protracted run, a run which had meanwhile extended to every other banking firm in California, including of course Wells Fargo and Adams. By February 23nd, every bank of consequence in San Francisco and their branches in Sacramento and the Sierra diggings suspended payment. At Placerville, Auburn, Coloma, Mormon Island and Sonora, there were mobs and threats of violence against the closed bank branches. All major business was at a standstill in San Francisco and Sacramento.

WELLS FARGO BANK

## IN OLD MONTGOMERY STREET

This is Wells Fargo's familiar offices on the northeast corner of California and Montgomery Streets in 1865, from an old stereopticon slide with an ornately decorated horsecar in the foreground. The two views on the page opposite depict the banking and express departments of the firm and are believed to be hitherto unpublished works of a well-known San Francisco engraver, D. Van Vleck. Van Vleck was at the time these were executed a partner of William Keith who later achieved fame for his landscapes and these engravings came to the hand of Wells Fargo executives in one of the artist's scrapbooks after his death.

WELLS FARGO BANK

Throughout these terrible days, however, Wells Fargo maintained its express services with commendable tranquillity and after a temporary receiver had been in control of its banking affairs for three days, its complete solvency and substantial credit balance were established and its doors were immediately opened to permit the withdrawal and deposit of assets.

Page, Bacon and Adams, however, were irretrievably ruined. The affairs of Adams had been so conducted that its express business was hopelessly involved with its banking branch. Adams never reopened for business of any sort in California. For two years an association of former employees of Adams attempted to carry on under the name of the Pacific Express, but in 1858 this company, too, was added to the already impressive list of minor firms consolidated in the near monopoly of Wells Fargo.

It had required but three brief years for Wells Fargo to set itself up in California and to dominate the express and banking business. In San Francisco, where in 1852 the express companies had been numbered by the score, it had in 1858 the entire field to itself without competition of any sort. With the collapse of Adams, Wells Fargo gathered in at one fell swoop almost every feeder company that had formerly done business in the mining camps with its rival. Its prestige was beyond reproach, its authority beyond question of obedience, and for the next decade and with scarcely any interruption, Wells Fargo was both literally and figuratively in the saddle, high, wide and handsome.

Some idea of the respect and even affection in which Wells Fargo was widely held after the great panic may be derived from a news item in the *Shasta Courier* announcing the firm's decision to establish a branch in the northern counties.

> Messrs. Wells Fargo & Co., our readers will be informed by reference to our advertising columns, *are about establishing* a branch of their very popular house in this place. During the financial explosion a few months back, Wells Fargo & Co. stood the shock without exhibiting the least quivering. They have, in consequence, the confidence of the entire commercial portion of the state. They have also, by their promptness and FIDELITY in attending all business entrusted to them, won for themselves a name as expressmen that is of itself the highest encomium that can be paid to their deserts. S. Knight is to be the resident in this place. Judging from a very short acquaintance with the gentleman, we are inclined to the opinion that he is possessed of one of the requisites of a good expressman, at least: that of being a good, clever gentleman.

Such flowery and naïve, but unquestionably valid, expressions of esteem may be counted by the hundreds in the yellowing files of the California papers of the year 1855.

In the East, the affairs of Adams Express Co., which bore to Adams & Co. of San Francisco much the same relationship that existed between the American Express and Wells Fargo, were not seriously affected by the tragic fiasco of its Western agents. Old Alvin Adams, however, who had been received "with such honors as might have been given to Cornelius Vanderbilt or John Jacob Astor" when he visited San Francisco, was acutely conscious of the criticism to which his entire organization had laid itself open and, although the company was to exist as an express in the Deep South until well into the twentieth century, he resigned its presidency in 1855.

In Montgomery Street the rout of Adams & Co. and the ascendency of Wells Fargo were symbolized in a single overwhelming gesture of triumph when Wells Fargo took over for its own quarters the counting house which Mr. Parrott had been at such pains to build for the joint occupancy of Adams and Page, Bacon. The numbered granite blocks from China and the humorous overtones of the Chinese strike became part of the Wells Fargo legend. Instead of merely stepping next door to get to Barry and Patten's, Wells Fargo's staff now had, however, to cross the street.

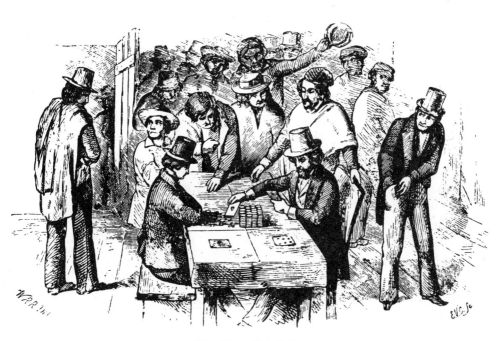

GAMBLING SCENE IN SAN FRANCISCO.

# CHAPTER III

## Mother Lode

BEFORE the coming of the first steamcars to California in the form of Theodore Judah's Sacramento Valley RR between Sacramento and Negro Bar, later Folsom, there were a number of modes of overland travel in common use. The ageless two-wheeled Spanish *carreta* drawn by oxen had largely given way to the lumbering heavy-duty mud wagon powered by as many as thirty-six mules. There were stagecoaches and diligences in an alarming variety of styles and designs, many without any springs whatever. For light fast country travel without revenue loads there were buckboards drawn by a span of ponies, of a sort still encountered in the horse-conscious reaches of the Southwest. In cities the size of San Francisco there were herdics or omnibuses with a sprung axle and lengthwise seats much like an opera coach. There was the six-mule-team Waverly omnibus on the San Jose-San Francisco run, and a photograph taken in the early sixties of the New Almaden stage shows a four-wheeled brake drawn by two span of fine horses, capable of carrying nine passengers inside and three on the box and decorated with a "fringe on the top" for all the world like the surrey in the ballad of a much later date.

And there was the incomparable stage which has become so closely integrated to the fabric of the American saga: the Concord coach, designed and manufactured in far-off New England by Abbot, Downing & Co.

Golden indeed is the legend of the Concord coach, as bright as the metal bars that were to be its most romantic of freights, and although the stage has disappeared forever from the high passes of the Sierra and although its yellow spoked wheels no longer dance and glitter down the old Spanish road into Tombstone, it still rolls bravely in the human imagining, wonderful and deathless.

The thorough-braced stagecoach manufactured by Abbot, Downing has engaged the attention of almost every writer on Western Americana, and deservedly so. It was, in its fullest perfection, a triumph of Yankee ingenuity and artistry, as beautiful a creation for travel in its special field as the clipper ships of Donald MacKay or the graceful Taunton-built eight-wheel locomotives of William Mason which for nearly a century were the motive power on American railroads and whose wheel arrangement was so universal as to make them known as the American Type engine.

Wells Fargo was to own or lease space in a great variety of conveyances spanning the earth's oceans and continents: sailing packets and steamships, railroad trains of astonishing diversity of gages, style and terrains covered, dog sled, muleback, horseback, oxen, buckboards, mud wagons, and sleighs, celerity wagons, trolley and interurban cars, and eventually automobiles and even airplanes. But the Concord coach is, in the public consciousness, the supreme symbol of Wells Fargo's romantic mobility and far-flung landfaring. The sparkling sound of wheels upon gravel and the clatter of the horses' hooves have become an integral part of the symphony of American sounds. At one time Wells Fargo was to be in the fast fruit freighting business by rail, employing its own specially built refrigerator cars through the Southwest. It was to carry treasure out of the last bonanzas in Nevada in Reo and Pope Hartford motorcars of fearsome design and seagoing proportions. One of its successor companies was to ferry vast sums in bullion across the continent in the invention of the Wright Brothers, but the six-horse stagecoach still is the hallmark of Wells Fargo's mastery of time and distance. Along with Sam Colt's patent equalizer, the Stetson hat and the diamond-stack railroad locomotive it was one of the essential properties of the Old West, immortalized in legend and literature, in paintings and eventually in motion pictures.

The first Concord to reach California arrived in San Francisco consigned to the California Stage Co. It came around the Horn, knocked down and carefully secured in the hold of a sailing ship, and its advent was of momentous implications to California generally and Montgomery Street in particular. Experienced stagers gave it the once over with knowing approval, and from that day until the meeting of the rails at Promontory it was to be the standard of excellence for overland travel, a classic artifact much as a Rolls-Royce is today and, in comparative terms, costing almost as much. A Concord cost a cool $1,500 f.o.b. on the banks of the Merrimac, back in the shady New England town where it was manufactured and after which it was named. A span of good coaching horses cost in the neighborhood of $3,000 delivered in California and it took three to power a coach. Throw in another $1,500 for harnesses and the bill per unit of staging comes into the Rolls-Royce bracket in money that was considerably more valuable back in the sixties.

Lewis Downing and Leon Abbot didn't believe in the industrial age and they had never heard of an assembly line. Concords were made throughout and exclusively by hand, down to the last detail, by a force of artisans numbering 300 who worked fourteen hours a day for six week days, and every man in their five-acre factory was a specialist. A minimum of metal was used in their joining and what there was had to be the best Norwegian iron. The spokes, smoothed and balanced to perfection, were of hand-hewn ash. The panels were made of countless layers of paper-thin plywood painstakingly laminated and dried. Oak and linden and other woods were aged four years before they were allowed to enter the Abbot, Downing plant. The thorough braces, the tough, heavy straps of leather which supported the egg-shaped body of the coach above its draft and running gear, were

## BY DOG SLED, RIVER PACKET, STEAMCARS AND COACH

Until the railroads came, the classic conveyance of Wells Fargo's treasure and sometimes passengers was the Concord coach, a completely utilitarian specimen one of which on the Shasta run is shown here pausing briefly at Trinity Center. Below is yet another means of conveyance in California's spacious days: the swift and graceful steamer *Antelope* on the Sacramento-San Francisco run. So much treasure was brought down to the counting houses of Montgomery Street aboard this packet that its express messenger's compartment was known as "the gold room" and its floor occasionally had to be braced against the weight of unusually heavy shipments.

## WELLS FARGO MOVED VARIOUSLY IN CALIFORNIA

When mules and horses foundered in the snowdrifts Wells Fargo's early-day messengers to the Sierra hill towns sometimes resorted to Towser power to speed the mails to their destination. Here a staff artist for Crofutt's *New Overland Tourist and Pacific Coast Guide* for 1880 depicts for its fascinated readers a tandem of Wells Fargo's fearless Fidos on their appointed rounds, obviously unstayed by rain or snow or gloom of night. About the time of the vogue of Towser, Wells Fargo was riding aboard its first steamcars, the Sacramento Valley RR which was opened to traffic between Sacramento and Negro Bar, later Folsom, on February 22, 1856. Above is the Folsom terminal in that year of transition.

FIRST WELLS, FARGO & CO.'S EXPRESS OVER THE MOUNTAINS.

One of the great notables on the long tally of Wells Fargo's messengers and stagers who ranked in contemporary greatness along with Billy Hamilton, Jim Miller and Curly Dan Robbins was "Old Charlie" Parkhurst who, in later years, came to be known as "One-Eyed Charlie" as the result of a horse's kick in the face. Charlie drove for more than thirty years for the California and Pioneer companies on such difficult and dangerous runs as the Stockton - Mariposa and Sacramento - Placerville routes and, while never known for recklessness, was still a skillful and daring horseman beyond the average. J. Ross Browne, a Western author and traveler of the period, reported that one indication of a bad road was when Charlie chewed an extra-large wad of cut plug tobacco and it was proverbial that the day after payday Parkhurst was usually insolvent as a result of whisky drinking and dice throwing for two-bit cigars. When, in 1879, "Old Charlie" died at Watsonville, it was discovered that Charlie was a woman and a physician's certificate attested that she had been a mother. She was buried in the Odd Fellow's Cemetery, for she was a member in good standing, at Watsonville and her grave is there today. Here is "Old Charlie" with a payday cigar and a passenger in pincenez, perhaps J. Ross Browne.

THE COACHMAN WAS A LADY

the product of master tanners of Lynn and Framingham down Massachusetts way.

Edward Hungerford writes that it required the hide of eight steers for the thorough braces and boots of a single coach.

The final touch was, of course, the work of the paintshop. Bodies were vermilion, running gear a bright, rich yellow with black trim. And the door panels were the work of qualified artists: John Burgum and his son Edwin. The decorations were mostly New England landscapes and were the calling cards of New Hampshire, posted and forwarded to Hangtown and Whisky Slide, to Virginia City, Grass Valley and Butte, Montana. The useful life span of a Concord was nearly that of a man and you can see one in all its wonderment to this very day in the Wells Fargo Bank's Museum in Montgomery Street. Film companies still use original Concords for Western thrillers and with a little bracing and reinforcing here and there by the property department they survive breakneck chases, Indian assaults and tumbles down mountainsides in the most approved Hollywood tradition.

An example of the indestructibility of the Concord was furnished when one was sunk in a shipwreck off San Francisco. After being wholly immersed in salt water for more than a month, it was recovered and remained in active service for fifty years.

The greatest single shipment of stages from the premises of Abbot, Downing was consigned to Wells Fargo at Omaha within two years of the completion of the Pacific Railroad. It comprised thirty coaches mounted on fifteen flatcars and four high cars loaded with harnesses and a caboose. The day of its departure was a holiday for Concord, but their purchase did not reflect too flatteringly on the judgment of the executives of Wells Fargo. In 1869 the Pacific Railroad was forever to remove the stagecoach from the transcontinental routes of travel and the number of these vehicles already in use was ample for the ever-diminishing requirements of the feeder runs of Montana and Oregon, Arizona and Nevada in the closing years of the century. Wells Fargo just didn't think much of the railroad until it was altogether too late.

The completed Concord weighed only a little over 2,000 pounds, little enough when one considers that it was designed to carry fifteen passengers and merchandise adding perhaps to another ton at high speeds over roads which were sometimes nonexistent and seldom good. The great coaching road from Carson City across the Sierra to Placerville by way of Strawberry was famous as the exception rather than the rule in Western highway construction; for it was maintained in immaculate smoothness winter and summer and in dry seasons its entire surface was constantly watered to allay the dust.

In those halcyon days of the fifties with which this narrative is momentarily concerned, San Francisco was the functioning center for all Wells Fargo's activities as the expressman of treasure. But its advanced seat of operations, the entrepôt of its treasure freight and the point of immediate departure and arrival of its messengers for the mines of the Mother Lode was Sacramento. And it was at Sacramento that Wells Fargo came into the immensely profitable contact with the great California Stage Co.

The California Stage Co., brought into being by shrewd Jim Birch in 1854, was one of the few million-dollar businesses besides Wells Fargo in California of that time. Its routes converged upon the front porch of The Orleans Hotel on the Sacramento river front from every imaginable town, hamlet and city in California: from Shasta far to the north, from Nevada City and Grass Valley, from Downieville and Rich Bar in the Northern Mines, from Mariposa, Bear Valley and Angel's Camp in the Southern Mines. Its coaches rolled in from Placerville and Jackson and Fiddletown and fared forth again at dawn for Whisky Slide, Rattlesnake Bar and Fourth Crossing. Until some years later when Wells Fargo could claim the distinction, it was the largest owner of horseflesh outside of the military organizations in the history of the world. At first it operated over 1,500 miles of California highways and byways and a year later its wheels traveled over twice as many. And Wells Fargo's treasure chests rode the boots of the California Stage Co.'s stages wherever they went.

## SEEKERS AND FINDERS

The universal mule, above ground and below and in a score of capacities, was inseparable from mining in an age innocent of machines. The seedy character above and his capacity-laden mule are the authentic article, prospectors in the California Mother Lode, from a photograph taken in the fifties. In the center is a placer miner panning for colors on some now-forgotten California bar, while below is a Wells Fargo messenger in the swift accomplishment of his appointed rounds, probably in the California sixties and in some foothill vicinage impervious to horses.

Three o'clock in the morning was the zero hour when all the California Stage Co.'s Concords were lined up in front of The Orleans, for this was the time of the arrival of the San Franscisco steamer with its varied assortment of freight and passengers.

There were often more than a hundred coaches — and their drivers crying their destinations, their hostlers waving lanterns and their passengers hurrying from the taproom of The Orleans and struggling into their great-cloaks and wrap-rascals made a fine tumult of ordered confusion in the darkness.

When all the passengers were aboard and the mail and express matter sorted and loaded, the mightiest coaching cavalcade of history started off up K Street. Most of the stages happened to be ready for the road at about the same time, so that their departure was a vast consolidated movement rather than a series of isolated departures. At the edge of town they began to separate into smaller groups, their running lamps resembling a congress of orderly fireflies in the false dawn and the noise and tumult of their riding diminishing down the rich, dusty highways of the Spanish ranchers. Such was the outward going of the treasure fleet.

At nightfall the stages began to drift their separate ways back to town, converging upon the landing where the night steamer bound for Clay Street wharf in San Francisco was getting up steam in her low-pressure boilers. Out of the boots and into the gold room of the steamer came the little green wooden chests with their wrought-iron hasps and ornate insigne of Wells Fargo on the lid. Sometimes when the gold dust had already been weighed and signed for in the Sacramento office, it came aboard in suède leather bags strung like fish on a pole and balanced on the shoulder of a messenger. The receipts issued by Wells Fargo's messenger on a single night steamer sometimes totaled more than a million dollars and sometimes the weight of dust and nuggets was so great that the floor of the treasure compartment had to be shored up by stout timbers braced against the bilges underneath and the rest of the ship's cargo trimmed to make her even on her keel before she left the wharf.

The tangible, instantly negotiable and available wealth thus freighted down from Sacramento aboard the steamers whose names are now but myths upon the river — *Yosemite, Senator, New World, Cleopatra* — staggers the imagination. When, as not infrequently happened in an era innocent of steamship inspection, the boilers blew up in terrific explosions as they did on *The Secretary, The Ranger* and countless other boats, Wells Fargo's gold dust was atomized beyond all recall along with engines, superstructure and passengers.

The supremacy of Sacramento as the nerve center of Wells Fargo's communications with the mines, camps and diggings of the Mother Lode was a relatively brief one and came to an end with the construction and completion in 1856 and opening for service of the Sacramento Valley RR running between the levee at Sacramento and the town of Negro Bar which was coming to be known as Folsom. The pioneer venture of iron-horse transportation in connection with bonanza activities was the conception of the

## "BLESS ME THIS IS PLEASANT, RIDING ON THE RAIL"

Newspaper reproduction in the fifties was not as nearly instantaneous as today and this woodcut version of the first run of the Sacramento Valley RR appeared in the Sacramento *Union* on January 1, 1856, or four and a half months after the event itself. When the road was complete from Sacramento to Negro Bar (Folsom), Wells Fargo rode the steamcars for the first time anywhere, an association which was to continue for more than seventy years.

great Theodore Judah, later to achieve fame in the surveying and construction of the Central Pacific. Its initial run was celebrated with the conventional great "railroad ball" at Folsom with the oratory, champagne and visionary promises dear to the hearts of the expansive citizens of the era. When the last busted plug hat and the last empty flask with the delightful inscription: "Hurrah For the Railroad" had been swept up, Wells Fargo was traveling by its first steamcars and Folsom, instead of Sacramento was the jumping-off-place for the Sierra's western slopes.

Great was the indignation of Sacramento when the stages which had lined up for the three A.M. arrival of the Antelope began to line up somewhat later for the arrival of the train brigade powered by the locomotives *Nevada* and *Sacramento* at the Folsom team track. The same drivers, on duty at the new stage terminal, shouted their destinations: El Dorado, Mormon Flat and You Bet, and set off on their appointed rounds on an appreciably accelerated schedule. By the year 1860, when all the world and his brother was off to the Comstock, the Sacramento Valley's timetables had started printing connections for the Washoe, and Folsom found itself a communications link with the fabulous Golconda of the trans-Sierra.

Wells Fargo's treasure now traveled from its branch offices and agencies in the northern mines by the traditional stage to Folsom. There it was stowed aboard the wooden baggage cars of the Sacramento Valley, forerunners of the many, many bullion cars and treasure vans to come, and again transshipped to the San Francisco steamers at Sacramento where the cars were run up Front Street to the K Street landing. It was Wells Fargo's first taste of shipping treasure by the agency of the flanged wheel and the (in this case) rolled-iron rail and it found it good. Holdups, wrecks or mysterious disappearances of gold shipments were unknown on the Sacramento Valley.

It is not within the proper province of these Taillefers of Wells Fargo to attempt any new cantos of the already well and truly sung saga of the Mother Lode. Its rich wonderments and gaudy destinies of hurrah and heartbreak have been the theme for many a literary prospector who has staked his claim to the records of Volcano, Downieville, Jamestown and Shasta, Dutch Flat, Angel's Camp and Sierra City. The literature of the Mother Lode from Bancroft to Joseph Henry Jackson and from Alonzo Delano to Walter Noble Burns is admirable and comprehensive. Its bibliography alone and even the chronicles of individual hill towns and hamlets have engaged entire books and the life efforts of scholars.

For our purpose let us select a single typical Wells Fargo town of the sixties and examine briefly the texture and excitement of its being and the wealthy commerce which gave it validity.

Take, for example, Columbia.

Columbia came into tumultuous being in the spring of 1850 as the mining community of Hildreth's Diggings in a landscape of such dark ravines and fantastic boulder formations as to give it to this day, an air of some remote and inaccessible never-never land of a lost geologic era. The pattern of its growth followed other California mining camps with such fidelity that it might be taken as a paradigm. Its first edifice was a tent housing a saloon; its second a tent sheltering a fan-tan game conducted by the inevitable Celestial, and the shacks, shanties and lean-tos which followed in civic succession were devoted to fandango houses, cheap hotels where the miners occupied the beds in rotation, and all the assorted temples of pleasure which came into being after each new strike.

Because its resources were richer and its consequent fame more iridescent, Columbia's assassinations were more frequent, its orgies more bacchanalian, its various communal dithyrambs more Dionysiac than those of less favored diggings. Patriotism dictated the change of name to Columbia after a few months of existence and to get "Columbia drunk" was to be more gone in wine than was the rule even in Hangtown, which was plenty. Columbia's early years were happy ones punctuated by a multiplicity of stabbings, garrotings, lootings, riots, holocausts, assaults upon female virtue when this commodity was infrequently available and of other forms of noisy outrage which delighted the simple soul of the "honest miner." Columbia in the early fifties was, in a word, a caution.

William Daegener came to Columbia to represent Wells Fargo & Co. late in 1852, the year the firm commenced operation, and remained there as agent for more than two decades. Tracing the early outlines for a pattern which was

## A SURVIVOR OF THE STORIED PAST

Although it has all the internal earmarks and correct period properties of a Mother Lode coaching scene in the fifties or sixties, an older generation of San Franciscans will remember this Concord as one of the attractions at the California Mid-Winter Fair of 1894 wherein passage around the fairgrounds could be had for two bits. The venerable coach bore under the headrail the original lettering "To All Points in the Southern Mines" and the legend on the forward boot reads "Poole's Stage Lines." The poster on the wall of the "Dance House" is a directory of the Mother Lode diggings originally issued by Wells Fargo and it is entirely probable that, at an earlier period in its life-span the ancient vehicle did indeed actually know the dusty highroad to Columbia as pictured on the page opposite.

## "TOWERING O'ER THE WRECKS OF TIME"

Like the banking house which to this day bears its corporate name, the Wells Fargo agency at Columbia was once the richest and is the most enduring of many hundred similar structures. Standing in Columbia's now-tranquil Main Street it sets a style of placidity and venerable repose for the best preserved of all the Mother Lode communities. The photograph below was taken in a livelier day, probably in the early seventies.

to become almost universal in subsequent mining communities in California and across the Sierra in Nevada, Wells Fargo's first counting rooms and express offices were located in a saloon, in this case the taproom of The Maine House. For some reason this arrangement proved unsatisfactory, but it would be entirely a case of wishful thinking for moralists to suggest that the proximity of his strongboxes to The Maine's whooping clientele was offensive to Daegener, for he shortly removed to a precisely similar premises in the American Hotel, where he again hung out his shingle next to the bush of the boniface.

By this time Columbia had all the technique of high life and low thinking that characterized the towns where Wells Fargo was most in demand. The municipal record shows that by 1854 in Main Street and its lesser byways were flourishing, four banks, a post office, print shop, an authentic Chinatown with all the conventional vices, a theater, an uncounted number of love stores, and an amphitheater where on Sunday afternoons the miners rejoiced to bet on bear and bull fights. At this early date no fiscal genius had yet evolved the scheme of paying for the public school system by a head tax on prostitutes, an aspect of municipal finance which was to be observed almost universally throughout the West until the late nineties, and no check was made of Columbia's madams until later.

Columbia, ever to the fore in all matters of municipal pride, could boast as frequent conflagrations as any other Mother Lode camp and their details were often more exciting. In 1854, the community was reduced to half a million dollars' worth of ashes, and again in 1857 it was put to the torch, this time even more expensively. It was after the latter conflagration, locally known as its counterpart was known in every American community worth mention in the nineteenth century as the "Great Fire," that the singed miners were able to buy the little hand pumper "Papeete," a fire engine originally commissioned by the King of the Sandwich Isles but which was somehow diverted and still reposes in its shed in Columbia as this is being written.

Like so many frontier towns of the American nineteenth century Columbia boasted its Antoine's French Restaurant where, as a miner wonderingly remarked after scanning its impeccable menu, "it was an education just to eat," and its resident Englishman, often enough a remittance man of Cambridge background and county family manners whose deerstalker hats,

## A WEEK END IN THE COUNTRY

Saturday night at the mines there was usually a ball. In the almost total absence of women, "lady partners" were indicated by the wearing of a handkerchief on the arm of whiskered miners. Sunday morning at the mines (lower) found the miners variously inclined, some toward remorse and the Scriptures, some to the repair of their wardrobes, some to further injudicious carouse. At the extreme left it is apparent that even in midmorning all hell is still manifesting itself at the scene of last evening's festivities.

## SOUVENIRS OF SPACIOUS TIMES

This is Wells Fargo's office at Columbia as it appeared at the turn of the century, practically unchanged since the sixties save for the introduction of an electric light. Its safes, gold scales, letter presses and other official furniture are the archetype of these things everywhere from Tombstone to Shasta, and the scales themselves are now in Wells Fargo's museum in San Francisco. Shorty Moore, posing at Columbia years afterward, in his hat of office was a Wells Fargo stage driver of the eighties.

60

single eyeglass and "Piccadilly weeper" whiskers delighted the miners. In the case of Columbia, the resident refuge from the stately homes of England was a lawyer named Nugent who lived at the American House above the weighing scales and treasure boxes of Wells Fargo & Co.

When the great fire of 1857 broke out Barrister Nugent was occupied, perhaps with the proverbial English obsession for bathing, perhaps seeking the solace of his couch, but in any event with something which for the moment obviated the need of his trousers. The horrid clangor of the tocsin brought him to the balcony outside his chambers overlooking Columbia's Main Street. Flames were already enveloping the roof of Knapp's General Store only two blocks distant and threatening the adjacent premises of the Big Nugget Saloon.

Columbians, buckets in hand, paused delightedly to gaze upward at the spectacle of the scion, as it was generally believed, of one of England's noblest houses, executing nip-ups in his excitement clad only in red flannel nether garments and a white top hat while pointing to the blaze and shouting with King's College overtones: "Conflagration, conflagration!" Not even long familiarity with the California idiom could bring him to the uncouth vernacular of "Fire, fire!"

It is interesting to note that, elsewhere besides Columbia, where Wells Fargo suffered the familiar calamity of being burned out and forced to open temporarily under canvas, its affairs were prospering mightily. California produced $43,000,000 in 1857 and of this creditable sum most was carried by Wells Fargo, an impressive increase over the first year's total shipments back in 1852. Wells Fargo maintained by now 87 express offices, almost all of them in California, and, purely as an experiment in promotion and publicity, was shipping to Los Angeles on regular consignment and for general use the first ice ever seen in that sleepy, Spanish ranching town. It was also in 1857 that a large steamer of the Pacific Mail Line sank en route to Panama and all Wells Fargo's express shipments together with original drafts valued at many thousands of dollars were irrevocably lost. Wells Fargo made capital of its decision to waive the legal sixty days' notice it might have invoked before paying the "seconds of exchange" and thereby won the praise of the *Boston Journal* which remarked in its editorial columns that "such instances should not go unrecorded in these days of financial difficulties."

The great days of expressing at Columbia were only a happy microcosm of Wells Fargo's affairs on every hand and constituted a sort of instructive curtain raiser to the fabulous drama of riches that began to unfold only two years later along the still undreamed-of Comstock Lode.

Fire was, of course, the constant and recurrent hazard of the mining camps just as it was of such comparative metropolises as San Francisco, Sacramento and, later, Virginia City and Hamilton. The cardboard shanties and tent settlements, almost explosively dry in the hot sunshine of the northern California summer, were accessible to combustion on the dropping of a lucifer or the emptying of a pipe bowl. They rose in splendid bonfires, evicting residents, bankrupting merchants and inconveniencing everyone, but the next week or the next month, at the latest, saw them rise in some measure from the ashes and ready to repeat the performance. Engine companies, where they were available, as they were in such progressive and richly endowed communities as Columbia and Placerville, were of no great avail. Usually the firehouse was leveled with the town before the tocsin could summon the volunteers from the diggings. Water was hard to come by in emergencies, the apparatus was primitive, and stone and brick construction infrequent. For months after the first railroads came to California the sound of the engine bells in the night would bring the volunteers pelting to the fire station to demand the whereabouts of the conflagration. Bells in the night meant only two things, fire or civic commotion.

Typical of the equanimity with which these holocausts were viewed by the natives and typical, too, of their resourcefulness in the face of catastrophe, is the story of Alonzo Delano, a Wells Fargo agent at Grass Valley who was widely known for his activities as an artist and historian of life among the miners at the diggings. His *Tales of California Life* is a classic item of Western Americana.

At the time of the Grass Valley Fire in 1855 — the date was always appended to any such conflagration to specify which one of many it was — Delano had been roused from his slumbers by shouts of alarm and the conventional ringing of bells and emerged from his sleeping quarters in the back of Wells Fargo's offices to find the front of his premises already in flames and destruction walking boldly in the midnight where only an hour before all had been tranquil security. On this occasion Grass Valley, then a township of some three hundred buildings, was burned as flat as an overcooked pancake. Within the community's radius the only standing landmarks in the morning were Wells Fargo's brick and iron vault and a dozen or so chimneys of brick which had not fallen into the ruins when the surrounding roofs collapsed. Even the vault had taken harm and Delano, who knew its every detail from long familiarity, was hard put to see in the center of its heavy door the outlines of what had once been a gaily painted representation of a Highland castle.

A scant hour after sunrise, however, a disreputable shanty on rollers was being drawn by two span of oxen down the still smoldering main street. As the rollers emerged from under its rear sills, the bearded conductor of the errant edifice picked them up, ran ahead of his team and slipped them under the front of the precariously balanced structure. Its doors flapped, its blinds slammed and the brick chimney threatened at every moment to come down around its jehu and his oxen.

At length Delano and his find achieved the barely cool ashes of Wells Fargo's agency of yesterday. The shanty was maneuvered into place and backed up so that one of its doors opened on the front of the vault, the rollers were removed and the oxen unhitched. Half an hour later a crudely lettered sign reading "Wells Fargo & Co.'s Express Office" appeared on its façade and by evening the vault was cool enough for it to be opened and commerce

## THER LODE VIGNETTES OF THE SIXTIES

When Lola Montez set out to keep an engagement in the Mother Lode she was accustomed to travel with not only her husband but also a Wells Fargo messenger as a guard against the highway perils of the era. This often reproduced photograph shows the incomparable Lola setting out from Grass Valley in 1854 with a trusty Wells Fargo agent complete in silk top hat and double-barreled shotgun, and highwaymen did well to keep their distance. Below is a once famous stager on the Wells Fargo run between Marysville and Sacramento. His name was James E. Johnston, and like Jim Miller and many other knights of the rein, he was a celebrated dandy. In addition to being possessed of a penchant for gaudy waistcoats, Johnston was known throughout California for his inflexible habit of wearing a new pair of fine kid gloves on every run.

## THE FUNCTIONS OF WELLS FARGO

The youth in the lower photograph is doing business with Wells Fargo in the manner of its transaction in a hundred camps and diggings. This one is a modern recreation and all the properties are present: the miner's poke in his hand, the Wells Fargo treasure chest with its massive padlock and the traditional gold scales attended by a grizzled ancient with a revolver close at hand. Above, another veteran posts a letter via Wells Fargo in the days when the express company had a better name for dispatch of communications than the Federal Post Office.

WELLS FARGO

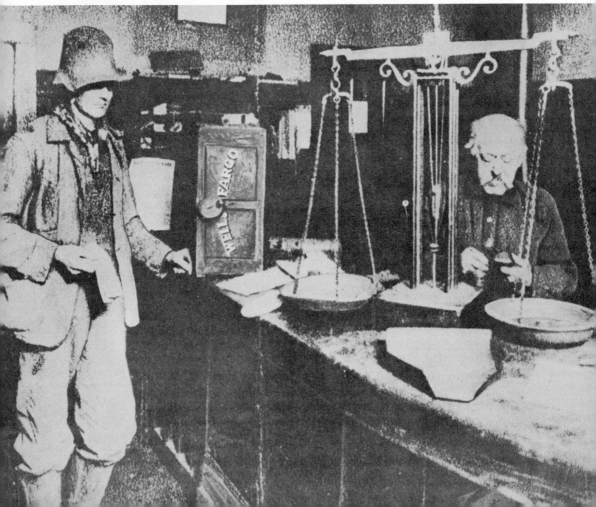

resumed as usual. Wells Fargo at Grass Valley hadn't missed a single business day.

It was after the great fire of 1857 at Columbia that William Daegener caused to be erected the beautiful express offices for Wells Fargo which can still be seen in the tranquil southern reaches of Main Street more than ninety years after they were built. The mellow red bricks were fired in the new kiln at Shaw's Flat; the graceful wrought-iron balcony was ordered from far-off Troy in New York State and transported around the Horn in sail, pausing perhaps at New Orleans on the way to acquire some of the atmosphere of the old French Quarter architecture which it invariably suggests to those who view it for the first time. The heavy iron door and window shutters, secured in their place by massive dogs and systems of interlocking bolts, were freighted up from San Francisco after a long sea voyage around the Horn and up the coast of South America.

And it was after Barrister Nugent's "conflagration" that its true golden age came to Columbia. Iron and brick replaced the shakes and shanties of the early years and wealth in positively astounding quantities began flowing through the rockers and long toms of the adjacent diggings and over Daegener's counters. Gold was close to the surface around Columbia and in the early years $87,000,000 of the precious metal was mined within its corporate limits and, after the advent of hydraulic processes, another $55,000,000 was washed to the surface. Wells Fargo, of course, handled the vast preponderance of this bonanza and during the busiest times of his agency Daegener kept his offices open on a twenty-four-hour-a-day basis because his clerks and cashiers were unable to transact all the business that came to his doors during the daylight hours.

Miners coming to town with heavy pokes and anxious for an advance estimate of their wealth but unable to gain access to a reliable scales borrowed teacups from Mrs. Barron, a Cornishwoman who served tea and saffron cakes every afternoon in her home in Fulton Street, just to get a rough idea of what they might expect in the way of a draft from Wells Fargo's chief clerk. Often the line of anxious sourdoughs would extend at three in the morning all the way from Wells Fargo past Knapp's Store and down Main Street past Sleeper's Gold Exchange, which was closed for the night, and some impatient depositors were willing to pay ten dollars for an advanced position near the head of the waiting throng.

When John Milton Strain brought to the scales in Daegener's agency a single nugget which he had uncovered in the shadow of Kennebec Hill on the very outskirts of town, which weighed thirty pounds and was appraised at $7,438.50, Columbia knew that it was the new El Dorado and that the wealth of the Incas was a mere shinplaster by comparison to what the future held.

There is a legend that during its golden hour Francis Bret Harte passed through Columbia, and paused outside the door of the Stage Driver's Retreat, so named because from its portals the stages with Wells Fargo's messengers

# CALIFORNIA MINING

At the earliest placers, the white miners were often content to whittle and smoke while hired Indian labor operated the sluices and long toms as is shown by the still from the motion picture *Wells Fargo*.

In later years came hydraulic mining with pressure streams from water guns which cut away the hillsides and filled many California rivers with so much silt as to render them unnavigable.

And most destructive of all were gold dredgers such as this one near Oroville which turned the landscape into a wilderness and floated ahead of its own destruction on a self-perpetuating lake of refuse.

## SATURDAY AFTERNOON IN THE DIGGINGS

The whereabouts of this barbershop scene is lost to the record but it could be any diggings in the Mother Lode and its properties fix it in the fifties. The interlude of home life shown below is even more atmospheric, including as it does a coffee mill, obviously home-made furniture and a week's collection of unscoured pots and tin plates. Note, in the foreground, the batch of pancakes reposing, for lack of better place, in the crown of the wide hat on the floor.

aboard set out from Stockton and Sacramento. There were 143 faro-bank games in progress at one time in the gambling apartments of the Stage Drivers' Retreat, a circumstance which never contributed notably to the tranquillity of Columbia after dark. At the Pioneer Saloon down the street the Cornish miners were accustomed to raise their voices in song on Saturday night so that the hurrah was reported to have been distinctly audible as far away as the Concannade Mine at Santiago Gulch. Bret Harte shook his head and moved on in the general direction of Broadway Street and the Long Tom.

The Long Tom Saloon was the pride of outrageous Columbia. It was the biggest in the county and reached from Broadway Street right through to Main Street, each of its portals guarded by two doormen and its whale-oil-lit interior constantly patrolled by ostentatiously armed bouncers or floormen who, on general principles, were opposed to the shooting out of lights and who subscribed to the management's theory that an absolute minimum of currency should be removed from the premises by the patrons. Such local notables as Jack White, Ad Pence, Doc Johns, Lou Alverson and Strain of thirty-pound-nugget fame were among the regulars at the Long Tom's twenty-four expertly dealt tables.

If Bret Harte sought further clues to the manner of life in Columbia in the middle sixties when 15,000 citizens thronged its streets, he might have paused profitably at George Foster's City Hotel, celebrated for its fine ales and English mutton chops, where undoubtedly he would have beheld the splendid whiskers of Barrister Nugent fluttering above a chalice of his native brew. He might have attended one of the Sunday afternoon bear and bull encounters at Ham and Hildreth's Livery Stables, a form of Sabbath diversion which caused excitement and satisfaction among the populace but which awakened only alarm for the state of public grace in such literary explorers of California as Hinton Helper, who later denounced bear and bull fights in stringent terms in his hilarious *Land of Gold*.

Or, as he took leave of Columbia, Bret Harte might have taken note of the last hundred yards or so of Washington Street where, as a local and obvious improvement on the mere scattering of "First and Last Chance" saloons which dotted the outskirts of most California mining towns, Columbia's departing guest had his choice of two solid city blocks where almost every premises on both sides of the street was occupied by a suburban oasis.

One shrewd pair of California eyes which remained fixed on the main chance in Columbia belonged to Darius Ogden Mills, whose name in another decade would be that of a titan of finance and whose banking houses, in their varying succession, were to be the mightiest of the nineteenth-century West. Banker Mills' offices in stone and iron as befitted their substantial and dignified purpose were located at Columbia. Like Wells Fargo, Mills had seen in the affairs of Main Street and the resources which lay so close to the surface around Kennebec Hill a jumping-off-place to greatness and a source and fountainhead for future wealth of fantastic proportions. Until many years later, when Mills tired of the Pacific coast and removed to New

## LANDMARKS OF OLD COLUMBIA

Down the street a block from the Stage-driver's Retreat shown below, which still functions as a going establishment, and handy to Wells Fargo, being removed but by a single door, was the first banking office of Darius Ogden Mills, greatest of California money-bags in the sixties and seventies. The picture of Mills shows him as a young man at about the time of his association with Columbia. His affairs interlocked with those of Wells Fargo for many years, and eventually he became a director of the company. Wells Fargo rode Mills' railroads; Mills consigned treasure by Wells Fargo; all were happily involved in stupefying profits, and there was always between them the bond of a common youth in pastoral Columbia.

WELLS FARGO BANK

York, a retreat from the West which was to cost him dearly in several notable transactions, his course and that of Wells Fargo were to run in grooves closely parallel and often identical in their interest.

Even today it is easy to see why Columbia was once the most stately and beautiful of California hill towns as well as the most wealthy and tumultuous. There was an inherent dignity in the Louisiana store fronts differing from those of the New Orleans' Vieux Carré only because there were great gold and green painted iron shutters instead of glass in the tall French windows. The arcaded sidewalks with their balconies above were cool in the noonday and invited the miners to explore shops where fine merchandise was available to every purse. There were then, and there are now, a multiplicity of magnificent trees, Lombardy poplars, locusts and weeping willows. The locusts grow richest around the balconies of Wells Fargo as they once clustered thickly around the portals of the Three Brothers Store, the great Columbia Brewery and Jim McChesney's Saloon. There is only tranquillity now where once there was a superb pageant of animation that caught the imagination of Bret Harte in a skein of color and vitality.

It is pleasant, in a generation of futility, to imagine the bearded sourdoughs gaging their dust and nuggets in Mrs. Barron's pretty china teacups that were on other occasions used for serving the wives of the Chileno miners, the wild fandangos on Saturday nights at Frank Vassalo's "first class saloon and billiard house," the tinkle of the little bells announcing the arrival of pack trains from near-by Yankee Hill and Martinez, and Agent Daegener's clerks, in beaver hats and green billiard cloth aprons, wrestling the wooden boxes of Wells Fargo up to the boot of the California Stage Co.'s Concords at the foot of Main Street amidst the turmoil of noontide traffic.

The Mother Lode was Wells Fargo's first great empire, the first taste of spacious days and golden vistas of profits mounting steadily in the buckram-bound double ledgers and "Boston books," in Montgomery Street. Wealth drifted wonderfully, almost as in a dream sequence, down the tree-shaded highways of Old California, converging upon the railheads, the loading platforms and the little wooden cars of the first railroads, piling high in the green, cast-iron safes in Wells Fargo's offices in the Transportation Block just down Second Street from the Orleans Hotel in Sacramento, and finally floating down the tranquil midnight Sacramento in the gold room of the *Antelope* toward the splendid fulfillment of its created purpose.

Of course the going of Wells Fargo's treasure was not always as serene and unmolested as may be suggested by these pastoral vignettes. Its very richness and seeming availability attracted the attentions of unwelcome parties in such numbers that Wells Fargo was forced to maintain a private police force and detective bureau far greater than those of any other organization or municipality in the Far West. The rogues and scoundrels of California's highways were to become the central figures of a legend as enduring as the legend of the highwaymen of Old England whose pistols and command to "stand and deliver" were a scandal to British coaching.

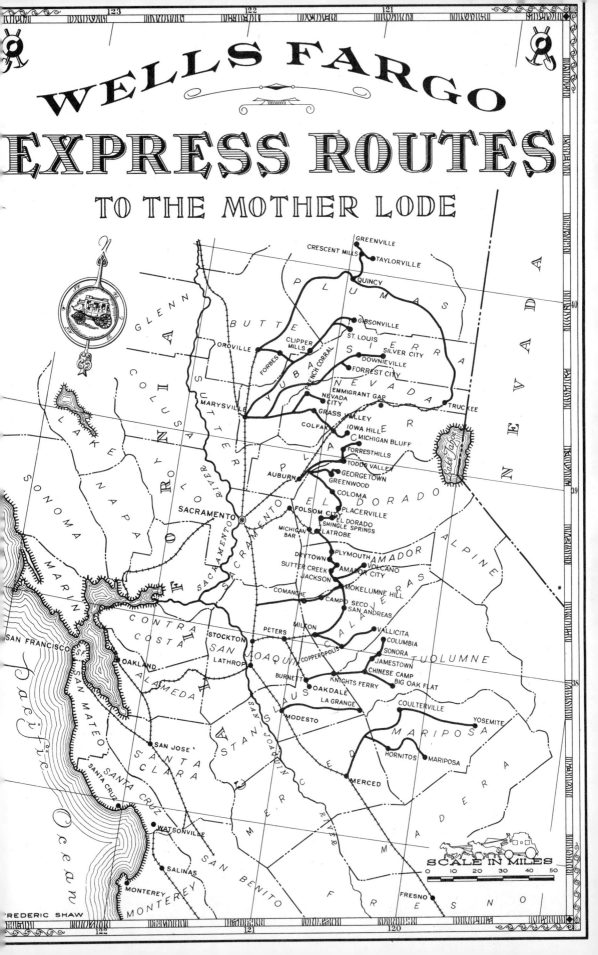

Exploits of some of the more engaging of the road agents who justified the salary of James B. Hume, chief of Wells Fargo detectives, will be found elsewhere in this narrative.

By the early sixties Wells Fargo was once again making headlines by the handling of perishable foodstuffs, not oysters this time for the nabobs of upstate New York, but fresh butter from Vermont for the well-heeled populace of San Francisco and for the clamorous miners of the Mother Lode. The butter was brought in merchantmen to the Isthmus, transshipped there to the Pacific side of Panama and rushed north in the steamers of the Pacific Mail Co. In a single shipment in 1861 Wells Fargo brought in 713 firkins of Vermont butter and San Francisco merchants made a point of advertising that their butter arrived by the express company. Some of the butter even reached the foothills of the Sierra and eventually as far as Carson Valley and Virginia City. The shipment over such distances at this remote date of highly perishable merchandise may come as a surprise to moderns who like to imagine that the expeditious shipment of foodstuffs is a strictly twentieth-century achievement. They may well ponder on the thought of butter from Montpelier traveling in coaches from Concord into the desolate Washoe.

Wells Fargo was agreeable to even more unusual shipments and when the city fathers of Sacramento purchased a fine new pumper from a fire-engine manufacturer in Baltimore, Wells Fargo drove it noisily across the Isthmus and delivered it on time.

Elsewhere in the Mother Lode hills, but nowhere as picturesquely preserved as at Columbia, there are vestigial traces to show how stellar was the role of Wells Fargo in California's mining years. At Mokelumne Hill, where mining properties were so rich in yield that the individual miner's claim was limited to sixteen square feet of ground, the three-story structure built by a native architect for Adams & Co., and which, following the pattern of its more celebrated prototype in Montgomery Street, was taken over by Wells Fargo after the great express panic, still stands. As the stoutest edifice in the neighborhood it harbored also several fraternal lodges and its façade bears a lantern with a swivel shade of glass whose four sides are engrossed with the emblems cf the four orders who used its meeting hall. On lodge night the insigne of the order whose session was about to be called was turned so as to be visible from the hill above. Next door was a celebrated tavern where the jack-booted miners sang:

> We're going to get drunk, by gum, by gum,
> In Shorty's Saloon tonight
> We'll guzzle our ale before it's stale
> And dance until broad daylight.

And they did, too.

The Wells Fargo Building still shows clues to its first occupant, and on one of the heavy stone courses of the second floor may be traced the carved letters "—AMS & CO." chiseled by a forgotten hand in the years when Adams was still in the running.

At Folsom the lettered legend of Wells Fargo is still discernible over the façade of a soft-drink bottling works, a mute and ironic commentary on changing times, and at one time the premises next door housed a campaign committee for a now almost forgotten chimera of unsound minds called the Townsend Plan. It is amusing if not profitable to speculate on what the

founding fathers of Wells Fargo would have thought of a plan for the state subsidy and support of all mendicants over the age of sixty. Parallel to the state highway into Folsom runs the pastoral right of way of the Sacramento Valley RR, now a branch of the Southern Pacific, where Wells Fargo first rode the cars. Over its grass-grown fills and gentle grades the enlightened fancy may still hear the hushed panting of the little wood-burning locomotives, *Nevada* and *Sacramento,* as they rolled their freight and sleepy passengers into the California dawn.

In many and many a township, however, the tangible traces of Wells Fargo have vanished, leaving the memory of their going in custody of the ancients who haunt the plaza and whose walking sticks tap their way uncertainly down the dusty lanes of yesterday.

"Right over there it was, the Wells Fargo office," they will tell whoever will pause to hear them. "I saw the gold dust carried out of there in fire pails. And right next door was the Howling Wilderness Saloon. If you'd like to wet your whistle now I'd be glad. . . ."

WELLS FARGO BANK

## WELLS FARGO IN THE MOTHER LODE

In the early fifties Wells Fargo shared the substantial stone structure of the Bear River Hotel, Applegate, on the heavily trafficked road between Auburn and Colfax.

The ancients are in the plaza of all self-respecting hill towns in California, their beards and Mormon hats a catch-me for the photographic tourists who ride the old wagon roads in cushioned ease on rubber tires. Of course the ancients never saw the gold in buckets, but there were ancients before them who had, and their impossible recollections are founded on legitimate fact.

Here and there the Boot Hill graveyards of California and Nevada bear on their headstones the warning legend: "Wells Fargo Never Forgets," but the passive is as valid as the active. Wells Fargo is never forgotten.

# CHAPTER IV

## Riding Pony

THE evolution, inaugural and brief lifespan of the fast overland mail service by mounted courier between Missouri and California which was known as the Pony Express and which has ever since laid hold on the imagination of the American people was successful only in an oblique manner. Its major purpose never was the fast transport of news dispatches and urgent mails between its terminals so much as the demonstration that the Central Overland Route to California was the most practicable, available means of communication and, eventually, the proper location of the Pacific Railroad. But these broad generalities could only be demonstrated to the public mind through some agency with highly dramatic overtones, and these the Pony Express, in a time and generation as yet entirely innocent of rapid continental communications, supplied in Sunday-feature abundance.

Wells Fargo became proprietor of the Pony Express only in the last few months of its highly expensive operations, but the galloping pony of the fast mail will be forever one of the most theatrical properties in the saga of Wells Fargo, one with the Mother Lode treasure shipments, the far-flung agencies of Washoe and White Pine and the shotgun messengers riding perilously out of Tombstone, Deadwood and Bodie.

The precise corporate history and the background agencies that brought into being for their brief riding the relays of the Pony Express are a nightmare of involutions which make the history of expressing a threat to the sanity of the amateur and a baffling farrago even for the historically informed.

The venture had its birth as an idea in the mind of California's Senator William M. Gwin when, back in 1854, he traveled on horseback from San Francisco to the Missouri over the Central Overland Route with B. F. Ficklen, then general superintendent of the monster freighting firm of Russell, Majors & Waddell. When, in the following year, Gwin submitted the proposed establishment of a fast mail service via this itinerary to Congress, it aroused scant enthusiasm; but when gold was discovered in Colorado in 1858 and there became apparent the need for some sort of mail service to the Rocky Mountain regions as well as to California the cause of the Central Overland route was materially strengthened.

Early in 1860, Russell, Majors & Waddell chartered a new company called the Central Overland California & Pikes Peak Express to operate a freight

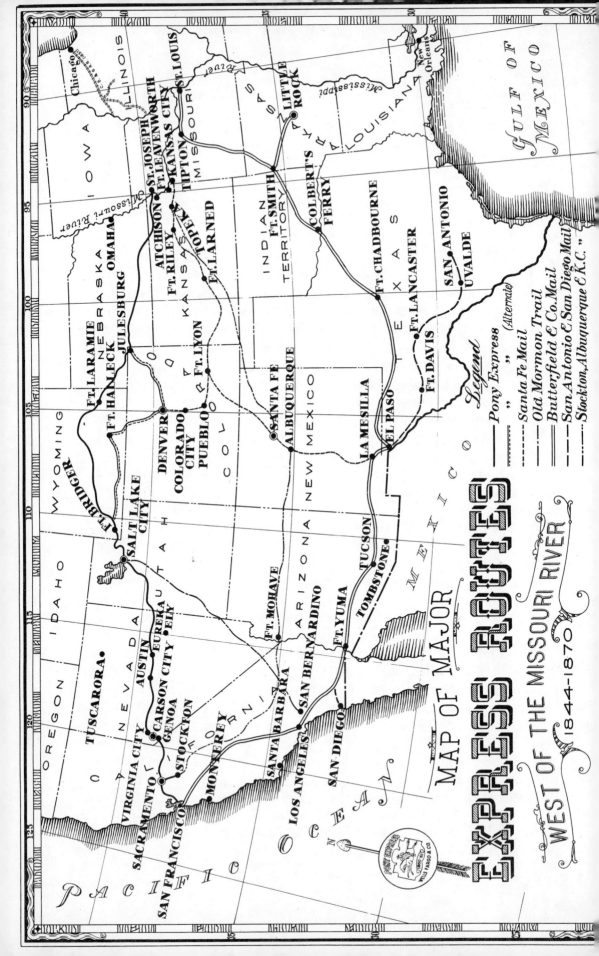

service and weekly overland mail delivery to California to be known as the Pony Express. The new firm absorbed the already functioning Hockaday & Liggett firm which for some months had been operating in the Rockies, and the stage was set for the emergence of the Pony Express. Russell, Majors & Waddell had already grown rich through the agency of ox trains supplying the army of Albert Sydney Johnston in Utah, and its management was quite agreeable to ponying up, literally, a cool million dollars to underwrite a transcontinental letter service starting at St. Joseph, then the most western of all railheads and the terminus of the Hannibal & St. Joseph RR, now part of the vastly embracing Burlington.

The real reason why Russell, Majors & Waddell was willing to risk such a vast sum of money and go to the trouble of inaugurating what was obviously from the first a losing proposition in fast mail transport was the hope, once the Central Overland was demonstrated to be the most advantageous route, of taking away from the Butterfield Overland Mail Co., then operating over the southern or oxbow route, the contract for the government mails. Possibly it also foresaw that the impending War between the States might sufficiently dislocate the affairs of Butterfield, operating as he did through secessionist territory, to make even easier the acquisition of his business by a concern already spanning a safer and more expeditious route.

From St. Joseph west the entrepreneurs purposed to supply mounted messengers riding in relays varying from fifty to 100 miles in length, equipped with fresh mounts every fifteen or twenty miles, and protected by armed stockades in hostile Indian territory; to begin with the schedule called for one trip a week in each direction. Eighty bold and trusty riders and 400-odd swift mustangs in conjunction with sail and steamer were to speed the mail between New York and San Francisco in the scarcely credible time of nine days if the telegraph was involved, in thirteen days if a written message was conveyed the entire distance. The Alta Telegraph was then in fairly reliable operation between San Francisco and Carson City (Telegraph Street in the Nevada capital commemorates it to this day) and between St. Jo and New York the railroads handled the mail.

The take-off of the first pony from St. Jo on April 3, 1860, and its antecedent excitement were national news. The take-off in the other direction was local news only because, until the horse and rider carrying it came through, there was no means of communicating its details to the East.

The Hannibal & St. Joseph RR was, in the nature of its kind, a cocky little pike of unballasted rails and engines, which, so far as their tractive force was concerned, were beautifully painted and stunningly brassbound teakettles. Thirty miles an hour was an alarming speed for those aboard its trains although the gentle whooshing of exhausts floating from its immense wood-burner stacks would seem like a tranquil pastoral melody compared to the thunder of today's locomotives. The terror of passengers and crew alike may be imagined on a run across the entire state of Missouri at an average speed of fifty miles an hour — almost a mile a minute!

For this splendid occasion the railroad's superintendent had selected his fastest motive power, a sleek Taunton-built eight-wheeler appropriately named *Missouri*. Coupled to its drawbar was one of the first of all mail cars and into its confines crowded the operating executives of the ambitious little road. They intended to share the risk of the crew and, not entirely innocent, they intended to share in the publicity and hurrah. They wore their best top hats and frock coats and if they were going to glory in the ditch or off a trestle they were going to be suitably dressed for it. Henry Kip, general superintendent of the United States Express, who had come out from Buffalo for the occasion, was especially notable for a fine white beaver and blue coat with gold buttons.

Operating timetables of the little Hannibal & St. Joseph RR of that remote period are before the authors as they prepare this chapter. Westbound passage over its 206 miles ordinarily consumed something in excess of fifteen hours, making all stops, so that when the *Pony Express Special* flashed from terminal to terminal in four hours flat, it is safe to suppose that along the line the citizenry to a man were lining the split-rail fences and cheering it through Palmyra, Bevier, Macon City, Laclede, Chillicothe and Utica.

All the switches had been spiked, fuel piles along the line were manned with picked crews who were to load the tender with fat pine in record time, and crossings were guarded by ancients armed with red flags to safeguard its passing. But the mails from the East were late and Engineer Addison Clark, who had worked on the Boston and Maine under that prince of speed, Superintendent Charlie Minot of the Western Division, had to open his throttle wider than discretion would have dictated. The little train fairly flew; its wake was illustrated with dead poultry which hadn't been fast enough and the brass hats in the mail car looked out at the flying landscape with mingled horror and fascination.

During all this commotion down the line, a slight contretemps was being remarked by observers in front of the Pikes Peak Stables in St. Jo. "A fine bay mare," in the language of the local newspaper, was being led up and down in readiness for the arrival of the mail, but at length her groom was compelled to take her inside and lock her in a box stall. The assembled spectators were pulling hairs out of her mane and tail with an eye to souvenirs and the proud steed was beginning to assume the appearance of a half-plucked chicken. Also it made her understandably irritable.

Pandemonium, it is reported, reigned in St. Joseph when cannon on the outskirts of town boomed with news of the train's approach across the countryside. The mail was already sorted and ready for delivery to the local postmaster who locked it into the three lock compartments of the rider's *mochila* and the first Pony Express galloped off from the Pikes Peak Stables and was quickly lost in the gathering dusk of the mysterious West. The *mochila* was a special type of saddlebag indigenous to the Pony Express. It had four almost watertight pockets, two on each side and fitted over the actual saddle so that it was held in place by the saddle horn and the weight

SOUTHERN PACIFIC RR

## IT'S STILL A WELLS FARGO TOWN

When the technical director of Paramount's film *Wells Fargo* was confronted with the necessity for recreating the scene at Tipton, Missouri, railhead of the West in the fifties, he sought authentic express-company atmosphere in the files and came up with a photograph taken at Cisco, California, in the sixties. Cisco came to live again as Tipton with a more suitable background than that of the Sierra and with a diamond stack on the engine instead of a "Dolly Varden." The similarity is still notable.

PARAMOUNT PICTURES

of the rider. It was a matter of seconds to remove it from one saddle and adjust it to another, and expert riders could do it with their horses on a run. Three of the *mochila's* cantinas were locked throughout the trip and carried the transcontinental mail, while the fourth carried the local post and the stationmaster at each stop had a key for it. Twenty pounds was the limit of the pay load and the rate was $5 per half ounce, but after Wells Fargo took over the Pony Express the rate was reduced to two dollars.

MADE FOR MAIL

This replica of a Pony Express rider's saddle and *mochilas* was made for Wells Fargo in recent years by the Wyeth Co. in St. Joe, original makers of all Wells Fargo's saddles during the fifties and sixties.

WELLS FARGO BANK

Great, too, was the excitement at the other end of the run when on the same day the first rider set out from San Francisco on the 1,966-mile run, the first stage of which was accomplished aboard the *Antelope* as far as Sacramento.

The arrival of the first pony at the western terminus of the run was the occasion of almost as much amiable turmoil as had been the departure of the original courier from the Pikes Peak Stables in St. Jo ten days before. The St. Jo rider [*] had made his connection with the special of the Hannibal Railroad at dusk on the 3rd of April. His relay arrived at Salt Lake City at about the same time of day on the 9th and the mail streaked into Carson City by midafternoon on the 12th. There wasn't any time for jollification at the Ormsby House if the sweaty and worn *mochila* was to be in San Francisco in ten days.

Warren Upson, whose father was a person of consequence as editor of the *Sacramento Union*, and who himself was a celebrated rider, firearms expert and trailsman in the Sierra, was going up Telegraph Street at a handy

[*] The records of the event were not kept with the scrupulous accuracy which could be exercised by the Associated Press today so that, depending upon source, the historian has a choice of no fewer that five riders: Johnny Frey, Alex Carlisle, Henry Wallace, Henry Richardson or Al Carlyle as having ridden the first pony west from St. Joseph.

WELLS FARGO BANK

## THEY RODE INTO LEGEND

Both literally and metaphorically these four period-design dandies rode into history as messengers for the Pony Express. Of the four shown in this 1860 photograph only two are today identifiable: Stephen Rowland on the extreme left and Harry Roff on the extreme right. Frock coat with whiskers and the handsome youth with jack boots are not known. There is some dispute as to whether or not Roff carried the first Pony mail out of San Francisco on the afternoon of April 3, 1860. Newspaper accounts credit another rider; many historians for reasons to themselves valid credit Roff, who later became Wells Fargo agent in Virginia City. This rare picture of the even then vanishing Western frontier came from the files of the Home Insurance Co. which Roff served for many years in capacity of general manager in San Francisco.

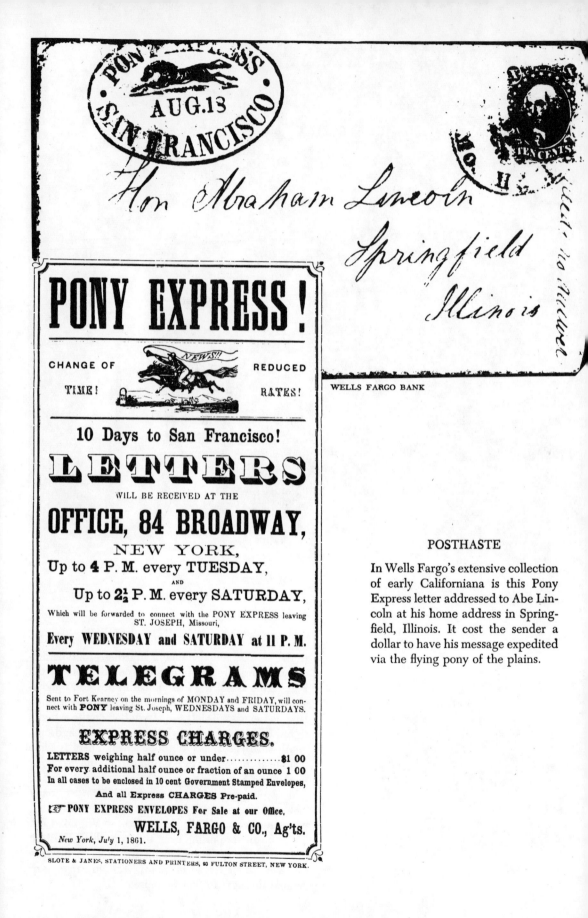

Hon Abraham Lincoln
Springfield
Illinois

WELLS FARGO BANK

## PONY EXPRESS !

CHANGE OF **TIME!**     REDUCED **RATES!**

### 10 Days to San Francisco!

# LETTERS

WILL BE RECEIVED AT THE

## OFFICE, 84 BROADWAY,

NEW YORK,

Up to **4** P. M. every TUESDAY,

AND

Up to **2½** P. M. every SATURDAY,

Which will be forwarded to connect with the PONY EXPRESS leaving ST. JOSEPH, Missouri,

**Every WEDNESDAY and SATURDAY at 11 P. M.**

# TELEGRAMS

Sent to Fort Kearney on the mornings of MONDAY and FRIDAY, will connect with **PONY** leaving St. Joseph, WEDNESDAYS and SATURDAYS.

## EXPRESS CHARGES.

LETTERS weighing half ounce or under..............$1 00
For every additional half ounce or fraction of an ounce 1 00
In all cases to be enclosed in 10 cent Government Stamped Envelopes,

**And all Express CHARGES Pre-paid.**

☞ PONY EXPRESS ENVELOPES For Sale at our Office.

### WELLS, FARGO & CO., Ag'ts.

*New York, July 1, 1861.*

SLOTE & JANES, STATIONERS AND PRINTERS, 93 FULTON STREET, NEW YORK.

## POSTHASTE

In Wells Fargo's extensive collection of early Californiana is this Pony Express letter addressed to Abe Lincoln at his home address in Springfield, Illinois. It cost the sender a dollar to have his message expedited via the flying pony of the plains.

gallop before his winded opposite number had been bought his first drink by the patriots of Carson, but the going was rough. There was a great deal of snow at the summit of King's Canyon, and eastbound wagon trains, part of the ever-crescent rush to the Washoe, impeded his progress. Bad-tempered freighters and profane mule skinners cared nothing for the mails from the Missouri with Gold Hill and the new Golconda of C Street just beyond the horizon, and a score of times Upson had to turn his mount off the road into the deep drifts. Today motorists on the granite-hewn superhighway between Tahoe and Strawberry can look over the edge and see how far horse and rider would have dropped in the event of a misjudged step.

At Sportsman's Hall Upson was relieved by Bill Hamilton and the word was already preceding him via the grapevine of magnetic telegraph. There was a reception committee out with bunting, bottles and the worst oratorical intentions by the Hanging Tree at Placerville and, due to the enthusiastic spectators, the change of horses was effected in front of the solidly built Pony Express Office with difficulty. Mayor Swan finally got Hamilton out of town without the loss of more than a few minutes.

From Placerville word had been sent ahead by wire, and the steamer was held at its pier in Sacramento. A slim wisp of steam emerged from its valve escape to show that pressure was being maintained, and every now and then the engineer turned her paddles with a slow gesture of the walking beam just to keep things limbered up for a quick getaway. The *Antelope* had figured in a great deal of California history but this was its rendezvous with national destinies.

There is one detail connected with the progress of the pony across the California countryside not entirely understandable at this late date. The superintendent of the Sacramento Valley RR, by then a reliable and established carrier, offered a specially chartered train to take the mails and their messenger from Folsom to Sacramento in record time, but the suggestion was declined with thanks by the agents of the Pony Express. Why? The little Hannibal & St. Joseph had performed valiantly in the East. Why should not the railroad contribute to speed in the West? Or did the Pony Express already feel the hot breath of steam and the "new mechanic birth" on its neck even before the competition of the Overland Telegraph, and was it resentful?

Sacramento, like Placerville but on a grander scale, was prepared with bunting and bottles. Bells pealed, cannon muttered and rumbled across the river surface, fire companies assembled in full departmental regalia on the levee and the *Union,* with Papa Upson in proud editorial mood, had an extra on the street with the latest news from St. Louis in a couple of hours.

The welcome of the *Antelope* in San Francisco was stirring but "a bit more decorous" according to Harlow, possibly because the steamer didn't dock until near midnight when a reasonable portion of the populace had retired even though the event had been announced in all theaters and the California Band had made night noisy since eight o'clock, marching up and down, dressed in full regalia, in front of the better saloons.

There was an impromptu parade, of the sort in which San Francisco takes pride and pleasure even today. Engine Companies No. 2, 5 and 6, Ladder Company No. 2, the California Band and the pony followed by a cheering crowd made up the procession. There were brief speeches, after which, according to the *Bulletin* the pony and its rider both looked sleepy; the twenty-five letters addressed to San Francisco were distributed from the steps of the Alta Telegraph Company in Montgomery Street and everybody went home to bed.

Before its last run the Pony Express was to bring to California Abraham Lincoln's inaugural address in seven days and seventeen hours; it carried the news of Sumter to Sacramento in eight days and fourteen hours and the details of Antietam came across the Sierra so far ahead of the working schedule that it earned the last rider a bonus of $300. History doesn't record whether or not he divided the money with the previous riders who had also hastened the *mochila* on its way across desert and mountain. Harpers Ferry, the President's call for volunteers and the first great Federal disaster at Bull Run were also to come West via the flying pony.

The Pony Express, despite the almost fabulous publicity it was accruing to itself and its manifest justification of its proprietors in their advocacy of the Central Overland Route, was also costing Russell, Majors & Waddell so much to maintain that by the end of the year 1860 their losses on its operation were reported to have been close to $1,000,000. Indian troubles in Oregon had occasioned the withdrawal of the military from the protection of the Pony Express and for several weeks during midsummer the service had been interrupted with increased loss to its proprietors.

Butterfield & Co., in which Wells Fargo by now owned a controlling interest, was still carrying the government mails at the turn of the year, but its service was being interrupted by Southern sympathizers and in February of 1861 its operations over the oxbow route were ordered discontinued and its equipment and resources moved north to the Central Overland. By the terms decreed by the Post Office under the new set up, the C O C & P P operated the Pony Express and a daily mail by stage from the Missouri to Salt Lake, while the Butterfield outfit, now in fact owned by Wells Fargo, operated the lines west of Salt Lake in conjunction with its Pioneer Stages from Virginia City to California.

Even as these complicated financial and operational maneuvers were being effected, the doom of the Pony Express was near. Late in the spring construction was started on the overland telegraph and the distance over which urgent dispatches were carried by the pony constantly decreased as the two ends of the telegraph system approached each other across the plains.

On April 15, 1861, Wells Fargo indirectly indicated that the management of Pony Express activities had passed into its hands by the insertion of an advertisement in the *Alta* announcing a new schedule of mail rates. Thereafter the mail was carried "From St. Joseph to Placerville Per Pony Express"

## THE PONY RIDES INTO HISTORY

When the river steamer *Antelope* from Sacramento docked late in the evening, April 14, 1860, San Francisco inaugurated what was perhaps the most exciting of all celebrations in the history of a community where they have been frequent and of impressive dimensions. The arrival of the first mail from St. Joseph by Pony Express is here shown passing the well-known corner of California and Montgomery Streets with Wells Fargo for a background and demonstrations of triumph on every hand. The pony is ridden by Bill Hamilton; ahead is Engine Company No. 2; somewhere in her carriage, perhaps shown following in the line of march, is the wife of John C. Frémont, eccentric agitator of California's earliest times. There were speeches and toasts and huzzahs and the California Band played *See the Conquering Hero Comes*. It was all very splendid and, after the fourteen letters addressed to San Francisco had been distributed from the steps of the Alta Telegraph Company, the town went to bed secure in the knowledge that a new day of super-speed was at hand. The East was only thirteen days by letter post from Montgomery Street.

85

in Wells Fargo's own privately franked envelopes and Wells Fargo was in actual fact owner and proprietor of the Pony Express for the last few months of its operations.

A few weeks later Wells Fargo inaugurated a short new link in the chain with a Pony Express service in its own name between Sacramento and San Francisco. Probably it was but a slight improvement over service aboard the steamers, but it seemed desirable from the point of prestige.

Up to the very end the volume of mail via the Pony Express continued to increase, and as late as the last week in August 1861 more than 150 letters were being received in San Francisco where but twenty-five had arrived in the first *mochila*. But by September 24th the pony was traveling only 500 miles between the ends of the telegraph as they approached each other, and a month later the electric circuits met and the Pony Express came to an end.

But if its treasury, almost from the beginning, was poor in profits, the annals of the Pony Express were rich in atmosphere and no chapter in its record was more robust than that of Julesburg, Nebraska. Here the Pikes Peak trail diverged from the through Overland and Oregon routes, and Julesburg, for the first decade or so if its existence, was rough and tough even by the standards of the time. Along in 1868, when the Central Pacific came through, Julesburg was the stamping ground of such numbers of undesirables that General Jack Casement, in charge of construction, hanged a few of the more determined scoundrels and ordered the rest out of town. The story has it that Julesburg's lower elements loaded themselves and their possessions, including residences, on flatcars and moved along with the end of track to Cheyenne, 140 miles up the line. The long freight train of flat-cars loaded to capacity with portable bagnios, roulette wheels, mobile saloons and frame honky-tonkys was received with glad acclaim as it rolled into Cheyenne yards, and the conductor, with a flourish, leaped down from among the cindery madams and other merchants of merriment and announced with a flourish: "Gents, here's Julesburg!"

That was some years later, and when the Pony Express was pausing there, briefly, Julesburg was even less sedate. Its founder and "bourgeois," as the headman in such frontier communities was then known, was old Jules Reni, a Canuck of uncertain disposition but undoubted capacity for strong waters. Arthur Chapman reports that when he was unable to absorb any more whisky by the normal processes devised by a benevolent Deity, Jules would bake himself a batch of "whisky bread" the constituent parts of which were mixed into dough with ardent spirits instead of the more conventional milk or water. Old Jules was a character, also, and in addition to his other practices, he stole the livestock of Russell, Majors & Waddell, and, locally, there was no one tough enough to say him nay.

Russell, Majors & Waddell set about finding the meanest man in Nebraska for the office of division agent at Julesburg and as likely as any seemed a Captain Joseph Slade, a veteran of the Mexican War and an expert with weapons of precision. Old Jules, apprised in advance of his advent, waited behind a convenient shelter — it happened to be the swinging doors of the Rawhide Rattler Saloon — emptied two barrels of a shotgun into the captain when he showed up for duty and then took to the sagebrush to await news of his enemy's demise. This should have been forthcoming on schedule except that Slade was even tougher than advertised. He went down to St. Louis for the week end and had the slugs pulled out of his internal economy by experts in such matters. Soon he was back with the casual announcement that, alive or dead, he was about to cut off Old Jules' ears as a lesson in manners. Slade made safari into the sagebrush and a few days later dragged Old Jules into town with a Winchester slug in one leg and tied him to a post in a prominent part of town. He then held practice with Old Jules as target and it was some hours before he tired of the sport and lodged a lethal ball in a vital part. True to his word, he removed Old Jules' ears and thereafter carried them in his jacket pocket as souvenirs.

Slade later came to a bad end himself up in the Tobacco Root Mountain region where he had taken to wantonly shooting up saloons and occasionally their inmates just because he liked to hear the guns go flash and bang. He did a good job, however, on the Pony Express' meanest division, upon one occasion shooting it out with four cattle rustlers and accounting for them all with no more than four cartridges, and there was a notably increased respect for company property wherever he was on duty.

The affair of Slade of Julesburg is one of the many powder burnings of resounding proportions involving Wells Fargo employees in line of duty or at least under closely adjacent circumstances. So was the great battle at the O. K. Corral in Tombstone which was to lend a blazing immortality to the Earp brothers, Wyatt and Virgil, and Doc Holliday. A third was the shooting at Rock Creek, Nebraska, which was to bring his first fame as a gun fighter to James Butler Hickok, later to become known as Wild Bill. Nobody seems to know, and the years have not disclosed, why Wild Bill Hickok found himself constrained to kill David McCanles and two other men at the Pony Express Station at Rock Creek. The records of the time are fragmentary and later chroniclers were to exaggerate the matter out of all conscience.

The stock tender for Wells Fargo at Rock Creek in 1861 was Bill Hickok. The owner of the ranch at Rock Creek was Dave McCanles, an emigrant from North Carolina who had built a little cabin and stable of logs in the Nebraska prairie and had subsequently leased it to the Central Overland Company as a stage post and Pony Express Station. On the morning of July 12th in the year in question there arose a difference of opinion in some matter which seemed important at the time, and when the black powder smoke had blown downwind Dave McCanles was very dead as were his two friends, James Woods and a rancher named Gordon, and Wild Bill Hickok was well on his way to fame in the letters of the West as well as in his own proper person.

## WELLS FARGO RIDES THE SOUTHERN OVERLAND

Antecedent to the organization of the Pony Express was the service of public necessity by John Butterfield's Overland Mail stages which was organized in 1857 to handle government mails on the so-called Ox-Bow Route between the Mississippi and San Francisco. Service was twice a week in each direction, the distance covered on the long swing through Texas, Arizona and southern California was 2,650 miles and the first trip with Butterfield himself on the westbound stage was accomplished in twenty-four days. It was believed at the time that the southern route followed by Butterfield's line would eventually be the survey for the Pacific Railway. From the beginning Wells Fargo forwarded its more urgent mail and express matter in the Butterfield stages and by the time the southern route was abandoned at the start of the Civil War Wells Fargo had bought heavily into the property. Part of the distance was covered in conventional Concord coaches while other stretches and branches were served by "celerity wagons" (above), a lighter type of express vehicle with canvas top. Below, a Butterfield stage is escorted by United States cavalry during prewar times of unsettlement along the route.

## 1864.

# OVERLAND STAGE LINE

*Carrying the Great Through Mails*
*Between the Atlantic and the Pacific States.*

**BEN HOLLADAY,**
*Proprietor.*

DAILY COACHES to and from ATCHISON, OMAHA, and NEBRASKA CITY via DENVER CITY; connecting at Denver with its Daily Line of Coaches for CENTRAL CITY, GREGORY and CLEAR-CREEK Mining Districts; also, with Tri-weekly coaches, for TAOS, SANTA FE, and other principal points in NEW MEXICO.

At SALT LAKE CITY, connecting with its TRI-WEEKLY LINE of Coaches for VIRGINIA CITY and HELENA;—BOISE CITY, WALLA WALLA, DALLES and PORTLAND, Oregon;— also connecting with the daily coaches of The Overland Mail Company, for AUSTIN, VIRGINIA CITY, Nev., SACRAMENTO, and SAN-FRANCISCO, CALA.

DAVID STREET
*(General Agent.)*

PAUL COBURN
*(Assistant Superint'dt.)*

NAT. STEIN
*(Agent at Virginia City.)*

JO. S. ROBERSON
*(Agent at Great Salt Lake City.)*

## THE OLD BEARDED KING OF HURRY

This hand-lettered poster from the Californiana collection of the historian Boutwell Dunlap gives some idea of the vast territory covered by the staging empire of Ben Holladay when that transportation enterprise was at its height. The photograph shows Holladay himself when he was about forty and has been pronounced by Wells Drury as the best picture of him he had ever seen. Grouped around him are his principal agents, David Street, general superintendent, Paul Coburn, assistant superintendent, Nat Stein, agent at Virginia City, and J. S. Robertson, agent at Salt Lake City. The lower photograph shows the Overland Stage Line's office at Salt Lake with a coach in front of it. This was the most important transfer point in the Holladay system. At their greatest extent Holladay's stage routes west of the Mississippi covered more than 2,700 miles.

The Wells Fargo stock tender was immediately acquitted by local authorities and it is presumed that there was scarcely an interruption in the servicing of the daily stages, east and west, and the twice-a-week passage of the Pony Express. But Wild Bill was en route to fictional immortality.

A few years later, while he was peace officer at the seething frontier town of Abilene, Kansas, where the Chisholm Trail ended at the stock-loading platforms of the Kansas Pacific RR, Hickok was to pick up a copy of *Harper's Magazine* and discover himself described as a "famous scout of the plains, William Hitchcock" who, single handed, had wiped out no fewer than ten members of "this McKandlas gang of desperadoes, horse thieves, murderers and regular cut-throats." Later in the dime novels this score was bettered, but it is safe to say that Hickok was surprised with even the modest ten ascribed to him in the pages of Editor Harper's presumably conservative family magazine.

There is one item of photographic evidence in the McCanles shooting: a daguerreotype in the California State Library showing Dave McCanles on horseback with a bottle in his hand in front of the Rock Creek Pony Express Station. No less an authority than Arthur Chapman says that the bottle contained whisky. The inference is tenable that, when the time arrived for McCanles to draw and defend himself, his hand and aim were palsied from a low way of life. No other available moral seems to attach to the affair at Rock Creek.

The saga of the Pony Express, though in many ways it was a fiasco and its lifespan was brief, has come to be one of the irreplaceable monuments to the old American West. It took hold on the fancy of its own time as the first real experiment in rapid communications; it demonstrated beyond question the general course of the Central Overland Route which was less than a decade later to become the location of the Pacific Railroad; it supplied the legend of the frontier with a theme that was more cohesive than the mere generalities of Indian fighting, exploring or prospecting for gold.

Probably the two most famous riders of the fleet-footed pony were Pony Bob Haslam and Buffalo Bill Cody, although there has been doubt in the case of Cody, as there has been throughout the entire tally of his achievements, as to where fact left off and imagination took over. He would have had to be no older than fourteen to have ridden pony for Wells Fargo.

As a sidelight, the *mochila* mail led to the printing of special editions on lightweight paper of Eastern newspapers comparable to the air-mail editions of a later generation. People also began writing letters on rice paper, a forerunner of air-mail sationery. They began to think in terms of fast communications between California and the East and newspapers were able to record events of national significance with a time lag that in its age was very brief indeed.

As with almost everything else in the West of its shining years, Wells Fargo was in on the Pony Express.

# CHAPTER V

## The Saga of C Street

THE great third movement of the symphony of Wells Fargo, played *allegro vivace,* is Virginia City, Nevada. This is the grand canto of the Eroica of the West, opening to the imperial thunder of drums on the eastern slopes of Mount Davidson and progressing into the fullest orchestration of a theme of wars and empires, the destinies of a hemispheric world. It is an unceasing movement of armed horsemen and coaches; the music of their riding and the thunder of their passage will echo forever in the legend. For in Virginia City there came to its fullest flower the most grandiose of all themes, the final opening of the illimitable West, the financing of an epic war, the justification of the American Union; and the players in its pageantry lived up to every florid implication, every heroic overtone of the script.

It was in Virginia City that the great tradition of staging reached its climax, both in the technique of its practice and the importance of its service. The last Pony Express brushed Virginia City with the wings of its going as the riders swept past the lower end of Gold Canyon, hastening on the business of kings with the destinies of empire in their sweaty and often blood-stained *mochilas*. The railroad, the most compelling and wonderful of all American dreams, came to Virginia City less than a decade after the last galloping pony had disappeared, and slowly but inevitably the stagecoach became a feeder service. Within a span of ten brief years, Virginia City was served by the three methods of overland travel which have laid the most powerful hold upon the imaginations of men of any age, and this circumstance alone and divorced from every other aspect of greatness would fix it forever in the firmament of mighty place names.

The year 1859 found Wells Fargo the supreme agency of express banking on the Pacific coast. Its 126 iron-shuttered and brick-vaulted offices and agencies with their ornately balanced gold scales and their Wells Fargo treasure boxes extended from the Fraser River to the Mexican border. The polished Henry rifles of their messengers represented everything that most remote communities knew of probity, security and law. In San Francisco the directors and executive heads of the firm were "warm men" in the Forsytean sense and in their fast horse rigs the silk-hatted magnates of the town might be observed streaking for the newly established resorts over-looking the Seal Rocks on Sunday mornings for substantial Sabbath break-fasts followed by long business conferences over illimitable quantities of the favored champagne of Mumm & Co. After 1863 Sunday breakfast at the Cliff House was to be a hallmark of San Francisco's financial and social respectability, and to provide a substantial gustatory basis for the champagne, Wells Fargo, following an earlier pattern in the matter of sea food, was supplying its own Lake Tahoe trout, packed in moss and ice and handled by a special service.

The urge for expansion dominated Wells Fargo and, with a patness not altogether conspicuous in its history, the Comstock provided an avenue for it.

It was in July of 1859 that a California rancher sent back for assay to Nevada City the samples of blue-black Nevada ore which were to be a turn-ing point in the history of the American West. It had been in the previous year that Old Pancake Comstock had browbeaten and swindled honest Pete O'Riley and Pat McLaughlin into sharing with him their discovery of gold-bearing ores near the head of Six Mile Canyon and only a little later that "Old Virginny," James Finney, had smashed a not irreplaceable bottle of booze while stumbling along the side of Mount Davidson and, with howls of alcoholic satisfaction, christened the wilderness landscape "Virginia Town."

It was only a matter of hours after the Grass Valley assay had shown the Comstock ores to run as high as $4,790 a ton in silver with a substantial lagniappe of gold that the reverse rush across the Sierra was on. Judge James Walsh of Grass Valley and his friend Joe Woodworth, the first to learn of the Mount Davidson bonanza, hardly had time to pack a pair of mules and set out for the new diggings before half the population of Nevada, Placer, El Dorado and Sierra Counties were on their heels bound for the Washoe. By the time they had reached Gold Canyon the rabble of prospectors had actually overflowed the Sierra passes and was in Carson Valley, half a day's stage behind them. Even the rush to the Frazer River had never been like this and it was only by the narrowest of margins that Judge Walsh and his partner were able to stake out claims and sites on the Comstock. Their closest pursuers arrived the same evening.

Until the first boom in the Comstock, Wells Fargo had been exclusively in the express-banking business and, although the vast majority of their ship-ments had been transported by stages, these stages had always been owned and operated by organizations other than Wells Fargo. Now, just in time to be in on the ground floor in Virginia City, Wells Fargo acquired a stage line in its own right extending straight over the Sierra from Sacramento to Washoe by way of Placerville. The route had been laid out and the line started by a pioneer stager named Jared Crandall, but he had become discouraged with its prospects and Louis McLane, general manager for Wells Fargo, had picked it up for the proverbial song. Nearest rival to the Pioneer Line, as Wells Fargo's fortunate acquisition was known, was the powerful California Stage Co. operating to the north through the pass behind Nevada City

## THE HIGHROAD OVER THE SIERRA

The classic stage run of the Old West, made famous by Hank Monk and a score of other drivers in the princely tradition of Jared Crandall, was the haul from Sacramento to Virginia City by way of Placerville, Lake Tahoe and Carson City. Travelers today can experience its breathless abysses and hairpin curves on the King's Canyon Grade out of Carson Valley almost as Horace Greeley knew them, save that in the sixties the entire distance across the Sierra was so heavy with traffic as to require being watered in summer over its every mile to lay the dust. Wells Fargo came into possession of the Pioneer Stage Co. on the eve of the Comstock's discovery and its early passengers numbered Mills, Sharon, George Hearst, Jim Fair and William M. Stewart. Below, a Pioneer Stage skirts Tahoe's Point of Rocks, now penetrated by a highway tunnel.

and Grass Valley. The Comstock seemed to inspire Wells Fargo to expand into fields of endeavor hitherto foreign to its experience, and a decade later the record discloses the express-banking-staging firm also involved in mines in Virginia City under the style of the Wells Fargo Mining Co.

Jared Crandall, once "the prince of stage drivers" who had been chosen by Governor Peter Burnett to take the tremendous intelligence of California's admission to the Union from San Francisco to San Jose, must have regretted selling out to Louis McLane!

Like almost everyone else, from future Senator George Hearst and future millionaire John Mackay to future manipulator William Sharon and future hobnobber with royalty Sandy Bowers, Wells Fargo arrived in the Comstock diggings with a whoop and a holler. The only member of the advance guard who was destined to be even closer to the ground-floor plan of Virginia City than Wells Fargo's first agent, Dave Ward, was Charley Sturm who located his Express Bar, one of the first on the slopes of Sun Mountain, in the cellar-age of the Wells Fargo Building. When Ward arrived on the scene in 1860 he had hung out the first Wells Fargo sign on the ridgepole of a tent directly across the corner of A and Sutton Streets from a similar tent of Penrod, Comstock & Co., codiscoverers of everything in sight. All of them forgathered in an identical tent of Sturm, pitched handily adjacent to both. They agreed that it was a shame a man had to drink under canvas which might leak without warning and dilute his drink. Ward promised Sturm quarters as soon as he should have one himself and Penrod, Comstock & Co. promised him their patronage which was practically a guarantee in itself of financial success.

Until Wells Fargo had a building of its own run up on the original site of Ward's tent, the managers of the Ophir, Mexican, and Gould and Curry had deposited their bullion with Lyman Jones, proprietor of a canvas hotel who maintained a strongbox under his bed, but when Wells Fargo's treasure vaults were in place, which was even before the last courses of brick had been laid in its ascending walls, they redeposited them with the community's first banker, and Wells Fargo was in business on the Comstock.

Also in the new building, the largest and finest in town, were located the offices of the Pioneer Stage Co. and the Overland Mail Co., and Sturm's slings and toddies passed across the bar with gratifying and ever-crescent acceleration. In the beginning there were three bullion shipments a week from the vaults by Pioneer Stage across the Sierra, but later, when the Comstock really got into its stride and Wells Fargo had a branch office just over the Divide in Gold Hill, the shipments were to become daily.

Still another feature of Wells Fargo's ever-expanding service between California and the Comstock was a schedule of fast freights the principal traffic of which was goods for the mines, both durable and perishable. Traveling with a speed somewhat abated from that of the express stages, but nevertheless one that was headlong compared to anything Washoe had known before, the freights moved in heavily constructed, canvas-roofed wagons drawn by six draft horses with consignments of tools and gunpowder,

## HANK MONK AND GREELEY PASSED THIS WAY

In the years when Strawberry Station (left above) was one of the most important staging posts on the Immigrant Route from Placerville to the Washoe, more than 120 tons of freight a day rolled through for the Comstock and the mines of Virginia City paid $1,500,000 annual toll charges on this road across the Sierra alone. Strawberry today (right above) has changed little in appearance save that

a modern luxury hotel occupies the spot where once the teamsters drank deep and slept on the floor of the coaching station of the sixties. Best known of all drivers on the run to change his horses at Strawberry was Wells Fargo's legendary Hank Monk who, by driving Horace Greeley over the hill in record time, became the central figure of an imperishable saga of staging. Monk (below), who drove many celebrities, was made famous by Mark Twain's account of Greeley's historic ride and was for a time the most famous of Comstock characters. When he died the Virgina City *Enterprise* remarked: "In the old days before the leathers under his coach were soaked with alcohol there was no better balanced head than his. . . . In his prime he could turn a six horse coach in a street with a team at a full run with every line apparently loose." The memory of Monk's driving and his brandy smashes still haunts the bars at Strawberry.

cables for the hoists, liquor for Virginia City's continuously expanding array of saloons, hotels and restaurants, household goods, groceries, dry goods and low-fare passengers wherever there was room.

But the come-on attraction in Wells Fargo's repertoire, which promoted the firm's fame to the ends of the earth and also contrived to gross $1,000,000 a year in passenger fares alone, was the Pioneer Stage Co. What the extra-fare transcontinental varnish trains like the *Twentieth Century Limited* and the *City of San Francisco* are to their railroads today, the twelve magnificent Concord-built thorough-braced stages of the Pioneer guided on split-second schedules by superlative drivers were to Wells Fargo.

The stage drivers of the Pioneer, from every contemporary account, were the ranking aristocracy of the Nevada scene in bonanza times. They took no nonsense from anyone, be it arrogant but honest and sagacious old Darius Ogden Mills, whose frown shook bank directors right down to their boots, or mannerless road agents who occasionally shot up the stages without first ascertaining if there were ladies on the passenger list. Their insignia of office were long dusters of immaculate white linen, white hats of the so-called "Mormon" shape with flat crowns and wide brims, or gleaming silk toppers and dude-yellow kid gloves that would have excited envy at Delmonico's. Added to the million dollars in passenger fares, Wells Fargo was in 1864 taking in something like $12,000,000 in freight charges over the Geiger Grade or over the old road through Six Mile Canyon. There were few flies on $13,000,000 in the middle sixties.

In gaining a foothold that was to amount to a monopoly of the express and banking as well as of the stage and freight business in Virginia City, Wells Fargo had gotten in on the ground floor of the greatest bonanza of recorded history and at a single stroke of enterprise became forever associated with the chapter of the Western saga that was destined to be most heavily adorned with romantic glamor.

Of another Western bonanza town of the approximate generation a Colorado poet wrote:

> For it's day all day in daytime
> And there is no night in Creede,

and this obtained in double measure in Virginia City.

"There were military companies," wrote Mark Twain in *Roughing It*, "fire companies, brass bands, banks, hotels, theaters, hurdy gurdy houses, wide open gambling palaces, political pow-wows, civic processions, street fights, murders, inquests, riots, a whisky mill every fifteen steps, a Board of Aldermen, a Mayor, a city Surveyor, a City Engineer, a Chief of the Fire Department with First, Second and Third Assistants, a Chief of Police, City Marshal, and a large police force, two boards of Mining Brokers, a dozen breweries and half a dozen jails and station houses in full operation, and some talk of building a church."

### THE GENTLE ZEPHYR OF WASHOE

Mark Twain deposed that once during a Washoe zephyr he saw a live and bray-
ing donkey carried away at an altitude of a hundred feet in the general direction
of the Sink of Carson with his owner following on foot and imploring him to come
down out of there. Once a Wells Fargo stage was actually blown over the edge
of the Geiger Grade by such a gust and early comers to the Comstock repeatedly
lost the roofs of their dwellings until they learned to secure them with stones at
the corners.

Not all of these identifying marks of civilization were available to Virginia
City when Wells Fargo first hung out its shingle and commenced business
transaction over the finely balanced gold scales on its front counter. There
was, for example, no newspaper, since the *Territorial Enterprise* did not move
up from Genoa, where it had been founded in 1858, to its office at the corner
of Sutton Avenue and A Street until the next year. To compensate for this
deficiency, dispatches from Sacramento over the grapevine telegraph, so-
called from the propensity of its wires to roll up into hopeless snares when
they became disengaged from the trees on which they were carried, were
dutifully posted every afternoon on a bulletin board on the Wells Fargo
Building, and the conveyance of news was added to the express-banking
business. This was all very well for a time; but the bulletins were sketchy
at best considering the magnitude of political events in the East and Wells
Fargo, for all its functions, was not an intelligence service. Dave Ward was

understandably relieved when Joe Goodman's Washington press came up Gold Canyon and the compositors began setting agate and brevier along with Rollin Daggett's six-point editorials.

Very little went on around Washoe in these well-heeled times that Wells Fargo didn't have a finger in, and special assignments were, in reality, only remarkable for their frequency. One of these was a special coach and armed messenger to transport Sandy Bowers and Eilley Orrum over the Sierra and into San Francisco on their way to call on Queen Victoria. Bowers, who was taking $10,000 a month out of the innards of Sun Mountain, and Eilley had risen from the simple life of the early days when Sandy's nether garments were laundered by the Washoe Seeress, and now, in her handsome mansion by the margin of Washoe Lake, she was not only a seeress but, indeed, a queen!

And what could be more normal in the life of a queen than to drop by for a friendly call and perhaps a cup of tea with the Queen at Windsor? Sandy had seen Chief Winnemucca and Governor Nye and tolerantly allowed that there might be characters almost as interesting in Europe. So off they went, after having taken over the entire resources of the International Hotel for an evening and reduced the community to a happy shambles with champagne and terrapin. They drew a quarter of a million dollars from Wells Fargo's vaults in Virginia City and filled a heavy oak chest with bars of gold bullion to give away as souvenirs when they had been bowed in by the better major-domos of England and the Continent. This, as it turned out, wasn't enough, and soon the bank was honoring additional drafts for fantastic sums to cover their purchases in the Rue de la Paix and Bond Street.

When it was time to go, a coach, complete with messenger as specified, drove up to the Bowers Mansion. A photographer was on hand to record the great occasion even as it would today be made imperishable through the agency of news photographers and their speed guns. The shotgun messenger accompanied them to the massive doors of Shreve & Co. in San Francisco where the bullion was converted forthwith into a fine tea service which Eilley purposed to present to the Queen on her throne six thousand miles away.

Unhappily Her Majesty's court chamberlain remained unimpressed by the wealth of Washoe and even Charles Francis Adams, recently appointed Ambassador to the Court of St. James's, seemed not to be available in this emergency. Eilley, however, secured cuttings from the vines of Westminster Abbey for her mansion and she and Sandy went on to Paris where history records that in a single day they spent $20,000 in the shops of the Place Vendôme and achieved a local fame as the prize shoppers of the 1861 winter season.

Aside from her ride with Sandy Bowers and the shotgun messenger across the Sierra upon the occasion of her travels abroad, the Washoe Seeress had but infrequent contact with Wells Fargo, an organization concerned essentially with tangibles and therefore removed from the unworldly realms inhabited by the spirits of Eilley Orrum. In later years, when the glory had departed from the Bowers Mansion and Eilley was earning an occasional fee by inspecting the future for selected clients, she evaluated some property adjacent to the Wells Fargo Mine along the extreme edges of the Comstock.

Asked, quite incidentally, about this property, the old lady went into a momentary trance and came up with the opinion: "In Wells Fargo the hardest sort of rock will be encountered, not in the main shaft, but in one of the drifts. Heavier machinery will be required for the development of the mine." Wells Fargo evidently felt that the heavier machinery was unjustified for the development of its only recorded venture into the mining of precious metals and the property was soon afterward allowed to lapse.

What tongue, be it ever so eloquent or so inspired with the potent sour mash of Bourbon County or the rich distillates of Cognac and Charente, shall tell of the saloons of Virginia City in the bright noontide of its youth, of the cheerful workingmen's taverns, of the all-night deadfalls, the gilded and floriated wonders of the splendid bars of C Street? The forests of Honduras and San Domingo were ravished for the rich mahogany that was at once the symbol and substance of their being; matchless masterpieces of fine arts, many of them devoted to pagan voluptuaries in diaphanous attire which caused palpitant symptoms in the breast of nabob and miner alike, adorned their walls; mustachioed servitors in genial waistcoats in patterns on which games could have been played and with solid-gold Albert watch chains which might have secured a team to a laden Concord, stood ready to dispense a bewildering array of choice matters at the sound of solid money on the bar. Washoe never placed much faith in folding money, but it was remarkable in what case a man could get himself and a friend to boot with a golden double eagle or with an even handsomer fifty-dollar slug minted in octagonal form by Belcher & Co.

In many of the bars there were also available the refinements of the muses. There were music boxes in which for the modest price of two bits a pleasing assortment of snares, fiddles, horns, lutes and cymbals snarled, sawed and emitted unidentifiable but satisfactory sounds of distintegration. Most of these triumphs of the cabinetmaker's art possessed glass fronts and as an extra added attraction it was possible to watch the hammers trip, the cymbals smite and the fiddles jiggle. In the coney traps and tourist boites of C Street to this day you may hear the identical melodeons that enchanted the ear of James Graham Fair with their altogether unreasonable facsimile of a discharge of dynamite in a plate-glass factory, abated in no detail of violence by the decades.

On clement evenings when the town's portals were wide, the uninhibited sounds emerged to envelope the bemused passerby like a symphony from Bedlam. If his sensitive soul revolted against such robust beguilements, the turmoil inside a single one of these premises assuredly was less deafening than the collective whole, and he entered. Did his senses delight in the

## INSTITUTIONS IN THE STORIED WASHOE

When Sandy Bowers and Eilley Orrum set out from their Washoe Valley mansion (above) to call on Queen Victoria, a Wells Fargo coach and messenger conveyed them across the Sierra and their departure, amidst glad bon voyage atmosphere, is shown in this old photograph. Below, Piper's Opera House at Virginia City was a setting in which Adah Isaacs Menken repeatedly played *Mazeppa* and Wells Fargo maintained a special service for transporting steeds for this melodramatic production. The right-hand stage box shown here was reserved on opening nights for John Mackay, the one on the right for William Sharon. Both these historic Washoe structures are still standing.

## WELLS FARGO IN UNCOMMON ASPECT

At various times and in a wide variety of places, Wells Fargo has been in several businesses: banking, express, staging, hotel management, the government and private mails and the conducting of tourists. The only venture of the firm in mining was at Virginia City in Comstock times, but whether this mine, located at the northern end of the Lode, was a formal venture by the directors of the firm or a flyer into finance undertaken by a group of employees who appropriated the company name is not known. Wells Fargo's archives contain no record of it, but on at least one occasion Eilley Orrum, the Washoe Seeress, was consulted by interested parties in the mine's prospects. The Seeress was not entirely favorable. Another aspect of Wells Fargo's activities in the Comstock was the Wells Fargo Band (below), much in demand on occasions of state and pleasure.

tumult, then for certain some fortunate establishment must happily be louder and more welcoming than any other, and he entered. Poet or peasant, the result was identical.

It is notable that when, on one of the many occasions fire overtook Virginia City, the conflagration started, inconveniently, in midevening, and most of the town was destroyed before the fire companies could be recruited from their favorite saloons. In some cases the first convincing proof they received of the inferno raging outside was when the resort they patronized was itself suddenly discovered to be in flames.

From such modest beginnings as the Express Bar under Wells Fargo's offices and the precariously maintained oases under canvas which illuminated the slopes of Mount Davidson by night, Virginia City came to boast a greater diversity of refreshment parlors than any community of comparable size on earth. Prominent in the roster was Pat Lynch's Place, a retreat famous for its barroom nude trailing a chaste vestige of gauze where it was appropriate and elevating in toast a dripping goblet of what might be presumed to be the wine of Champagne. A slight excursion down the street would bring the venturesome thirsty to Hennessey and Breen's Saloon, the latter of the proprietors being popularly reputed as ancestor of today's Breen in San Francisco's Third Street.

Next he might pause to lay a gold piece or two on a favorite number at Gentry and Crittenden's roulette parlors or at the Roadside Club without fear of abnormal suffering from thirst, since a bar was always available in all temples of chance. He could stop for oysters and brandy, that favorite combination of Dan'l Webster, at Barnam's Restaurant and then saunter comfortably to the taproom in Jacob Wimmer's Virginia Hotel, a hotbed of secessionist sympathizers where most of the guests, whether they espoused North or South, arrived fully armed with Colt's Navy pistols and derringers for reserve. The Howling Wilderness, too, was what its name advertised and at Johnny Newman's Saloon in Sutton Street he could be sure to run into superintendents from one or more of the mines, aristocrats of Washoe society who dressed in fashionable broadcloth and whose ladies drove abroad in the afternoon in magnificent coaches with liveried footmen.

Should the pilgrim tire of these delights there still remained the Cafe de Paris, El Doracho gambling rooms and Chuvel's French Restaurant where the antelope steaks nestling on beds of genuine Strasbourg foie gras, another Wells Fargo importation, were a gourmet's dream and the champagne was said to be available in as great a variety as it was in the Lick House in Montgomery Street over the hill. And, should he be minded for the play, there was nothing to prevent his strolling into Maguire's Opera House or the Melodeon Music Hall where well-upholstered bars obviated the inconvenience of stepping out during the intermissions, which, thoughtfully provided by the management, were long and frequent. The Crystal Bar in C Street, still available to tourists, was an all-night resort for the more fastidious customers in the hours between supper and breakfast. It never closed.

And last of all, but only of course if a man were one of the Comstock's upper tendom, securely established in the community's top financial and social brackets, there were those two superlative resorts of masculine luxury and fashion, the Washoe Club and the International Hotel. Far beyond the reach, but not the aspirations, of common miners who passed their fabled portals every day, it could never be said that fortune might not the very next week place them within the reach of the most casual whim of a winch tender at Cholar or subterranean stable hand at Ophir. Hadn't such present ornaments of these gilt and cloisonné establishments as Sandy Bowers and John Mackay arrived without more than a single shirt to their powerful backs? And weren't they now, at this very minute, seated in deep armchairs of tufted red brocade, wearing beautifully fashioned tailcoats of English broadcloth and sipping Comet Year Cognac costing five dollars a glass while smoking clear Havana stogies from Nob Hill tobacconists?

It is difficult, three quarters of a century later, to stand in the weed-grown lot where once the International Hotel rose six amazing floors with the only elevator between the Mississippi and the Pacific to imagine the splendors which once unfolded themselves there, or to climb the rusted circular iron staircase which still leads to the rooms of the Washoe Club and envision the opulence of vanished times. No trace remains of the International save on the glazed surfaces of the picture post cards the tourists buy at the Bucket of Blood. The apartments of the Washoe Club are untenanted and through the broken skylight of the condemned building the winter weathers have descended to rot the woodwork and mildew the handsome papers on its walls.

But once, in both these ghost bars in a ghost town, there had been life and vitality at full flood tide, and soft coal-oil light, and municipal gas had shone from floriated chandeliers on the starched shirt fronts and gleaming evening studs of rich men and kings. Silver collars on crystal decanters proclaimed the names and styles of whiskies which have been long forgotten by the oldest steward in the oldest club, and the double eagles minted at Carson City with fabulous dates under their liberty heads which once slid across the gaming tables are now secured in velvet trays in the vaults of numismatists.

Only the imagination can recreate the interiors of the Comstock's inner sanctums of wealth and success, but, knowing the taste of the times, it is not difficult to summon to the mind's eye the crimson looped and fringed curtains, the French clocks, the avalanches of ormolu, cloisonné and marquetry, the Flemish paintings under protective glass panels and the determined elegance of marble statuary which on every hand and especially on the newel posts of staircases depicted classic characters adjusting wreaths, trailing long vestments and touching marble lyres with upraised eyes. Everything, of course, that was available to metal was made in Comstock silver: plumbing fixtures, ash trays, cuspidors and doorknobs. In some of the art French taste prevailed, depicting in engraved steel the charge of horsehair-

## THE GRANDEUR THAT WAS

Virginia City in the early seventies was a community of such world-shaking importance that New York and San Francisco newspapers maintained news bureaus there and there was a Presidential suite at the International Hotel. When the *Territorial Enterprise* published Dan De Quill's news story of the Big Bonanza in Con Virginia and the California Mine, thrones tottered in Europe, panic seized the bourses of the world and the date line of Virginia City eclipsed that of London, Paris and Washington in a thousand newspapers. Life seethed in a quintessence of vitality in the town's drawing rooms and restaurants, saloons and stock brokerages. Ladies of the evening wore diamonds that would have been the envy of dowagers on Murray Hill and the menus at the Washoe Club glittered with terrapin, foie gras and rare tropical fruits. Booth, Barrett, Salvini and McCullough played regular engagements at Piper's and there was overnight sleeper service over the fabulously rich Virginia & Truckee RR to San Francisco. Mine superintendents' wives ordered their landaus with footmen on the box to call on next-door neighbors at a fashionable hour in the afternoon; luxury shops of jewelers, florists and furriers thrived, and drinkers in the better bars seldom asked for change from a five-dollar gold piece. That was Virginia City, Queen of the Comstock, in 1875.

## THE GLORY THAT IS GONE

Three quarters of a century after the Big Bonanza, Virginia City is not a ghost town, but the ghosts are there, and the magic of its name brings innumerable summer tourists who drink, vicariously, with Jim Flood and George Hearst at the Crystal Bar and rub shoulders, metaphorically, with Joe Goodman at the Sazarac. A paintless, shabby, wind-sprung town, dreaming incurably of the opulent yesterdays when the great and famous of the earth rolled up to the porte-cocher of the International Hotel and when champagne in double magnums was used for brushing their teeth by the Bonanza Kings, Virginia City still is possessed of a wonderment and flavor owned by no other community. It is remarkably easy, late at night, when the gambling tables are crowded and the smash of indestructible music boxes rolls into C Street, to imagine that the past has never really vanished and that the great days are still current. An uncommonly Bohemian populace simply refuses to allow illusion to die and although the requirements of the community are served by a single omniscient telephone operator the concentration of hurrah is notable even by Nevada standards. Unchanged since 1875 are Six Mile Canyon, Sugar Loaf in the distance and the symbolically everlasting Church of St. Mary in the Mountains.

105

RANCHMEN LOOKING AT LADIES IN STAGE C

## MARKED FOR SPECIAL HANDLING

Frontiersmen gazing with rapture upon female travelers. Consignments of rare goods destined for Virginia City's Sporting Row often elicited such profound interest when Washoe-bound stages paused at post stations.

plumed chasseurs in forgotten battles and grenadiers off duty flirting with Directoire maidens.

The millionaires of the Comstock loved every rococo smidge that could be rolled up the Geiger Grade in creaking vans, and always sent for more to the ateliers of Fifth Avenue and Bond Street.

Wells Fargo was even associated with the tremendous trade enjoyed by the love stores and houses of mirth which flourished along "Sporting Row" just down the hillside from C Street. Until the coming of the railroad and throughout the decade of the sixties all the "fair but frail" were consigned to the care of the stage drivers and were ferried in avalanches of lace, feathers and fringes up the Geiger Grade or Six Mile Canyon to be received at their destinations by the fashionable madams who were eagerly awaiting each new shipment from their agents in San Francisco and Sacramento. The arrival of particularly large and sensational bills of these choice goods was a signal for public rejoicing throughout the length and breadth of the town, although the virtuous married women of Virginia City twitched a haughty and disapproving bustle on such unseemly spectacles.

Queen of the more stylish strumpets in Virginia City during the middle sixties was Julia Bulette, a merry Jezebel whose wit and other resources of charm had established her firmly in every masculine bosom of the community both figuratively and literally. She was even an honorary member of the Virginia City Engine Company, a social honor which was considered a wanton outrage by the elderly female element of the town. She rode in all the parades, was the toast of every bar and her horses and equipages with their uniformed flunkies were the envy of the less favored sisterhood of "Sporting Row."

Wells Fargo was forever delivering mysterious packages to the door of the fair Julia, some bearing the imprimatur of Shreve & Co., the ranking diamond merchants of San Francisco, some the names of the more expensive furriers of Post Street. They were the tributes of Julia's more ardent and solvent admirers and she wore them in a rich profusion of sunbursts, stomachers, earrings and little fur cloaks in the current fashion.

But Julia's finery proved her undoing, for one cold winter's morning her maid found her murdered in her hospitable bed, her closets and jewel cases robbed of their costly contents. Her funeral and the subsequent grand ceremonial hanging of her murderer, when he was eventually apprehended, were two of the greatest days in the history of the Comstock and her memory was kept perpetually green in a saga of purple passion which waxed and grew with the years and the telling. At one time the management of the Virginia & Truckee RR had a club car on its roster of rolling stock named *The Julia Bulette* but the messengers and agents of Wells Fargo felt that if they hadn't delivered so many exciting packages to her house she would have been around longer to enjoy life as the queen of all Comstock courtesans.

By the summer of 1872 the reports of the Big Bonanza and its attendent tumults, by the time they arrived in New York, were assuming such fantastic proportions that the managing editor of *The New York Daily Tribune* detailed a feature writer to file an extended account of the state of Virginia City in all its various aspects, metallurgical, financial, social and municipal. By a singular coincidence, the anonymous correspondent, for this was in the days before by-lines were generally accorded staff members, the *Tribune's* Virginia City man delivered his copy, which ran well in excess of 10,000 words, to the Overland Telegraph Office on August 26th, the fateful date of the suspension of payments by the Bank of California. The next morning's front page was what amounted to a Comstock edition of Uncle Horace Greeley's daily, with the stop-press news of the death by misadventure of Ralston just in time to make the last run of papers for metropolitan distribution.

The *Tribune's* estimate of Virginia City in its superficial aspects reads like good reporting more than three quarters of a century later.

"The restaurants of this community [it read] are as fine as any in the world although not so extensive as some or as elaborate in their appointments. There are drinking saloons more gorgeous in their appointments than any in San Francisco, Philadelphia or New York, and there are shops and stores that are dazzlingly splendid. I have never seen finer shops than there are here and the number of diamonds displayed in their windows quite overwhelm the senses. The people here seem to run to jewelry.

"The club rooms (The Washoe Club) are nearly as well furnished as those in New York except in pictures, books and bronzes, and the manner of life of the inhabitants generally is on a high scale. It is as difficult to get along C Street in the evening as it is to go along Broadway in the neighborhood of Fulton in the afternoon. Every young blade or old one for that matter has his fast horse or his pair and, although he may be clad in rough attire, you may be satisfied his pockets are full of money."

Twenty-five years later the once gala International Hotel was owned by a Chinese; the celebrated hydraulic elevator that had charmed the miners off duty from Ophir and Chollar-Potosi was only a mobile memory and guests were charged in reverse ratio to the number of floors they had to ascend to reach their apartments. On a still summer night in 1914 the International Hotel went up in a sheet of flame and a towering cloud of the most expensive smoke which brought patrons from the saloons in Reno's North Virginia Street to speculate on what was ablaze. The flames were visible far across the Carson Sink whence the first Mormons had come to the foot of Gold Canyon. It was said that in the light of its burning, the finest newsprint was clearly legible on the very peak of Sun Mountain, although just who was there to observe this phenomenon does not appear in the record.

It was in the saloons of Virginia City that a pleasant custom, unknown elsewhere, was established: the first drink of the day was on the house. The theory was that if a man had done his drinking in a given oasis the night before, he might be shy of funds the next morning and reluctant to ask for credit. Also he would almost inevitably be in need of a hair of the dog. This worked greatly to the advantage of peripatetic drinkers who had patronized a number of public houses, and Wells Drury recalled that experts in free loading could promote as many as fifteen eye openers on this basis, but that four or five was generally considered the limit for conservative businessmen before breakfast.

In the golden noontide of Wells Fargo's greatest flowering during the seventies and eighties, San Francisco was known as a "Wells Fargo town" and California as a "Wells Fargo state" and it was an even tossup whether the Central and Southern Pacific Railroads were "Wells Fargo railroads" or whether Wells Fargo was the railroads' express company, but from the very beginning Virginia City was a Wells Fargo community, even more than old Columbia had been over in the Mother Lode country.

Wells Fargo's Comstock agents, anxious to lend the new boom town every vestige and appearance of early greatness, improved on old Virginny's original christening and began to insist that it be called "Virginia City." It took some little time for this stroke of press-agentry to catch hold, since every tent and shack town in the Old West had insisted on the word "city" being added to its postal address, and over in San Francisco, which had never bothered to call itself a metropolis by name, it was always Virginia and nothing else.

Homer S. King, Wells Fargo's first agent for banking in the Comstock, became a ranking local nabob, and George Anson King asserted the family prestige by building what was at that date, 1863, the show place of the town, a mansion high on Sun Mountain above A Street which survives to this day

## BONANZA INN, 1875

Today the International Hotel in Virginia City is but a fragrant legend but once it was the show place of the West. Grant and Sherman gloried and drank deep in its palatial apartments and privileged guests descended to its fabled cellars below C Street to draw their own Bourbon right from the wood. When it was built it boasted the most celebrated elevator west of Chicago's Palmer House.

GRAHAME HARDY COLLECTION

BUNDY, CARSON CITY

## BONANZA INN, 1949

When Homer S. King came to Virginia City as Wells Fargo's head of the banking department in 1863, his brother, George Anson King, built this stately Victorian mansion with ten-foot ceilings, paneled walls and a breath-taking view down Six Mile Canyon. In 1949 it is still a show place as the Bonanza Inn, an exotic and expensive restaurant where champagne still flowed and pheasant was on the menu in the grand manner of the old Comstock.

as the Bonanza Inn, the only luxury restaurant now in the Comstock. Its matched walnut panels in the vestibule, magnificent frosted-glass fanlight and door panels, ten-foot ceilings and still unblemished marble fireplaces testify to the position occupied in the community by its first owner.

It was at Virginia City, according to legend, although there is no documented evidence to support the belief, that James B. Hume first ordered a headstone for a dead bandit who had specialized in Wells Fargo holdups to be engrossed at the company's expense with the legend, thereafter a commonplace throughout the Western frontier: "Wells Fargo Never Forgets."

Wells Fargo had shown its good judgment in the Comstock and it intended to capitalize on it in every way possible. It was Wells Fargo by which blasphemous miners swore. "By God and by Wells Fargo" was a combination of consular dignity. It was Wells Fargo's superintendents who drove the finest horses with silver-trimmed harnesses, drank the best imported champagnes in the bars of the International Hotel and the Washoe Club and wore the longest frock coats and creamiest gloves at noontime in C Street. Wells Fargo's stake in Virginia City was the greatest it had ever played and it sustained it with a flair for magnificence that has never since been exceeded and seldom duplicated by American commercial enterprise.

In an age more or less innocent of calculated press-agentry and high-pressure promotion, one of Wells Fargo's happiest devices for advertising its expeditious services was the institution of fast mail delivery between Reno and Virginia City in competition with a similar service maintained by the Pacific Express, soon to prove an adversary for far greater stakes.

The daily races between the two agencies provided tremendous excitement throughout the Comstock during the two years between 1868, when the rails of the Central Pacific first ran into Reno from San Francisco, and 1870 when the completion of the Virginia and Truckee between Reno and Virginia City rendered the buckboard service obsolete. Wagers ranging in comprehensiveness from a round of drinks to thousands of dollars in minted gold attended every sprint of the matched ponies up the Geiger Grade and provided the most effective form of advertising for the name and functions of Wells Fargo in the Nevada bonanzas.

The route of these spirited and spectacular contests lay from the banks of the Truckee down what is now South Virginia Street in Reno, past Steamboat and up the old Geiger Grade. Mail for Silver City and Gold Hill was carried in the hurrying pouches, and citizens of these communities hastened across the Divide each afternoon to witness the conclusion of the contest in Virginia City. In the dash from the Truckee to the slopes of Sun Mountain, a distance of twenty-one miles, the Pacific expedited the mails consigned to it by pony and rider with the pouch strapped to his back, while Wells Fargo favored a light two-horse buckboard of the high-wheel type that still may be seen around Reno's North Virginia Street each summer at rodeo time. The buckboard could accommodate both mails and light express matter and upon occasion, as we shall see, a cash fare to boot.

At this time, before the coming of the Virginia and Truckee RR, the train from San Francisco was accustomed to roll its smoky way down Truckee Canyon in the early afternoon, although later when transcontinental schedules came into effect most passenger traffic passed through Reno in the middle of the night as indeed it still does.

About the time the engine whistled for the yard limit a mile of town, the Pacific pony and the Wells Fargo buckboard made their appearance at the lower end of the depot platform where the mail cars would be braked to a smoking halt. A crowd would gather for the fun and a minute or two later the light wooden bridge over the Truckee would resound to the thunder of three sets of ironshod hooves, at this point practically abreast of one another.

A favorite of the sporting element was William P. Bennett who drove for Wells Fargo. Another notable of the highway who carried the pouches for the firm was Pony Bob Haslam, while the champion jehu of the Pacific Express stables was Frank Henderson, a daring driver who could make five changes of horses along the twenty-mile run with all the speed of a Pony Express rider of the older tradition who changed his steed and transferred his sweaty *mochila* at a dead gallop. There was a telegraph in those days at Steamboat and the positions of the racers as they approached the Geiger Grade would be wired ahead by way of Washoe City, Ophir, Carson, Mound House and Six Mile Canyon so that sports in beaver hats flocked to the saloons in these back-of-the-mountain communities and cheered their favorites as the telegrapher in his eyeshade and black alpaca sleeves of office decoded the dots and dashes from his relays. Great was the excitement among the faithful at the bar as the news came through that Wells Fargo had thrown a tire and gone into the ditch or that the Pacific's pony was a nose ahead as they passed through the vaporous precincts of Steamboat.

A few years later George Francis Train would have had his private palace car routed over the Virginia and Truckee in the wake of such notable private car fanciers as Senator Sharon and George M. Pullman. But when Train arrived in Reno for a lecture in Virginia City in 1869, the obvious means of getting there in time for his rendezvous at Piper's Opera was the Wells Fargo stage, to whose driver he addressed himself.

The driver that day was Bill Bennet who had confirmed prejudices against the extra weight and conversational inclinations of passengers, but Train was armed with the authoritative name of Latham, the Wells Fargo agent at Virginia City, and was hoisted aboard with a minimum of ceremony!

> There is no time to think or joke
> On such a trip as that
> Train, do not let your hold get broke,
> And watch out for your hat!

WELLS FARGO BANK

## TRANQUILLITY IS HERE

In 1863 (above) the Devil's Gate between Silver City and Gold Hill boasted a hotel, several saloons, a stable, a tollgate and numerous residences. It was a favorite place for stage robberies and at one time, during the Indian scare of 1860, there were cannon mounted there to protect the approach to the Comstock. Today the rock formations of the Devil's Gate are unchanged, but vanished forever is the animation of teaming and the bold, rough life of staging.

CHARLES CLEGG

## "LO, ALL THY POMPS OF YESTERDAY . . ."

Gold Hill in 1875 (above) was rich and populous and shared the resources of the Comstock Lode with Virginia City and, to a lesser degree, Silver City down Slippery Gulch and beyond the Devil's Gate. Wells Fargo maintained an office there to forward the treasure from the hoists and mills of Crown Point, Yellow Jacket and other bonanzas, and there were saloons and fire companies, newspapers and sporting houses, all the paraphernalia of the frontier, in abundance. In the lower left is the celebrated Crown Point trestle of the Virginia and Truckee RR. Gold Hill as seen today from the identical spot (below) shows only the abandoned railroad depot (left) and the ruined hoists of the Yellow Jacket in the foreground. The rest is legend.

There was a cheer from the onlookers as the buckboard started with a jerk which threatened the eccentric lecturer's neck with dislocation in a day before there were chiropractors available in Reno.

Train clutched at the grabirons of the buckboard and endeavored to establish conversational rapport with Bennett.

"Perhaps you would be interested in the substance of a most enlightening interview I had yesterday in San Francisco with the Emperor Norton?" he began.

"If you lose that silk hat I won't stop for it," replied Bennett as the careening buckboard grazed a sleeping dog with the near front wheel and brought an excited group of patrons to the door of the First and Last Chance Saloon on the edge of Reno meadows.

"The Emperor, a most interesting fellow, believes that I am a menace to the peace between the United States and Great Britain," continued the Cicero of the lecture platform.

"Mind your tile," screamed Bennett, who himself had $500 on the race in the hands of a stakeholder in a C Street bar.

"He proposes that Her Britannic Majesty cede the Island of Vancouver to the United States for the sum of $1,500," shouted Train whose hat, at that very moment, parted company with its owner and sailed into the dust of the Carson Road.

Tried beyond Christian endurance, Bennett nevertheless reined in his horses. Half a mile behind he could discern the pony of the Pacific rider through the dust at Huffaker's Station and if God and Latham sent him this cross to bear he still had a tolerable lead on the opposition.

"Tie the goddam thing on somehow. I won't stop again," he admonished as George Francis, disheveled and perspiring, regained his seat. "Only a damn fool would wear a hat like that in these parts!"

At the Six Mile House at the top of Geiger Grade, Train made one last attempt. Cupping his hands he bellowed into Bennett's available ear: "The Emperor had the audacity to call me a humbug. Said I was an agitator and wrote an order banishing me from his empire. It was published in the *Herald*. Can you imagine that! No responsible editors nowadays. Print the most unconscionable rubbish. Norton is no Emperor. Never will be!"

Bennett said nothing eloquently and suddenly turned the buckboard off the highway to take a short cut through the sagebrush and amongst the prospectors' holes of Sun Mountain. Train screamed as loudly as Horace Greeley and Bennett continued driving like Hank Monk with no more than two wheels of the buckboard on the ground at any given time. With the Pacific rider a scant hundred yards behind them they rounded the last curve and the smokestacks and mine hoists of Virginia City came into view.

In C Street the verandas and housetops were black with cheering thousands. The multitude overflowed the sidewalks and tossed their hats as the buckboard raced for the porte-cochere of Wells Fargo, past the Bucket of Blood, past the International Hotel, past the brewery and the stables of the

## CAMELS IN THE COMSTOCK

Not only did Wells Fargo have to contend along Nevada highways of the sixties and seventies with road agents, blizzards, flooded fords, washed-out bridges, Indians, avalanches, alkaline water and rapacious tollkeepers. There were also the camels. Camels existed in California and Nevada during the nineteenth century in numbers dismaying to those who came in contact with them. Bactrian camels were imported from Tartary especially to haul salt between Austin, Eureka and Virginia City. Others were brought West by the Army at the time of the Civil War. Over the Sierra near Sacramento there was maintained a stable of racing camels. Eventually many were turned loose as useless to their owners and haunted the Nevada deserts as late as 1912. In Lyon County there was a law providing a thirty-day jail sentence for allowing camels to stray. Stagers and wagon-train men hated them, as horses and mules were understandably terrified of these great alien beasts. In Virginia City they were only allowed to pass through the streets at night. They attacked strangers with flashing teeth and ate the laundry of domestic washlines. Wells Fargo's drivers complained of camels all the way from Tahoe to Ely, since their teams, on encountering a stray Bactrian or dromedary, took off across the countryside in uncontrollable panic. Children had the horrors and alcoholics got religion when they strayed into the outskirts of Silver City or Six Mile Canyon. Camels were never popular in Nevada.

lower town. Train raised his battered top hat in graceful response to the wild acclaim. Seldom in his travels had he met with such a welcome. Surely this was an answer to the infamous attacks he had received at the hands of the Emperor Norton. This would show the *Herald!*

It was only minutes later that it dawned upon him that the excitement was not in honor of his arrival, but attended the race with the mails. It was noted by auditors that his lecture that night at Piper's was in a less than usually robust and florid vein. The viols of his oratory were muted. There was no reference at all to the Emperor Norton.

Bennett was not the only stager of the era who was celebrated, in a pre-Calvin Coolidge age, for his lack of loquacity. James Blake, a notable jehu on the run between Pioche and Hamilton, is reported upon occasion to have been beset by a chatty party who wished to snare him into enlightening conversation. No provocation seemed to suffice. Blake was indifferent to the affairs of state in Washington. The splendors of the Palace Hotel which William Ralston was building, of all places on the south side of Market Street in San Francisco, left him unaffected. Flattery of his technique in handling the coach evoked no response that was audible to the chatty party.

Finally the passenger hit upon a device which, he was sure, must at least call for a civil answer of some sort. He asked Blake the time of day.

"There is a clock in the Wells Fargo office when we get there," was his answer.

Stage robbery on the Virginia City runs, while not exactly sanctioned either by law or conservative public opinion, was an industry of no small proportions. Wells Fargo's policy of payment of all losses sustained while property was in their trust or conveyance was in itself a provocation to dishonesty by shippers of coin or bullion who, knowing that their consignments were completely insured by company policy, sometimes tipped off highwaymen when they were planning a rich shipment. The haul was then divided between the crooked shippers and the gunmen and the shipper was, of course, indemnified by Wells Fargo.

Not unnaturally Wells Fargo failed to see the virtues of such arrangements and took to putting heavily armed shotgun messengers on bullion stages and then, when a single guard was found to be insufficient to cope with bands of several armed robbers, the stages were made part of a cavalcade with armed riders going before and behind. It was this unfair practice, so deposed the Verdi car robbers, that forced them out of the stage-robbing business and into hijacking the steamcars.

Generally speaking stage robbery seems to have occupied in the public's moral consciousness approximately the position of prohibition in a later era. Robbery was deplored but even the best people never seemed to be outraged by it. A song about one of Wells Fargo's often robbed stagers, Baldy Green, came to be a part of the folklore of the Comstock, and ballad singers who strolled through the saloons and music halls with banjos were sure of a receptive audience when they sang *Baldy Green.*

## BALDY GREEN

I'll tell you all a story,
    And I'll tell it in a song
And I hope that it will please you,
    For it won't detain you long;
'Tis about one of the old boys
    So gallus and so fine,
Who used to carry mails
    On the Pioneer Line.

He was the greatest favor-ite
    That ever yet was seen,
He was known about Virginny
    By the name of Baldy Green.
Oh, he swung a whip so gracefully,
    For he was bound to shine ——
For he was a high-toned driver
    On the Pioneer Line.

Now, as he was driving out one night,
    As lively as a coon,
He saw three men jump in the road
    By the pale light of the moon;
Two sprang for the leaders,
    While one his shotgun cocks,
Saying, "Baldy, we hate to trouble you,
    But just pass us out the box."

When Baldy heard them say these words
    He opened wide his eyes;
He didn't know what in the world to do,
    For it took him by surprise.
Then he reached into the boot,
    Saying, "Take it, sirs, with pleasure,"
So out into the middle of the road
    Went Wells & Fargo's treasure.

Now, when they got the treasure-box
    They seemed quite satisfied,
For the man who held the leaders
    Then politely stepped aside,
Saying, "Baldy, we've got what we want,
    So drive along your team,"
And he made the quickest time
    To Silver City ever seen.

117

Don't say greenbacks to Baldy now,
It makes him feel so sore;
He'd traveled the road many a time,
But was never stopped before.
Oh the chances they were three to one
And shotguns were the game,
And if you'd a-been in Baldy's place
You'd a-shelled her out the same.

Wells Drury in *An Editor on the Comstock Lode* reported that old Judge Mesick, Colonel Bob Taylor and a group of impious cronies used to sit together in a stage box at Piper's and whenever Charley Rhoades, a local favorite, obliged with *Baldy Green* they would whoop and stamp their approval and pound the edge of the box with their revolver butts until they created such a disturbance that Piper would give them their money back and ask them to leave the house. As for Baldy himself, the ballad irritated him so that he retired from staging and became a justice of the peace, an occupation which lent itself less readily to irreverent balladmongers.

Now and then, but only infrequently, treachery raised its head within the Wells Fargo organization. It seldom prospered and the following case in point is cited by Robert Laxalt, an old-timer of Gold Hill who collects Nevada legends both as a business and a pastime.

"In that year, the year of 1870," deposes Mr. Laxalt, "stagecoach robberies were by no means uncommon things in Nevada, and so, when driver James Rickey came riding into Gold Hill with the news that he had been held up and relieved of his strongbox, no one was very surprised.

"Rickey came riding up to the Gold Hill station of the Wells Fargo, the company that owned and operated the stagecoaches and also paid the bills when shipments were lost, and told the agent, Enoch Jensen, a sad tale of woe. He told of driving along one of the trails to Gold Hill and being held up by three bandits who had even been dastardly enough to take the two dollars he had in his pocket. Jensen listened resignedly, heaved a sigh of despair, and prepared to notify the San Francisco office that another robbery would require immediate repayment by the company. Then he dismissed Rickey and went to bed.

"The next morning, Jensen decided to take a ride out to the spot where the driver had said the bandits had lain in wait for the coming of the stage-coach. He had no special reason for doing so, because he certainly didn't expect to find anything, but he hankered for an early morning ride, and so he went.

"After riding for some time, he came to the scene of the robbery and dismounted to examine the ground. He saw the imprint of where the strongbox with its heavy load of gold coin had landed in the sand, but for the life of him, he could not see the tracks of three horses. Instead, he saw the tracks of only one horse leading into the desert. On closer scrutiny, he noticed that the horse

## WHERE THE WASHOE ZEPHYRS BLOW

"The Divide" separating Gold Hill from Virginia City was a densely populated city in 1880. Here once, while returning from a midnight supper, Mark Twain was held up by masked miscreants and robbed of his cherished gold watch. Through its streets fire companies raced when disaster threatened, which was almost daily. Wells Fargo maintained banking and express offices in both communities and the Virginia & Truckee RR ran under part of "The Divide" through a tunnel. Below is "The Divide" as it appears ninety years after the first discovery of the Comstock.

was missing a hind shoe, and this made the trail very easy to follow.

"With nothing better to do, Jensen patiently followed the trail deep into the desert. Finally, he came to the place where the bandit had dismounted and pried the lid from the iron strongbox which still lay baking in the desert sun, mute testimony to stolen loot.

"Jensen almost turned back to retrace his steps, but something made him follow the trail still deeper into the desert. There was a chance in a million, he told himself, just one chance in a million. . . .

"And sure enough, three hours and many miles later, Jensen saw where the rider had dismounted again, at the foot of a rock formation. At the side of a peculiarly shaped boulder, the ground had been disturbed. Hardly daring to trust his hopes, he dug furiously and came up grinning with a sack filled with golden coins.

"He loaded the gold into his saddlebags and followed the trail of the horse with the missing hind shoe as it twisted back across the desert towards Gold Hill. Finally, it swung into a well-beaten path and it was impossible to follow it further.

"Jensen rode slowly to the Wells Fargo office, unstrapped the saddlebags and carried the gold to the safety of the company safe. Dusk had fallen over the Comstock and Jensen ate his evening meal with the quiet satisfaction of personal success. Afterwards, he strolled back to the Wells Fargo office.

"Then Rickey came in, still wearing the disconsolate expression of yesterday. Jensen could hardly refrain from telling him of the recovery of the gold, but first he wanted to kid him about the three big bandits, when in reality there had been only one. But Ricky spoke first. He sat down on Jensen's desk, tilted back his wide-brimmed hat, and said he was going to quit. The strain of stagecoach driving plus the shock of the robbery, was too much, Rickey said. He planned to move on to San Francisco.

"Then he walked to the door and said he would be back for his pay in a few minutes. Again Jensen opened his mouth to tell him of the good fortune, but Rickey's parting speech made him clamp his lips shut, made him summon the sheriff when the driver had gone. For Rickey had said he would return as soon as the blacksmith replaced the missing shoe on his horse's hind foot."

The same style and elegance which characterized social life and manners in Virginia City during its great years obtained among the knights of the road, and holdups acquired *ton* if not downright formality. When five masked miscreants held up the stage from Reno at three in the morning at the very top of Geiger Grade in 1866 the affair took on airs and graces that would not have been out of place at a stylish picnic at the Bowers Mansion. A young lady traveler who had been on a shopping trip to San Francisco was discovered to be among the passengers, and buffalo robes and blankets from the detained coach were spread for her comfort by the robbers at a removed spot near by giving a fine view of Steamboat and Washoe Meadows in the

## IMPERIAL PROGRESS OF WELLS FARGO

The years of supremacy of the Concord as a conveyance over vast continental distances had come to a close when this photograph was taken in 1878, but on innumerable runs in regions as yet impervious to the railroads, Wells Fargo still rode the six-horse stages. The High Sierra, where this team was halted for its portrait, was still a Wells Fargo empire and the symbol of its authority is visible in the persons of no fewer than three armed guards amidst the luggage on the stagetop. On the rear boot is a voyager in the hard bowler hat which shared the sartorial conquest of the frontier with the Stetson and even earlier coonskin hat of Dan'l Boone tradition.

moonlight. A case of champagne, discovered on the roof of the vehicle where it had been appropriately chilled by the night air, was broached, sandwiches were broken out and the fair passenger engaged in polite small talk by the younger members of the robber band while their companions dynamited the strongbox and extracted $4,000 in newly minted double eagles. The parties then separated with gallant adieus and the despoiled coach toiled on into Virginia City with the sunrise.

One of the more successful Wells Fargo employees who served on the Virginia City run in the combined capacity of driver and armed messenger and who for many years scorned other protection than that which he was able to provide himself, was a character known as Shotgun Bill Taylor. Taylor had been held up so frequently on the Geiger Grade and in the shadows of Six Mile Canyon and had found the offices of the conventional shotgun messenger provided by the company to be so ineffectual that he evolved a unique and singularly effective device for protecting Wells Fargo's treasures while still handling the three span of horses.

The next time a masked scoundrel appeared around a bend as Taylor's horses were slowing for the top of the grade, the driver obligingly put his hands in the air and at the same time raised his right foot as though for an application of the brake, the beam of which was handy to the driver's dexter boot. There was a terrific explosion; the bad man and his head rolled in separate directions over the edge of the grade and Taylor cheerfully picked up his reins and urged the horses into their collars. A wisp of smoke was observed to be emerging from the driver's trousers. He had secreted a short double-barreled shotgun up his trouser leg and with a cunning attachment of wires had secured the triggers to the fingers of his hand. All he had to do was point a foot over the dashboard while his hands were in the air, sight across his boot tip, and there was an end to another whilom bad man. Since no holdup man ever survived an encounter with Shotgun Bill, none returned to tell of the ambush and the device was a major success for many years.

At the Chicago World's Fair in 1893 Wells Fargo caused to be erected, as part of their exhibit, a statue of Shotgun Bill Taylor, his right leg jauntily, if stiffly, elevated in the position that had written so many popular and well-deserved obituaries on the Comstock in years gone by.

The opening years of the seventies put a term to Wells Fargo's most magnificent venture in staging. For a brief decade its Concords with their celebrated drivers, their rich freights and glittering assortment of passengers had rolled grandly up the Geiger Grade, up Six Mile Canyon and up Slippery Gulch in Gold Hill. Their arrivals and departures from the great brick structure in C Street were daily events of momentous import, swift interludes of drama and dispatch in a community where both of these things were urgent. Now the Concord on the Virginia City run was to be nudged, at first gently and remotely, and then rudely and abruptly by the iron horse whose presence for the past year or so had been dimly perceived high in the wester-

## VIGNETTES OF CARSON

By the middle 1870's the roundhouse of the Virginia and Truckee RR was alive with the activities of engines for as many as forty trains a day between Carson and Virginia City and Reno, and Wells Fargo was riding the gaily painted yellow and green combines and bullion cars of this most romantic of all American railroads. Here a Washoe sunrise finds seven engines with steam up at the dispatcher's disposal ready to roll the varnish cars. Above is Carson City's St. Charles Hotel, of fragrant memory, George Tufley proprietor, at approximately the same period. Coaches for Tahoe and other Sierra points via the old King's Canyon Grade made famous by Hank Monk, and for Mormon Station and other Carson Valley points met the trains of the V & T at the depot in Washington Street and picked up other fares at the St. Charles. The small picture shows the St. Charles today.

ing Sierra. In 1870, no longer remote and hypothetical, the railroad came to Washoe and the era of staging was done.

William Sharon, proconsular Virginia City agent for the mighty Bank of California, evolved what was later to become the world-famous Virginia and Truckee RR as part of a grandiose and inclusive scheme to take over the Comstock, lock, stock and barrel, for his principal, Darius Ogden Mills, over the hill in San Francisco. Mills, a frosty despot whose banking ethics in any age would be respectable but which in the whooping sixties were practically saintly, would have nothing of the Comstock as it was represented in San Francisco at the time by staggering stock swindles, hysterical speculation in mining properties and the high-pressure promotion and rigging of worthless securities. He believed in solid, tangible property and nothing else, and Sharon was well aware of the prejudices of his superior.

Many of the mines in Virginia City were, at the end of the sixties, in borrasca, unable profitably to mill their low-grade ores because of the cost of transporting any but the richest down to mills along the Carson River and unable to mine below the 800 or 900-foot level for lack of costly machinery and wood with which to shore up their forever sagging stopes, galleries and winzes. Lean days were at hand and Virginia City was in danger of becoming a ghost town half a century before its time.

In this pass, shrewd and canny Sharon knew the answer lay in a railroad. By a series of bold financial strokes he acquired for his bank control over the most important mills engaged in reducing Comstock ores, secured a charter from the states and set about the construction of a railroad which should make the hitherto despised low-grade ores cheaply available to the mills he owned and which should cut by a decisive one third the cost of wood being freighted up the precipitous slopes of Mount Davidson.

When the Virginia and Truckee was completed, at first between Virginia City and Carson City and later as a connection of the Central Pacific at Reno, Wells Fargo moved aboard its bright yellow baggage and express cars with a practiced ease acquired from previous experience on the Central Pacific and other railroads in California. Its agents and shotgun messengers stepped down from the boot of the Concord and boarded the cars, and from that time forward, until the unhappy day in 1938 when the Virginia City branch of the railroad was abandoned, the treasure of the Comstock rolled down to the mint at Carson and the countinghouses of Montgomery Street by rail and until the First World War through the agency of Wells Fargo.

For eighty years the Virginia and Truckee was to be the golden girl of American railroading. It was the most famous short line in the world. Its operations, motive power and rolling stock were studied and copied by railroads everywhere and the rich and celebrated of two generations were carried up to the Comstock over its rails, rolled in the seventies in Sheffield at the fiat of William Ralston. Its legend is rich with memories of Generals Grant and Sherman, Modjeska, Patti, McCullough, Adah Isaacs Menken and Salvini the Younger.

## FRAGRANT AND IMMORTAL, THE V & T

No railroad in history is so perfumed with romance and gilded with wealthy memories as the Virginia & Truckee which was built to carry down the wealth of the Comstock from Virginia City to the stamp mills along the Carson River and, eventually, to the strong rooms and countinghouses of San Francisco. Its principal owner was Darius Ogden Mills, and it was only natural that Wells Fargo, of which Mills was a director, should ride its bullion cars. Here the artist, E. S. Hammack, shows the V & T's beautiful No. 11, the engine *Reno,* in the silver seventies against the background of Gold Hill with Wells Fargo's bullion car in tow, just as it noses its pilot out onto the great Crown Point Trestle. Below are the hoisting works of the Yellow Jacket Mine; over the Divide in the background lies Virginia City, Queen of the Comstock, wonder of the mining world.

WELLS FARGO BANK

## THE WHEEL OF WELLS FARGO COMES FULL CIRCLE

Before Wells Fargo built its most famous of all agencies on the east side of C Street in Virginia City, the site was occupied, as is shown in this rare photograph taken on July 4, 1862, by Scholl & Roberts, the gunsmiths, Light & Allman's Livery Stable, Young America No. 2 Hose and the Young America Saloon. The picture, taken at nine that historic morning, shows the Virginia City fire companies assembling for the day's parade. Below is Wells Fargo's great Virginia City agency as it rose on the same site later in the sixties and remained a landmark for seven decades. Facing south in C Street are two stages of the Pioneer Co., Wells Fargo's staging line from California to the Washoe.

GRAHAME HARDY COLLECTION

WELLS FARGO BANK

From the turn of the century on, after Wells Fargo had departed the Comstock, its once stately offices in C Street remained a monument to the departed grandeur that had been Virginia City in the bonanza years. As the timbers of the vast subterranean stopes and winzes in the abandoned mines crumbled from the earth's pressure, entire structures in Virginia City commenced to tumble down the slope of Mount Davidson and by 1930 the ruin of Wells Fargo's office (above) was largely accomplished. By the forties it had been entirely razed as a measure of safety while still remained to view the towering spire of St. Mary's in the Mountains, an allegory to who will read it as such of the enduring qualities of the Church of Rome, quite literally "towering o'er the wrecks of time."

CHARLES CLEGG

And among its other qualifying superlatives, it was for many years the wealthiest and most profitable railroad property known to the record. At first for Mills, Sharon and Ralston, and after the death of the last of these for Mills and Sharon, it not infrequently netted $110,000 in gold double eagles every month. This was in addition to the fact that it was carrying ore in which the partnership was vitally interested down to the mills which it either owned or controlled and hauling on return trips lumber from stands of timber which also were the property of the "bank crowd." Now and then some boorish fellow in the state legislature raised a mannerless cry of "monopoly" but at least it was a monopoly which immeasurably enriched the entire economy of American life and made possible the fullest mining of the Comstock Lode to its eventual total of nearly three quarters of a billion dollars in precious metals.

Nine decades after its first tumultuous flowering, Virginia City is still a bonanza, to be sure of a minor order, and in commodities far removed from the first silver sulphurets in the Nevada City assay office across the Sierra. Its traffic is in souvenirs of the past both tangible and sentimental, and every fair day in summer the new Geiger Grade swarms with tourists en route to drink in the faded saloons, to unleash the monstrous symphonies of its melodeons, still functioning as fearsomely as they did in the age of John Percival Jones, and to tread the board sidewalks of C Street, vicariously, with Flood, Fair, Mackay and O'Brien. For the more determined amateurs of *temps perdus* there are shops overflowing with Victorian objects of *virtu:* cruet sets for the table, beds with half-ton mahogony headboards, coal-oil banquet lamps with globular shades in floriated patterns which sell for Madison Avenue prices and disappear from stock almost as soon as they are retrieved from some decaying residence in A Street.

The stately King Mansion high on the slope of Mount Davidson is now the Bonanza Restaurant, the first "by reservation only" establishment in Virginia City in many years, and the town even has a part-time resident literary celebrity in the person of Roger Butterfield, author of *The American Past* and a mighty student of Comstock things and times.

Although the reverse can never be said, perhaps the tourists don't get all they might out of Virginia, since they come up the new Geiger Grade from Steamboat, never knowing that just below and parallel to it is the original Geiger, a far more adventurous highway with hairpin turns and vistas that shame the broad, safe auto road of modern construction. Nor do the tourists know that the road in Six Mile Canyon is still available, preferably in a downward direction toward Sutro and Dayton, with its incredible ruins of stamping mills and foundations for stupendous hoists and its site of Park's Mansion where an Italian artist was specially imported to paint sunlight into a dark stair well as the merest incidental of the half million dollars that was spent on its decoration.

But this is not a guidebook and perhaps it were better if the many do not discover Six Mile, leaving it an untraveled highway shrine for true believers in the Comstock Faith.

# THE SAGA OF C STREET

Sometimes the dead, too, return to Virginia City, also vicariously, in the form of descendants of the original Comstockers. They visit the hoists whence emerged their palaces in the Rue Tilsit, their directorates in Montgomery Street and their lawns and hourglass elms on Long Island, and they visit the cemetery which, at sunset as its shadows lengthen toward the purple east and the Sink of Carson, is the quintessence of all imaginable desolation and loneliness. Perhaps they lay a wreath, in part for their forefathers, in part for the ruin of the irretrievable past. In C Street, where Wells Fargo was, there is nothing. But deep down in the heat and darkness that shall last forever in the sealed stopes and winzes of Gould and Curry and the Mexican, the treasure that resisted all comers in bonanzas incalculable to mortal geologist is still secure, as inviolate as it was on the evening of the world's first Saturday when creation had been accomplished.

129

# CHAPTER VI

## *Silver Suite*

### I: THE BAD MAN FROM BODIE

**T**HREE quarters of a century ago the Bad Man from Bodie was one of the familiar properties of everyday American conversation and literary experience, like Macassar hair oil, the Wild Man from Borneo, the Grangers and wedding trips to Niagara Falls. He was the subject of sermons with obvious morals in churches in Boston's Park Street and Manhattan's Madison Avenue and he was frequently encountered in the pages of Frank Leslie's *Illustrated Weekly*. Had Bodie remained in the public memory down the decades it would be safe to imagine him in imperishable cinema celluloid along with Destry and the Durango Kid. Bodie was just as remote from firsthand experience and as unavailable to general access then as it is today, which is considerable, but everyone had heard about Bodie, and it was very much one of the Wells Fargo towns which lent overtones of galloping melodrama to the greatest of all expresses.

Bodie today gives no least hint of the epic excitements that once convulsed its being and made its name a synonym for outrage and violence throughout the West. Three or four miles south of Mono County's beautifully maintained Victorian Gothic courthouse at Bridgeport, toward Bishop, on U. S. 395, a gravel coach road turns off to the east so abruptly and so hidden in a stand of trees that the hastening motorist may more easily override than discover it. In the sixties and throughout the seventies it was populous with traffic from Bodie, Aurora and Hawthorne to central California over the old Sonora Pass, but now its pleasant way leads upgrade through meadows green in summer and across upland tangents so devoid of travelers that it is possible to traverse the fifteen miles to Bodie a dozen times and never encounter another pilgrim bound for the Esmeralda. For Bodie is one of the ghostliest of all ghost towns. Today its sole inhabitants are a watchman for the mines and the proprietor of a haunted general store whose only stock in trade, for tourists who never come, is warm bottled beer.

Where now are the robust wonderments of the Occidental Hotel, "Rooms *En Suite* If Desired," the May Lundy House and the Grand Central Hotel:

"The Best of Everything Adorns Our Table"? What ghosts inhabit the ruined cellers of the Can Can, the Chop Stand and Antelope, wining, in forgotten vintages, the memories of vanished yesterdays?

The Esmeralda outcroppings were discovered in the last year of the fifties of the nineteenth century by William S. Body, "the Dutchman from Poughkeepsie," who, true to the best mining-camp traditions, uncovered the Bodie Lode while digging for a wounded rabbit which had run to earth. Within a year a mining district had been organized and named after the discoverer who, in his proper person regardless of spelling, had perished in an outsize blizzard. His skull, rescued from the receding drifts and refurbished for the purpose, was fascinating customers from a place of honor on the back bar of the Cosmopolitan Saloon.

At about the same time, ten miles to the east, up a violent canyon pass at the confluence of the ravines of Silver, Middle and Last Chance Hills, there came into being the adjacent mining camp of Aurora. The *Sacramento Union* was able to report on March 6, 1861, that Aurora was possessed of "eight places where food is for sale, four blacksmiths, two bakers, two cobblers, one saddlery, six saloons and four gaming places. There are 67 graves from sagebrush whiskey and poor doctors." Aurora took the lead in the matter of metropolitan characteristics at the beginning, but it was not long before Bodie had far outdistanced it. In a decade its population rose from twenty to a reported 20,000 persons.

Among other generalities obtaining in the record of almost all the mining camps of California and Nevada is the exaggeration of their population figures by eager partisans or mere generous historians. In eastern Nevada at the time of its greatest hold on public attention the town of Pioche was claiming 10,000 inhabitants although well known to have a scant 3,000. Hamilton claimed 25,000 and had, at a generous estimate, half this number. Eureka had 4,000 by sober count, but was fond of talking about a populace of 8,000. Rawhide, the last of the bonanzas and not a very rich one at that, proclaimed grandly that its population was "going on 20,000," but unfortunately it existed in a period when more precise methods of determining the size of the populace were available and the record shows a mere 8,100. In the case of Virginia City it is more difficult to arrive at even an approximation of truth. Beyond all question it was a tremendous city for the Nevada desert of its time, but its wealth and resources of luxury were those of a great metropolis and for once quality was probably mistaken for quantity. Then, too, great numbers of travelers came and went each day by stage and by the V & T RR as well as by private means of communication. Informed old-timers, not given to drawing the long bow, incline politely to discount the reported population of Virginia City at 40,000 and to place its maximum number of residents at any one time at 20,000.

This 20,000 is also the legendary population of Bodie at its great hour in the early seventies and is probably, along with other such optimistic estimates, subject to some slight judicious trimming at the edges. Bodie was quite a place, and its index of violence, noise and gunfire was well above the general average, but it is doubtful if even its thirty mines, some of them not employing more than two score workers, could have supported as many people as the fantastic Comstock diggings.

It is pleasant to note that in the midst of these practical excitements the name of the Esmeralda diggings was bestowed on the two camps by a local admirer of Victor Hugo who took the name from a gypsy character in *Notre-Dame de Paris.*

Wells Fargo moved into both Bodie and Aurora at an early date as it was apparent at once that they were proven camps, and that both had great need of ironbound treasure boxes of the most resistant construction and of express messengers of more than average durability. In Bodie, Wells Fargo first took up offices in the Windsor House, whence the Concords of the United States Mail Stage Co. departed for Hawthorne at two in the afternoon, daily. Wells Fargo's boxes also went out to Bridgeport and the north at six forty-five aboard the stages of Fairfield & Co. which set out from Barney Clarke's Wine Rooms.

At a somewhat later date Wells Fargo was to remove its banking offices from these attractive and practical surroundings to share the building and massive vaults of the Bank of Bodie, but the express and treasure shipping end of the business continued for many years to be transacted among the demijohns of Treble Crown Old Noble Whiskey and the cold cuts of the free lunch.

By the year 1877, the *Sacramento Union,* ever fascinated by the news which came out of the Esmeralda mines, was able to report to its startled readers that Bodie was widely known as "a shooter's town" and that its saga was even then embracing "the widest, maddest years the West has ever known." Naturally Bodie was swollen with pride and making every effort to justify this ferocious repute. The local shootings, bludgeonings, stabbings, hackings, horsewhippings, gougings and more casual mayhem vied in the fine agate print of the *Bodie Free Press* with almost daily accounts of larceny on a grand scale and assaults of frightening frequency upon tangible property of every sort. There was hardly room for the minor local calamities, most of which seemed to concern the death of miners by all manner of violence in the pursuit of their lawful occupation.

At the high noon of its great days there were thirty mines in operation in Bodie alone, and the saloons, pothouses, restaurants, gin mills, ale stoops and allied and adjacent deadfalls averaged, according to the advertising columns of the *Bodie Standard,* something better than one to a mineshaft. Having dined at Stewart's Hotel, the Arlington, the Bodie House, Brown's or the aforementioned Occidental, Grand Central or Windsor, the workman off duty was confronted with a bewildering choice of oases on which to lavish his patronage. He had his choice of Wagner's Corner, the Parole Saloon, the Rifle Club, the Cabinet, the Senate, the Commercial, the Champion, Peters and Aldrige's, the Gymnasium Hall, Marks' Saloon or the Bonanza. At all of these the products of the town's three breweries — the Bodie, the Pioneer and Pat Fahey's — were the favored chasers.

Did his whim incline to the muse? There was almost sure to be a company of *East Lynne* or *Ten Nights in a Bar Room* both prime favorites in the Old West, performing at Miner's Union Hall. And after the show, at an hour when high life was really in order, the prudent reveler could save his final and best thirst of the evening to be dissipated at one or both of the town's ranking resorts of quality and fashion: the Maison Doree Restaurant, where the best quail in aspic in all the Esmeralda region was served for supper, or the Philadelphia Beer Depot, "Opposite to Wells Fargo, the Handsomest Saloon in Bodie and Patronized by all Classes. Sandwiches for Customers at All Hours." The river of life flowed very full in Bodie, both around and through its citizens.

As a result of this rich background of rompin' and stompin', Bodie was rough and tough and the Bad Man from Bodie was to take his place in the alliterative legend along with Pistol Pete, Deadwood Dick and any number of ballad brigands dear to the hearts of Beadle's Dime Library connoisseurs. Wells Fargo, shipping gratifying quantities of bullion out of Bodie and Aurora both over the Hawthorne Road and down the Geiger Grade, surveyed by the locator of Virginia City's more celebrated Geiger Grade, was very much aware of the Bad Man from Bodie. "Throw down that box!" was almost as much a commonplace of roadside conversation as "Here's how" was in the Philadelphia Beer Depot, and, inevitably, steps had to be taken.

Wells Fargo's most invulnerable express messenger of the period, Eugene Blair, and Mike Tovey were brought into Bodie, and their Annie Oakley exploits were given the benefit of a wide and exclamatory press. Every time Blair fought off an attempted holdup, the company presented him with a new weapon of precision, somewhat as it presented other stage drivers with handsomely engrossed watches. Blair was a firearms collector of heroic proportions and defended his coaches with such Gettysburgs of gunfire that he soon boasted an armory whose walls sagged under their weight of Henry rifles, Starr's Navy pistols, Allen and Wheelock's revolvers, Griswold and Grier's Army ordnance, Leech and Rigdon Model Colts and the terrible sure-shot Shawk and McLanahan eight-inch cavalry revolvers made at St. Louis and warranted to have the accuracy of a carbine. Most of these were selected with an eye to Blair's well-known Confederate sympathies and had been sold to the South during the War between the States. When Blair went into action the Confederate armory was represented by everything but the heavier field pieces from the Tredegar works.

Another messenger on the Bodie run was named Woodruff and, on one occasion when he had been slightly injured while Tovey, his companion, was seriously wounded, Woodruff was suspected of being in cahoots with the banditti. A Wells Fargo investigator, Aaron Y. Ross, came in from Carson and found one of the robbers who had been slain in the holdup had been buried nearby by ranchers who had discovered the body by the roadside. Exhumation was by no means beyond the call of duty to a Wells Fargo detective and, when some time later, the body was unburied, clues were discovered which led to the arrest in San Francisco of the man's confederate and to the

## VIGNETTES OF OLD, BOLD BODIE

These four *boulevardiers* of Bodie in the sixties are prospectors in search of further true fissures and other profitable discoveries in the Esmeralda district. The archetype of all the Shorty Harrises and Jim Butlers, it was such whiskery and whiskified fellows as this and their burros who prospected the Old West until the Model T Ford made the burro obselete along with their primitive methods. On the page opposite at the top are the Post Office and the Bank of Bodie as they appeared until the great fire of 1932 which virtually obliterated the town. Wells Fargo maintained its offices in the Bank of Bodie but had long since ceased to function in Aurora. Below is Wells Fargo's vault as it still stands, while at the bottom is the rubber-tired hack which conveyed so many of Bodie's bad men on a one-way trip after they had skirmished with Mike Tovey or Eugene Blair.

FRASHERS, POMONA

LUCIUS BEEBE

FRASHERS, POMONA

exoneration of Woodruff. The grave yawned in those days in Bodie, but it wasn't often that it gave up the dead at the behest of the express company.

In the roaring camps stage robbery was often facilitated by the understandable desire of mine promoters to boast of their rich recoveries from underground and the naïve advertisement of their wealth in hand. The whereabouts, routing and precise amounts of bullion in transit were even recorded in the public prints as when the *Esmeralda Union* for April 6, 1867, triumphantly reported: "Over three tons of bullion from the Cornucopia Mine, Partzwick, are lying in Wells Fargo and Company's office waiting for shipment. Over 150 pounds of bullion from the Diana have been shipped within the past week and plenty more at the mine is awaiting transportation, also $3,500 worth of bullion has been shipped from Aurora in the meantime." In a handily adjacent column, as a paid insertion, were featured the schedules of C. Novacoveich's Wellington Stages and the happy circumstance that they were carrying the Wells Fargo treasure shipments.

Often these news paragraphs read like a sort of à la carte menu for hungry gunmen. They occasionally carried a warning note as well, as might be inferred from an item in the *Bodie Standard* which read: "... it looked like old times in Aurora at Wells Fargo & Co.'s office last Thursday night. There were ten leathern sacks — five from Bodie and five from Benton — lying on the floor while three messengers armed with shotguns and self-cocking revolvers sat behind the counter."

More often, however, the notices were of an accomodating and entirely specific nature, such as the paragraph from the *Reese River Reveille* for December 8, 1876, under the caption "Bullion Shipment": "Manhattan S. M. will ship today twelve bars of bullion weighing 853 lbs., and valued at $12,471.14." In the next column an advertisement for the United State Mail Stage Line to Eureka and White Pine rejoiced in the exclusive carriage of Wells Fargo shipments out of Austin. If this sort of advance notice caused any worry on the part of Eugene Blair, who by this time had graduated from the Bodie school of gunnery and was functioning as Wells Fargo's crack messenger and bandit killer in the White Pine region, he apparently made no mention of the matter to the *Reveille's* editor.

Very soon, however, the banditry which had for a spell been abated by Blair's sure-shot conveyance was again on the increase and the community was rising to the heights of wickedness so vividly reported by the *Sacramento Union*. So fearsome indeed was its name becoming that when a miner in neighboring Aurora decided to move down the canyon to Bodie in search of better employment, his little daughter's tearful prayer at her mother's knee that night ended with: "Good-bye, God. We're going to Bodie!" The impious *Bodie Daily Free Press* acknowledged the validity of the sentiment claiming only that there had been a typographical error in reporting and that the moppet's quotation should have read: "Good! By God, we're going to Bodie!"

Bodie, the bad and Byzantine, was not only unabashed by its own wickedness, it never tired of bragging that it was even tougher than Candelaria, eighty miles to the east, where common report had it that miners with a toothache simply tamped home a charge of giant powder and then chewed on a fulminate cap to eliminate the offending canine or biscupid. Wells Drury, in "An Editor on the Comstock Lode," reports a remark made by a Virginia City undertaker which enchanted Bodie. "We never get any breaks in this business," lamented the shroud merchant. "As soon as the local talent get to thinking they're tough they go try it out in Bodie and Bodie undertakers get the job of burying them." John Hayes Hammond was later to recall that in 1879, during the first week he spent within the municipal precincts of Bodie, when the town was really feeling its oats, there were six fatal shooting affrays, or an average of one a day with the Sabbath exempted. The less lethally maimed were constantly encountered in the streets, bandaged and groaning and in search of sympathetic auditors to whom to relate their side of the argument.

While Bodie gloried in its bad renown and took inordinate pleasure in such shooting matters as involving Ed Ryan and Dave Bannon who burned powder against one another at such close range and with such precision of draw and discharge that each shot the other through the heart, Bodie's mines were not only producing bullion for the expressing of Wells Fargo, but were also consuming the woodstands of Esmeralda and Mono counties in the same voracious manner that was elsewhere denuding the hillslopes for the mines of the Comstock, the Reese River and White Pine districts.

The Tioga, the Standard Con, the Boston Con, the Silver Bulwer, the North Noonday, the Homer, the Blackhawk, the Red Cloud Con, the Champion, the Oro and the Bodie Tunnel were engulfing such quantities of timber that at length, as elsewhere, a railroad was constructed, not so much for the export of Bodie's products, a move which would have been frowned on by local stagers with fearful frowning, but for the elevation of timber from the lowlands for its stopes and galleries.

The little Bodie and Benton was a narrow-gage railroad, thirty miles long, which was planned to connect at Benton with Darius Mills' orphan, the Carson and Colorado, but today even most railroad historians have forgotten its very existence. In the pleasant manner of a more personalized age, each of its little locomotives was named *Mono, Inyo, Como and Yolo,* and a wicked resident observed that, when business warranted it, the line would probably purchase "three or fomo." The Bodie and Benton was one of the few Nevada railroads of the nineteenth century which carried no Wells Fargo strongboxes, since all the express company's bullion was headed the other way and since, in any event, it never did reach Benton depot on the Carson and Colorado. The local family which best remembers the Bodie and Benton are the Hunewills of Bridgeport whose freighting of lumber by oxcart was rendered obsolete by the railroad and who have been ranchers ever since.

Up the precipitous canyon at Aurora, a far more orderly and rightliving community than bedlamite Bodie, the *Esmeralda Union* was demanding that steps be taken to protect the coaches and their occupants. One of Wells Fargo's passenger stops in Aurora was at the Aurora Stage House, W. A. B.

## AURORA WAS FADING IN 1890

Although Aurora's fortunes had been declining since the mid-sixties when most of the population had moved down canyon to wicked but more prosperous Bodie, there were still enough voters left in Aurora to make it worth while for R. K. Colcord, candidate for and later governor of Nevada (in wagon), to campaign there for office in 1890. Below is the cabin Mark Twain occupied briefly when he lived in Aurora while prospecting in the Esmeralda.

## AURORA WAS THROUGH IN 1949

Because, when it came into being in the early sixties, stone and brick were more easily available than wood, Aurora survived the conflagrations that wiped out its neighbor, Bodie. But despite its substantial appearance, and from a distance, Aurora had no single inhabitant when these pictures were taken in the middle years of the twentieth century. In even better preservation than the town itself is its cemetery overlooking the scene of departed glory from a neighboring hillside.

Cobb, proprietor, "conducted strictly on temperance principles," which gives some clue to the state of grace of Aurora. If further evidence is required it can be found in the sort of news which occupied the *Union,* between the insertions for Robert J. Berry's and Henry Pennington's rival bathing and shaving saloons, which were waging a price war, and the advertisement of Ward's India Rubber Enameled Paper Collars, "The last word in style." It read that "Mr. Tennyson has contributed a poem on the subject of Lucretius to the May issue of MacMillan. It is positively announced that this effort will not be drivel." That was Aurora for you: law and order and Mr. Tennyson.

Wells Fargo again called a meeting of its best minds including, of course, Tovey and Blair; and a few evenings later, after it had been circulated that a particularly rich cargo of bullion was in transit, a strange thing was observed to happen in the conduct of the Hawthorne stage. Out in the meadows, between the fringes of Bodie and the halfway house, the evening stage halted in the gathering dusk and a number of resolute-looking men with a prodigious armory about their persons took over. The passengers were asked to dismount and identify their luggage and were then escorted to a light passenger wagon or carryall which was at hand. Their places were taken atop and within the Concord by an equal number of guards of similar appearance to the disembarked fares, and the little cavalcade set off in the direction of Aurora with the passengers at a discreet distance bringing up the rear as a sort of second section.

A mile or so on into the night the familiar command echoed from three masked figures waiting in the middle of the road. Like the armor of a battle cruiser, the Henry rifles and short snouted shotguns on the coachtop swung onto their target in the darkness and there was a blast of concentrated gunfire which would have done hurt at Shiloh. There was insufficient tangible evidence left to indentify the three bandits and formal burial was out of the question. For quite a while Wells Fargo was unmolested in the vicinage of the Five Mile House.

Despite Aurora's pretensions to a state of superior civic grace and low index of homicide compared to Bodie, it was Aurora that found itself famed overnight as the scene of the most sensational one-man jail break of its generation. Milton Sharp, an accomplice in the case of the disinterred highwayman down Bodie way, and finally run to earth in San Francisco by Chief of Detectives Hume, had been lodged in Aurora's jailhouse while awaiting transportation to the State Prison at Carson whence he had been sentenced on an indictment for armed robbery of Wells Fargo. During a gelid November night he made an escape by breaking through the brick wall of his cell and disappearing into the Esmeralda snowdrifts still wearing a ball and chain or, as it was locally known, Oregon boot. The excitement which followed is still remembered in western Nevada. Wells Fargo offered a handsome reward and overnight the countryside swarmed with the express company's police. The Aurora authorities, the County Commissioners and the State posted additional offers with the result that mines were closed and businessmen put up their shutters while half the populace went on an armed bandit hunt in much the spirit that ranchers in prairie states convene for a wolf drive. All bullion shipments out of the Esmeralda were suspended while he was at large. A week later Sharp gave himself up, at Candelaria, half starved and almost frozen.

Sharp was critical of the Aurora jail. "Anybody can get out of the cells," he said rudely. "The only part of it you can't escape from is the tank where they keep the Mexicans."

Not all the dramas which had their focus at Wells Fargo's various Bodie offices ended in the graveyard on the hillside behind Miner's Union Hall. There was, for example, the affair of the lady with the horsewhip which occupied space in the *Bodie Free Press* of February 3, 1882, and for several days thereafter.

On this approximate date, at the close of school (the scene of the outrage still stands, having survived all of Bodie's several conflagrations), Miss Florence Molinelli returned to her family hearthside with the tearful report that as she was departing from the classroom a number of wicked boys had even more wickedly pursued her with epithets which they may or may not have learned in the less refined vicinage of the Parole Saloon. The terms of these infamous accusations, breathed into the outraged ear of Mrs. Molinelli, caused that good woman first to reach for the ever-present square-faced bottle of Stoughton's Bitters, a family remedy which occupied a permanent place between the ormolu French clock and the vase of pussy willows on all best mantels, and then for her shawl and bonnet.

Mrs. Molinelli paused briefly at the home of a neighbor, Dr. J. W. Van Zandt, who, since her husband was underground at the North Noonday Mine at the time, consented to escort her on a mission of justified vengeance. She then made a small purchase at the hardware and undertaking establishment of Charles Kelly, "Coffins, Caskets and Shrouds Always on Hand, Also English Bulldog, self-cocking Revolvers and Hercules Giant Powder." The purchase was later described by witnesses as "a small dog or pet whip four or five feet in length," and it was just outside Wells Fargo & Co., banking offices in the premises of the Bodie Bank that she encountered the youth named by Florence as her loudest traducer.

The whip cracked ("smartly," the *Free Press* said) across the youth's face and Florence's mother announced between smitings that when he, Phil Evans, should "again address himself to her daughter in vile terms she would reduce him to the estate of a corpse." Young Evans screamed and sought shelter within the august doors of Wells Fargo. Dr. Van Zandt, agreeably employed as an accessory in the achievement of justice, dragged at his coattails. A crowd of small boys, friends and allies of Evans, gathered from nowhere and set upon Mrs. Molinelli and Dr. Van Zandt with loyal fury. The entire tumult seethed across Wells Fargo's threshold amidst the sound of smashing glass as the door crashed open, and Major Atlee, the manager, summoned in haste from a rear room, joined battle with a massive double-entry ledger which he prudently snatched from a handy letter press.

A MOMENT OF REPOSE IN BODIE

The tranquil interlude in a Bodie pothouse depicted here was not specifically the commotion in which Wells Fargo's front window was shattered but it is evidence that the gentle sex had no hesitancy in taking up arms in a just cause. Obviously the good woman with the domestic broom is about to chastise severely the vandal intent on oversetting a jorum of Old Noble Treble Crown 100 proof.

With the aid of the ledger and a shrewd tactic or two learned from Fighting Joe Hooker in the Valley of the Shenandoah, Major Atlee was able to clear the room and in time the dust settled as the participants in the affray went home to bandage themselves.

Bodie thought the matter at an end, but two days later it chanced that young Evan's mother, pausing at the window of Fred Webber's Harness Store, was seized by an idea, and again the sale of "dog or pet" whips boomed in Bodie. Nursing a smoldering sense of family wrong, Mrs. Evans addressed her footsteps to the door of Dr. Van Zandt. The doctor was taking a nap on his office sofa when he was rudely awakened by the avenging entrance of young Evans' maternal parent. "The subsequent conversation is of little importance," reported the *Free Press*, but Dr. Van Zandt told the reporters that "when a woman puts herself on a man's level she must take the consequences, and the whip now occupies a position on the doctor's desk next the skull of a deceased politician."

142

The stage of the Wells Fargo theater was sometimes set for comedy as well as for melodrama.

Seventy years, more or less, after these commotional doings it is difficult to believe that Bodie was once the scene of such sensational wickedness that as far away as New York it served as a synonym for Babylon in sermons. Four successive conflagrations, the most recent in 1932, have reduced most of its business sites to grass-grown cellarages and heaps of rubble dotted with the shells of ravished safes and vaults. By some irony of chance the little firehouse in the main street has survived, still sheltering in its primitive economy the handdrawn hose cart that served in holocausts of the seventies. The Miner's Union Hall, a museum, now is open to the public if the town custodian can be discovered. It boasts a raffish and disordered collection of pioneer Bodieana: badges from fireman's balls and church festivals, ancient Singer sewing machines, the daybooks of the Bank of Bodie, a watchmaker's diminutive chest of drawers still filled with hundreds of assorted watch crystals that never were fitted to timepieces, the town fire chief's trumpet and the gaily feathered bonnets of women who may have been the town's fair but frail in the bold, bad days of its youth.

The fair but frail themselves are buried on the hillside in "the outcasts cemetery," removed a few paces from holy ground, as shameful evidence of Bodie's sanctimonious churlishness of heart. "It's just as good land." said the ancient who pointed us to the wooden markers returning to elemental earth, "and I'm sure they're just as comfortable. But those stinkers up there" — he pointed to the ground sanctified by Holy Church — "must of been powerful sure of themselves."

Up canyon in Aurora where Tennyson and Lucretius made the news there is more visual evidence of the past than at Bodie, though in 1949 no single person made his abode in the ghostly town. Aurora was built of brick and granite and the big general store with its cellars and verandas and the Mazda Saloon might serve again if only they had roofs and customers. There is still wallpaper in some of the houses at Aurora — gay, gracious patterns that would command collector's prices were they available in Madison Avenue or Sutter Street to amateurs of Victorian antiquities. There are vast mounds of empty champagne bottles in the grass, evidence that the patrons of the Court House Restaurant in Silver Street, "Meals at All Hours and Oysters Special," and of the Exchange Hotel in Pine Street, whence Wells Fargo went out via Wellington, Dorsey's Stages for Fort Independence, lived well in spite of their devotion to Mr. Tennyson. At Aurora as elsewhere, it may be assumed, the miners were more or less allergic to the sparkling wine of Rheims and Épernay, even though the phrase had not yet come to their attention. Champagne was French and it was expensive. Aurora was rich and things French were in fashion then as now and champagne was consumed in heroic quantities on public occasions even though tastes at private symposiums were more robust.

Behind what had been a drugstore, or at least a pharmacy, a few brown bottles that had once contained chemicals lie amidst disintegrating bricks and mortar. They may have held palliatives to rival the virtues of R. Gibson's Dispensary whose discreetly worded insertion in the *Esmeralda Union* had read: "A sure cure for the effects of personal diseases or virus absorbed into the system will be sent for $10. in a plain envelope by registered letter or through Wells Fargo & Co." Here was one more office and function of Wells Fargo in an age innocent of penicillin.

At the corner of Pine and Antelope, in the ruins of Peter Job No. 2 Restaurant (ah, fetching name of long-forgotten significance!*) there is a coffee mill irrevocably smashed and beyond mortal recall, posing as it must to the philosophical the question of whether the gods of proverb or the management of Peter Job No. 2 Restaurant ground the smaller.

## II: ALONG THE EASTERN MARCHES

A cursory study of the map of Nevada will disclose to the interested beholder that almost without exception its bonanzas and mining excitements lie in the lower half of the state, growing in density and intensity as they approach, parallel and, in places, overflow the northwest to southeast tangent which is the California boundary. Until the building of the Pacific Railroad, the main transcontinental route across Nevada lay, not as it now does in a northerly curving bow through Wells, Elko, Battle Mountain and Winnemucca, but along a far more direct parallel across the very center of the state via Ely, Eureka and Austin.

After 1869 the mining districts of the Reese, the White Pine and Ely were all, at various times, connected with the transcontinental main line by short-line railroads of great character and charm. Even after the construction of the Nevada Central to Austin and the Eureka and Palisade, the many mining communities in mid-Nevada were not directly located on one of the railroads; Hamilton, Treasure City, Pioche, and others of less celebrated names were part of a complex of intercommunicating stages. On almost every one of these routes Wells Fargo operated express services and maintained agencies.

Pioche, it might be remarked parenthetically, also had a railroad of its own at one time, the Pioche and Pacific, but it reversed the procedure of every other short line in the state except the Las Vegas and Tonopah and the Tonopah and Tidewater, and ran southward for its main line connection with San

---

* A yellowed handbook of San Francisco restaurants and places of entertainment in the seventies mentions a French restaurant of remarkable discretion and conservative clientele opened by a Peter Job. This may well have been a branch of the San Francisco venture.

Pedro, Los Angeles and Salt Lake RR at Caliente. Like the lonely Bodie and Benton across the California line in Mono County, it has been forgotten by all but the most informed connoisseurs of the legend of vanished railroads in the West.

The first falling off of great revenues from the Comstock came in 1865 with the exhaustion of surface deposits and, although undreamed bonanzas were yet to be uncovered on the eastern slopes of Sun Mountain, there was, as the year progressed, a not inconsiderable exodus from Virginia City.

Most of it was eastward in the direction of the Reese River and White Pine districts where new and promising bonanzas, including the world's richest deposit of surface silver at Treasure Hill near Hamilton, were daily being reported with all the naïveté and enthusiasm which has accompanied the discovery of precious metals everywhere. Miners were departing from the Comstock. The mills along the Carson River were shutting down in such numbers that in a single day half a thousand stamps fell silent, not for years again to dance in the mad tarantella of silver. Lyman, in *The Saga of the Comstock Lode,* reports that the first International Hotel in Virginia City was pulled down, loaded on freighters and set up again in Austin complete in every detail of swinging lamps, green-topped tables and bowl and pitcher sets, but there seems no other evidence to this effect. The current owners of the International Hotel in Austin pronounce the tale a complete canard and believe that their famous property acquired its name but no more tangible assets from Virginia City's most opulent hostelry.

Be that as it may, the eastward progress of the prospectors which had started six years previous when the Comstock began luring men from the Mother Lode made mere way stations of Virginia City, Silver City and Gold Hill, for the moment at least. Wells Fargo had far too great a stake in the Comstock for any such simple and spontaneous abandonment; and, in any event Louis McLane, like Mackay and other deeply sagacious believers, looked into the Comstock future with unimpaired optimism. But the eastern marches of the state offered new fields for the freighting of treasure and Wells Fargo joined in the migration.

Austin, the nearest of the eastern Nevada bonanzas to the Comstock, was particularly a Wells Fargo town and, although it was not a new town when boom times arrived, it was popularly reported that the first valuable ore in the Reese River region had been uncovered by the flying hooves of a Wells Fargo steed in the old Pony Express service on whose route Austin had been a station as well as, later, a relay point on the transcontinental telegraph. By 1863 it boasted two hotels and a post office, and in later years it became celebrated in the annals of the Old West as the home town of Mme. Emma Nevada, as the home of the *Reese River Reveille,* one of the greatest of pioneer newspapers, and as the setting for the colloquies of the Sazarac Lying Club, one of the most notable of all congresses of raconteurs and merchants of mendacity. Austin was also the point of origin of the sack of flour which, when repeatedly auctioned off during the War between the States, was to

The Wells Fargo & Company receipt:

WELLS, FARGO & COMPANY

Office of WELLS, FARGO & Co., [Stage Department.]

GENERAL EXPRESS FORWARDERS TO ALL PARTS OF THE WORLD,

and Carriers of the Great Overland Mail between the Atlantic and Pacific

AUSTIN N. Feby 9' 18

Received of John Cummins the sum

Ninety Six Cur 100 DOLLA

in full for One passage from AUSTIN N Salt 4443 #38

to Salt Lake, in Coach leaving Feby 9 180

In consideration of the price paid for this Ticket, it is expressly stipulated and agreed between the holder thereof and WELLS, FARGO & COMPANY, that said WELLS, FARGO & COMPANY shall in no case be held responsible for loss of Gold Dust, Coin, Bullion, Bank and Treasury Notes, carried by said p

$96

W. E. Sibell, Stationer, No. 3 Wall Street, N. Y.

## A FARE FOR WELLS FARGO

In 1868 it cost a passenger $96 to ride on Wells Fargo's coaches from Austin to Salt Lake, which is a tariff of over $.25 a mile. A celebrated driver running out of Austin at the time was Jim Miller and one of his fares one day in the late seventies was Bill Wixom's daughter, Emma, who was going to Europe, it was reported, to study for grand opera. The *Reese River Reveille* said she would go far, and she did, as Emma Nevada, a soprano of some note in her generation. Adjacent is a professional photograph of Mme. Nevada, the original print of which is inscribed: "To my darling 'little brother' from his barefooted 'little sister' Emma Nevada Mignon, J'ai foi."

raise many hundred thousand dollars for the Sanitary Fund, predecessor of today's Red Cross.

In the hot years of its heady youth, when town lots were selling for as much as $8,000, when all transactions of whatever magnitude were arranged in terms of twenty-dollar pieces because no smaller currency was available, and when private schools gave instruction in French and classic dancing to the daughters of miners, Austin lived high. Its saloons and restaurants, outside whose rapidly swinging doors Emma Wixom, later Mme. Nevada, used to sing for silver dollars tossed to her by the enchanted inmates, included Smyth's, which shared premises with the United States Post Office, Gandolpo's Sazarac in Main Street, scene of the great bending of the long bow, Barovitch's "Next Door to the Engine House" and therefore and obviously advantageous meeting place for the volunteer fire department, the Magnolia, the Crystal, Luetjen's and The Confidence, "Patrons Served by Polite and Accomplished Bartenders." Louis Loustalot's Lafayette Restaurant introduced frog's legs Provençal to Austin, and Austin, somewhat to its surprise, found itself taking kindly to the strange ways of French gastronomy.

Long after the days of the Pony Express Austin was still an important agency for Wells Fargo, whose treasure boxes were carried by the United State Mail Stage Line between Eureka and Austin, by Clark's Fast Freight to Battle Mountain and also to Battle Mountain aboard the Concords of Tuller and Clugage's service.

When responsible talk of a "Pacific Railway" began circulating in Nevada, Austin took it for granted, as did Eureka, that the line would be surveyed smack-dab across the center of the state from Ely to the Canyon of the Truckee and that the two towns would become centers for a network of rails radiating to all the camps in the region with direct connections for Chicago and San Francisco right at the foot of Main Street. Where else, in heaven's name, would anyone think of locating a railroad?

When, in actual fact, the track gangs of the Central Pacific spiked down the first light iron a hundred-odd miles to the north, Austin and Eureka were livid, if not exactly inarticulate, with anger and each eventually built their own little railroad, the Nevada Central connecting Austin with Battle Mountain, and the Eureka and Palisade with the two terminals of its corporate title. The Central achieved its southern terminal at Clifton a mile down the hillside from Austin town, and passengers were pulled the last mile up the grade by mule power over the rails of the Austin City Railway, the only streetcar system in all Nevada. One evening the inordinately daring engineer of the down passenger train from Battle Mountain, conceivably in a hurry to get his own special decanter of Treble Crown Old Noble Whiskey at the International Bar, didn't stop at the Clifton depot, but kept working steam right up the middle of Main Street, past the Court House to the Manhattan Mill. After that the mules were retired and a steam dummy known as "The Mule's Relief" took passengers to the very swinging doors of the International. Austin was that modern!

## LIFE CYCLE AT AUSTIN

Austin, Nevada, by the early eighties (above) was the kind of town Wells Fargo admired to serve. Twenty-dollar gold pieces were the standard of currency and there was no smaller change. House lots were bringing a fantastic $8,000 apiece. There were a score of mills in day and night operation and the barmen at the International Hotel were serving quart-size whisky slings to miners whose children went to private schools teaching dancing, French, instrumental music and calesthenics. Wells Fargo from Austin was serving Eureka, Hamilton, Ely and Pioche and connecting with the Central Pacific over the Nevada Central RR. Almost none of these wonders obtain today although the International Hotel is still in operation and Austin (below) has largely returned to the sagebrush.

## WELLS FARGO RIDES THE HIGH IRON

Between the booming bonanza town of Austin, Nevada, and Battle Mountain on the Central Pacific's main line, after its completion in 1879, Wells Fargo rode the exciting little combines and bullion cars of the narrow-gage Nevada Central RR behind the brightly painted locomotives *Sidney Dillon, Anson P. Stokes* and *General Ledlie*. Another scene on this wistful and now-vanished railroad depicted by the artist, E. S. Hammack, is visible in the front matter of this book where it illustrates the half-title page. The photograph shown above is a rare item of Western Americana, not only because it shows a Nevada Central mixed consist pulling out of the Battle Mountain terminus, but because it shows a wooden combine in the foreground bearing the insigne of Wells Fargo on the freight compartment. Another merchandise car bearing the legend of Wells Fargo rode the first train (below) of the Oregon and California RR which, in 1884, ran into the Rogue River region of southern Oregon.

Elsewhere in the eastern landscape of Nevada Wells Fargo was playing a stellar role in the melodrama of mines and money. Over by the Humboldt the Eureka and Palisade, a narrow-gage railroad with the backing of San Francisco's Darius Ogden Mills, had gotten itself built as far as the tough, rough and swaggeringly affluent town of Eureka. Lacking a depot site the road set up a ticket window in Buell Street's Corner Saloon. The Atlantic and Pacific Telegraph Co. installed itself there too, among the decanters and beer pumps, and inevitably so did Wells Fargo. The possibilities for doing business, arranging for transportation and dispatching the news of new gold strikes were conveniently adjacent and all could be conducted in an atmosphere at once stimulating and congenial. The Wells Fargo stages were so frequently held up on the Eureka run that guards were required by company regulations to ride into town with the muzzles of their shotguns resting on their boots so that an inclination to doze might cost them a foot. But in the Corner Saloon business was conducted under more refined circumstances, and the miners and local magnates patronized the bar, the bank, the telegraph company and the railroad with fine impartiality, signing drafts with one hand while nursing whisky slings with the other.

One of the earliest holdups, or rather attempted stage robberies, in the White Pine region involved the celebrated Uncle Jim Miller, and the tangible evidence of it may be seen to this day in the display cases of the Wells Fargo Museum in San Francisco. Jim Miller was, beyond all cavil, the Berry Wall and sartorial beau ideal of all Nevada stagers of whatever generation. Even in an occupation notable for its regard for the formalities of attire and splendid accessories of dress, Uncle Jim was a famous dude. His hats were the widest "Mormons" available anywhere and were specially fabricated to his exacting measure by a San Francisco hatter. His resplendent Ascot ties were held in place by stickpins as big as a lady's brooch. His Inverness driver's cloaks with their sleeve-length capes were worn in a manner to shame the deportment of a grand duke at court, and his whipstock was bound with bands of pure gold from the diggings of the Mother Lode. In his later years, when his fame and dignity allowed him a measure of eccentricity, Uncle Jim took to wearing a widebrimmed hat ornamented with gold stars like an Uncle Sam of the plains.

Jim Miller had started out as a stager out of Virginia City, operating his own Concords under the name of the Overland Stage Co., but when the rush to the Reese and White Pine regions commenced during a low ebb in the fortunes of the Comstock, he joined the eastward trek and started another company with service between Austin and Battle Mountain (until the railroad came) and from Ely to White Pine. Wide was the fame of Miller's stages and splendid were his goings and comings. Of course he carried matter for Wells Fargo, and so it befell that one noontime in the middle sixties he set out from Ely on the Eureka run with six horses, five passengers and $30,000 in minted gold to pay off the millworkers at the end of the haul.

The daylight hours passed pleasantly. The weather was more than clement, the company aboard the stage was entirely masculine and so provided none of

### CLASSIC JEHU

Jim Miller was almost as celebrated in the annals of the Wells Fargo years in Nevada as was his big silver watch, a gift from Wells Fargo for saving a treasure consignment on the run between Ely and White Pine in the dangerous staging days of the 1870's. The watch and chain may be seen to this day in Wells Fargo Bank museum in San Francisco.

the inconveniences to its conduct implicit in female fares, and one of the travelers who was, perhaps by shrewd selection, invited by the driver to share the box, was provided with a square-faced bottle of Lawrence's Medford rum from far-off Massachusetts, no common fare in the Nevada sixties. Not until nightfall, when all his passengers were sleeping soundly under Buffalo robes in the interior of the coach, did Miller think of danger. Then, just before moonrise and as the Concord was climbing a steep reverse curve, there came out of the darkness the accustomed hail and command to "throw down that box."

Without hesitation Miller aimed a swinging blow with his buckskin lash at the near-wheel horse and in the same movement drew a heavy dragoon revolver from his cloak. There was a roar as of cannon fire from the dragoon. The horses leapt as though the devil was driving, the Concord lurched with terrifying abruptness, and the answering gunfire from the ditch lodged hot lead in the expensive painting on the door representing the Lakes of Killarney in springtime. The passengers cowered on the floor, sharing the remains of the Medford rum, and the entire entourage thundered off into the dark with Wells Fargo treasure intact and no great damage done.

What would Uncle Jim Miller like to receive for saving the treasure? inquired the general superintendent over the Eureka telegraph, and the message came back over the looping wires to Montgomery Street: "The damndest biggest bullion watch and chain in Nevada." There was nothing small about Uncle Jim. And so, at the command of Wells Fargo, J. W. Tucker, a San Francisco watchmaker of fair repute, went to work with a four pound bar of bullion from the Comstock, and artisans at Shreve & Co. started to forge the grandfather of all watch chains from a similar bar of metal. Together they produced a masterpiece of useful ornament.

The watch itself weighs two pounds and the chain the same weight again and the metal is so soft that the design on the case had to be recut three times during Uncle Jim's lifetime, which was a long and hilarious one. The chain has sliding shields with the name of its owner and the catch is a miniature of the patent safety hook used for letting down iron pails into silver mines. The design on the watch — and you may see it for the asking in Wells Fargo's Bank — shows the great holdup, with the Nevada mountains in the background and Jim Miller beating the bejaises out of his horses as plain as if it had been daylight and the artist had been there to see.

All his life Jim Miller's watch and chain were the hallmark of his fame and person. In the files of the *Reese River Reveille* for 1878, the issue of February 19th still tells how a traveling magician in Austin gave an evening performance and requested a member of the audience to surrender his watch and chain to be shot out of a blunderbuss and, presumably, restored in good working order as evidence of the magic of the practitioner. A grave, precocious teen-ager named Pat Lemmon, son of a miner, was asked to descend into the audience and return to the stage with the sacrificial watch, but when he discovered what he was carrying up the aisle, he returned with dignity and

## SCARCE COMMODITY IN THE DESERT

The water wagon was a factual reality in all early Nevada mining communities. This one, posed before the office of the Ruby Hill Water Works, was in Eureka.

restored it to its owner with the announcement that "he wouldn't allow any man to shoot Jim Miller's big watch at him out of any blunderbuss because it wouldn't be safe." He didn't say for whom.

The morbid potentialities of railroad travel in Nevada at this period are recorded for posterity in a paragraph in the *Eureka Daily Sentinel* for April 9, 1878, which read as follows:

G. W. Wright, President of the Bank of Nevada, had a rather ghastly experience on his recent trip to San Francisco. Just after getting started out from Oakland, a tramp's legs were cut off, the result of an attempt to steal a ride. Between Lathrop and Sacramento a sick man yielded up the ghost. After leaving Sacramento a son of William M. Evarts, Secretary of State, died a victim of consumption. Mr. Wright had just arrived in Eureka when the crack of the playful pistol announced another tragedy and he saw the body of Gus Botto, murdered at Bigelow's Music Hall, borne past to his residence. Fearing that his arrival at Pioche might be the signal for a general immolation, he tarried the night with us.

Wells Fargo at a later date maintained its own offices in Eureka. Only a slight departure from the convenience of Buell Street's Corner Saloon they were located with Matt Kyle's Saloon on one side, while right through the party wall on the other side was the Court Exchange. The treasure boxes went out in Gilmer and Salisbury's triweekly stages to Hamilton and Pioche as well

## THE GLORY OF THE NEVADA HIGHR

Wells Fargo's Ely-Eureka stage, w
beaver-hatted driver at the ribbons
the numerous family of some substa
citizen on top, poses for its portrait
side the Bureau Hotel at Eureka in
In 1949 the structure that was the B
is still standing as is the substantial
warehouse in the background. The
cord in the upper photograph was
of the more ornate masterpieces of
bot, Downing's manufacture and a
bottom of the page is shown in
detail the ornate and elaborate de
tive devices which delighted the
alike of stager and traveler in the a
glittering coaches.

## EUREKA CHANGES WITH THE YEARS

Sometime between 1880 (above) and 1949 (below) the Nevada State Highways Department straightened the road out of Eureka and, except for the conformations of the landscape, the town became almost unrecognizable. In the foreground of the upper photograph the tracks of the little Eureka and Palisade RR lie beside a cache of 15,000,000 lbs. of lead awaiting shipment.

as in the boots of the Eureka, Tybo and Belmont Staging Co., both of which picked up passengers at the Court Exchange, so that although Wells Fargo was able to shelter its letter presses and vaults under its own individual roof, the atmosphere was much the same as in communities where it shared facilities with less austere tenants.

Some notion of the urbane and civilized resources of Eureka in its years of wonderment may be derived from the following insertion in the *Sentinel* during the month of February, 1878:

Removed ————— Removed
BRANDT'S
Bavaria and Boca Beer
DEPOT

Is removed to the San Francisco Hotel or Red Light Lodging House Building, East side of Maine Street, Eureka,Nevada, where Louis will keep on hand a constant supply of the celebrated Boca and Bavaria Beer, also Vineyard, Prop & Co's Sazerac de Forge, and other well known brands of brandies, Bourbons and Rye whiskies, some of them 24 years old and all of the finest liquors at 12½ cents the drink. An elegant elevator of the latest pattern is employed in hoisting the beer filled in glasses, cold from the cellar, at a tick of the bell. Free lunch from eleven o'clock daily, also sandwiches, herring caviar, Westphalia ham, etc. Cigars a specialty. In connection with the bar he will conduct a first class Lodging House at which the weary can ever find repose in comfortable rooms and clean, downy beds. A share of the public patronage is solicited.

Still another fantastic bonanza in eastern Nevada during the sixties and seventies was that of Hamilton and its adjacent diggings at Treasure Hill in the White Pine Mountains. Located at so great an altitude that it was frequently above the clouds or shrouded in dense mists, Hamilton cut a caper of Dionysiac proportions in 1868 when two prospectors who had thrown up a rock windbreak against the inclement elements discovered that the walls of their bleak shelter were built of a cool $75,000 worth of nearly pure silver chloride. Overnight more than 15,000 people (this is probably the correct figure although local statisticians at the time claimed half again as many) converged on Hamilton, first on buckboards and with burros from Eureka, Pioche and Austin, and later among the Wells Fargo treasure boxes which rode Gilmore and Hamilton's stages to Pioche and the Concords of Woodruff and Ennor which operated to Wells, more than a hundred miles to the north on the Central Pacific until the completion, in 1879, of the Eureka and Palisade RR.

Old-timers at Wells recall that even this distant staging terminal was a scene of activity and bustle, never since duplicated, during the White Pines "excitement," and Hamilton, while its brief candle burned, was a metropolis in miniature whose main street afforded as much glamor and tumult as San Francisco's Market Street. All the prototypes of the mining West were visible at Hamilton: the top-hatted gambler with his starched linen and manicured hands, the sweating teamsters of incredible vocabulary, the flannel-shirted miner, the Eastern newspaper reporter in ratcatcher suit and curly-brimmed derby, the blowsy madams and their fair but frail and, of course, the trustee of all frontier wealth, the forwarder extraordinary, Wells Fargo & Co.'s agent whose Albert watch chain, broadcloth tailcoat and wide-brimmed black hat were the hallmark and superscription of trust, authority and unchallenged probity.

So rich were the superficial ores at Treasure Hill that representatives of an Eastern syndicate were empowered to offer $4,000,000 cash on the barrelhead for the leading property of the camp. "Maybe we can make a dicker after we've paid off the national debt," said the owners grandly.

For two years, during which time ore worth more than $3,000,000 actually was removed from this single-strip mine seventy feet long and less than twenty-five feet deep on the Eberhardt property, the stages out of Hamilton averaged two holdups a week and frequently there were two or even three in a single day. Aaron Ross, one of Wells Fargo's most fearsome bandit fighters, was imported and put on the various runs out of Pioche; Mike Tovey, who had been educated in matters of gunfire and coachtop strategy in the graduate schools of lethal arts and sciences in Bodie and Aurora, was ordered to the precincts of Hamilton, and Eugene Blair, by this time the possessor of a fabulous arsenal of engraved express rifles, each the memorial of an enemy of Wells Fargo now securely lodged in some local Boot Hill, was riding out of Hamilton on the Ward run of Gilmore's six-horse stages with the treasure box held to the floor of the boot with welded stay bolts.

From Hamilton to the Humboldt and from Austin to the great salt flats of western Utah, Nevada was ablaze with gunfire. The rich odor of burning black powder merged with the smell of sagebrush and greasewood, and back in Hartford and Bridgeport in New England the output of brass-cased slugs for the chambers of Winchester 40-82s and the Universal Colt's .45 equalizer was achieving a record peacetime level. In Central and South America, dictators and would-be political *jefes* were forced *faute mieux* if only temporarily, to postpone revolutions and *coups d'état* because of a shortage of ball ammunition. It was all going to Nevada.

Of all the Wells Fargo messengers of the time, Blair was the meanest bandit slayer and shootingest man to ride the Concords. During an attempted holdup between Hamilton and Ward, a rash amateur named Jimmy Carlo lost an arm to Blair's redoubtable aim and died a few hours later from the resultant loss of blood. His partner, one Jim Crawford, had momentarily escaped and Blair had taken six days off from riding the coachtops to follow him and brought him back from the sagebrush, a saddened bad man with his wrists in chains.

Between Eureka and Tybo, the stage carrying Jimmy Brown and Blair, a

## ABODE OF MEMORIES AND HOME OF GHOSTS

When the great Hidden Treasure Mine was in operation on desolate Treasure Hill behind the town, Hamilton was a mining center for 25,000 persons and itself had a population of 10,000. Two pioneers in the first rush to this now ghostliest of all ghost towns reached the diggings in 1868 and threw up a little stone shelter against the bitter winds of the White Pine region, shortly to find that they had built it with $75,000 worth of silver ore. Hamilton roared, flourished, and burned with a greater intensity of roaring, opulence of flowering and frequency of burning than almost any Wells Fargo town in the record. The great Withington Hotel, shown in this photograph, was built of sandstone and imported Oregon pine, and brokers' offices in this lonely region stayed open all night to transact business in White Pine shares listed at $70,000,000 on the exchange. One mining firm maintained an open telegraph circuit for weeks at a time to consult a female fortune-teller in New York as to where to sink its shafts. This photograph was taken about 1912 when Hamilton had two inhabitants. Today it has none and even the names on the headstones in the graveyard at Mourner's Point have been erased by the elements.

double guard for the run, drew into Willows Station after dusk one evening in 1870 and from the darkened stable came the accustomed command to up with the hands and down with the box. To point the argument, two shots blazed out of the dark, one of them nipping Brown painfully in the calf of his leg and making him intolerant of people who fired at him from ambush. Blair grappled with a gunman in the darkness, spun him into the yellow glare from the big storm lantern on the side of the coach and, though piqued, deliberately emptied first one barrel of a shotgun and then the other into the fellow. When they picked him up it was still possible to identify him as Big Jack Davis, lately of the state prison at Carson and one of the still-surviving members of "the Verdi car robbers" of exciting memory.

Hamilton was a city of recurrent and, indeed, almost constant misfortune. On various occasions the city's mayor, then its municipal treasurer and later the county treasurer departed from its civic midst with what turned out to be the public funds in their Gladstones, while fires were so frequent that it was impossible to obtain insurance anywhere in the neighborhood save at usurious rates.

Upon one occasion a local tobacconist with an eye to a nice, unobtrusive insurance fire amongst his panatelas and cartons of Danish snuff took the precaution of turning off the municipal water supply, and the resultant conflagration, surpassing even his wildest expectations, burned Hamilton to the ground. The fire of 1872 was followed by the burning of the county courthouse with all its records, which was in turn followed by a spectacular combustion in 1878 which destroyed what was left of the town's business district. By the time the great fire of 1886 came along to remove Hamilton in its entirety from the map, there was hardly anyone around to care.

When the last great fire came, a number of the old mills in the district which had for years been abandoned but on which taxes were paid by the San Francisco owners were in the care of a local character, Colonel Joseph Grandelmyer, an aged valiant who was inordinately proud of his extensive wardrobe. As the fire was still raging the Colonel sent a telegraphic dispatch to the San Francisco owners saying that he was saving their property (which proved emphatically not to be the case) and that his precious frock coats and Ascot ties were in terrible danger. The answer promptly came back over the wire to save his wardrobe if possible, but by all means to let the mills burn. The Colonel took his principals at their word.

## III: PREDICAMENT AT PANAMINT

EW persons today aside from students of the most detailed chapters of the Western legend ever heard of Panamint City. Still fewer know where it flourished, and almost nobody in the present generation has visited its site. And yet for a few brief years in the lush seventies, coeval with the bonanzas both of the Comstock and the Reese River, Panamint City was a roaring carnival of excitements, a minute mountain metropolis complete with all mining-town institutions in their most robust form, a road company from hell whose geographic locale not so very high above the floor of Death Valley contributed powerfully to the physical aspects of this illusion.

Travelers today between Lone Pine in the Owens Valley in eastern California and Stovepipe Wells and Furnace Creek, in Death Valley, after entering the floor of Panamint Valley can imagine its location if they look southward from the long tangent leading up into the western ramparts of the Panamint Mountains, and elevate their gaze almost to the top of this lifeless and shimmering barrier. The sad, vestigial traces of Panamint City are up there, two miles above the desert floor between Death Valley and Panamint Valley. Now and then a pilgrim in a jeep or a Model T Ford makes his way up Surprise Canyon to stare in incredulity at their presence. In 1948, a stock promotional scheme, later identified by constituted authority as strictly larcenous in practice and intent, brought the name of Panamint City to the attention of the stockbrokers in faraway Manhattan and to front-page mention in the evening papers when its sponsorship was abated by the district attorney of New York County. Otherwise Panamint sleeps in the heat of August midnights when even the State Police are reluctant to leave their air-conditioned barracks at Furnace Creek. It was always a city of Plutonian nightmares.

Like Aurora, Bodie, Darwin, Cerro Gordo, Greenwater and indeed all the camps of the Inyo and Mono Counties and along the lower reaches of the Nevada-California boundary, Panamint was sired by the legend of the ghostly Gunsight Lode and the myth — or fact, if you prefer to rank as a believer — of the Holy Grail of all true fissures, the lost Breyfogle Mine. For in their search for the Breyfogle, activated by a thousand whiskered Galahads packing rifles and smelling powerfully of strong waters, the prospectors of two generations uncovered as incidentals most of the minor bonanzas of these desolate and unhallowed regions.

The Breyfogle — Grail, will-o'-the wisp, swamp fire, actuality and figment of wealthy dreams and barroom drawings of the long bow, all synthesised into a saga of Paul Bunyan proportions and Semiramis appeal — had its origin back in the sixties. Setting out from Austin on a southerly landfaring there ventured one Jacob Breyfogle, blacksmith by trade, prospector by preference and fated to become an incandescent fragment of folklore by purest fortuitous circumstance. In later years his name passed into the language of the Far West as a verb, and to Breyfogle became a universally accepted synonym for the search for mineral wealth in desert places.

Somewhere between the Armagosa and Owens Lake, or perhaps some hundreds of miles to the north, in the vicinity of the craters of Mono, Jacob struck an outcropping of transcendent, fabulous richness. To prove it he brought back samples to his native Austin where they were treasured for years. The second unsolved wonder concerning them — the first, of course, was their place of origin — is that, with samples of bullion of such incredible purity in hand, nature had not already milled and minted them in the coin of the Republic.

But the whereabouts of Breyfogle's private mint never became known, for during his landfaring in the Panamints or the Cosos or the Funeral Mountains, wherever it may have been, his pack horses strayed and he wandered for days in the Nevada — or was it California? — sun without water. When found and rescued by Indians his mind was forever clouded and, despite all prompting — and one may readily imagine what a world of this commodity was placed at his disposal — he never recalled the location of his undoubted bonanza. Only the samples of his ores remained and these drove several generations of prospectors most unquietly mad.

The Gunsight legend was of even earlier origin but maintained quite as unshakable a grasp upon the imagination of the frontier. During the fifties a party of Mormons, California-bound, had crossed the Panamints where one of its number, chancing to knock loose the foresight of his rifle, replaced the missing bead with a fragment of soft metal which he chipped from a near by rock. Later it proved to be pure silver, but again the discoverer had no recollection of the whereabouts of his argentine gunsmithy, save in the most general terms, and the search for the Gunsight Lode was to cost many lives in the ensuing years.*

Even as the members of the royal houses of Europe were inextricably interlocked by marriage and community of interest (or disparateness of it) so the mines of Nevada and the eastern marches of California were all in one way or another connected either by succession, by juxtaposition, joint management and exploitation, by similarity of behavior patterns or, in some cases, by the simple process of transferring a community almost intact to a new and more promising location.

---

* The Gunsight, like the Breyfogle, was constantly being "discovered" during the prospecting years around Death Valley and the news of its locating printed in good faith by optimistic editors. A dispatch to the San Bernardino *Guardian* in April, 1875, announced the discovery by a prospector named Frink, of the authentic and undisputed Gunsight on the edge of Death Valley, halfway between Panamint and the Cerro Gordo. "The specimens sent us will go up in the thousands of dollars," said the *Guardian*, "and we congratulate Mr. Frink on his splendid luck. He and Lucky Baldwin will have to run in couples."

Panamint, even as German princes might claim descent from the legendary heroes of Norse legends, was related to the mythical Breyfogle. It was off the Breyfogle latitudes, but it was while searching for the elusive Breyfogle and its antecedant Gunsight that prospectors, fifty miles to the east, above Owens Lake, discovered the Cerro Gordo, Panamint's nearest neighbor of truly heroic stature. By 1872 the Cerro Gordo was producing an annual $1,500,000 in silver bullion and shipping it to Los Angeles by steamer across the then navigable waters of Owens Lake. Local report has it that a barge of ingots was overturned one stormy night in midpassage and hopeful persons have been looking for it ever since in the now alkaline flats which is all that remains of Owens Lake after the Owens River was diverted into the Los Angeles Aqueduct.

Later the Carson and Colorado narrow-gage railroad was built by San Francisco's puissant Darius Ogden Mills to connect the Cerro Gordo with his Virginia and Truckee, three hundred miles away and across Mount Montgomery Pass to the north. The Carson and Colorado still survives, in wistful three-foot gage, as the Owens Valley branch of the Southern Pacific RR, and the Cerro Gordo is still sending ore over its sixty-five-pound rails, but only from Keeler to Owenyo and thence by standard gage to Bakersfield.

Panamint was also connected by ties of closest consanguinity with the Comstock far away on the slopes of Mount Davidson, for Virginia City's first citizen, William M. Stewart, became first citizen of Panamint for a time and Senator John Percival Jones, the rich and powerful superintendent of the Crown Point mine in Virginia City, was Panamint's moving genius. Panamint in the family of bonanza royalty, at one time had ducal if not actually regal pretentions.

At the head of Surprise Canyon, midway between the declivities of Death and Panamint Valleys, Panamint City came into boozy and boisterous being early in 1873 when a mining district was organized there by its first tenacious discoverers, Richard Jacobs, Robert L. Stewart and W. L. Kennedy. Lacking precise assays, they still knew from crude tests conducted on the spot that the outcroppings they had monumented were rich in silver and copper, and in no time flat word spread through the adjacent camps and deserts, even to far-off Austin, Hamilton and San Francisco, that something "richer than the Comstock" was in hand. "Richer than the Comstock" was a slogan which, in its time and place, transcended in potency of appeal almost any battle cry since "God for Harry, England, and Saint George!"

Immediately interested were John P. Jones, hero of the fearful Crown Point holocaust in Virginia City, and Virginia's own Senator William M. Stewart, by this time proprietor of the most staggeringly opulent senatorial mansion in Washington's Dupont Circle and, until his death in 1909, a character of the heroic mold of the Old West. With two such backers of consular influence and dignity, Panamint came into florid and emergent being almost overnight with all the gaudy hooray of the flush and fortunate mining camp of the time.

The town mushroomed. The tarts and the teamsters, the greenhorns and

162

the gamblers, the soiled and the solvent, one and all toiled up the chasm of Surprise Canyon, at times only six feet wide, to the unbelievable settlement perched and tottering both figuratively and factually on the ragged edge of hell itself.

So tempestuous was the commotion of Panamint's coming and so fantastic the reports of its wonders that Virginia City, until now serene in its supremacy to all competition and secure in the inexhaustible treasure of the Big Bonanza, was forced to take notice. "Panamint," snapped the *Territorial Enterprise* ungraciously, was "no more than another opening in the Base Metal Range." Less than a hundred miles away, up Owens Valley, Independence, too, was in a civic huff. "Independence is becoming a deserted village," complained the *Independent*, "as everybody is off for Panamint." The horizon at every point of the compass was clouded with the dust of erstwhile Galahads of the Gunsight who had in a twinkling become the embattled and onsurging pilgrims of Panamint. Fearful for its subscription list, the Pioche *Record* spread its biggest Cassandra-bold italics to report that "the fever is still raging in Panamint." But in Austin the *Reese River Reveille* flanked its paid insertions proclaiming the glories of the Magnolia Saloon and Clarke's Fast Freight to Battle Mountain with the dolorous editorial admission that it had never encountered anyone with sufficient resolution to resist the call of a new strike and that folk, for all it cared, might be off for Panamint and be damned.

Panamint seethed in an ecstasy of combined expectation and fulfillment. Senator Jones was planning a railroad from San Bernardino to the very mouth of Surprise Canyon and soon the dusty freight teams and swearing mule skinners would be a thing of the past even as they had been rendered obsolete in the Comstock by the Virginia and Truckee, and were soon to be supplanted in nearer Bodie by the rails of the Bodie and Benton. On paper the Surprise Co. had a thirty stamp mill and in a few months juniper-fired boilers would start the ponderous machinery in its thundering pavane of prosperity. But Panamint's forty-odd saloons and their complementary roulette parlors, bagnios and other deadfalls were alarmingly popular with the local equivalent of the Bad Man from Bodie, and the sale of weapons of precision at Jacob Cohn's store to characters who were not even dubious was of frightening proportions.

What to do until the railroad and comparative security of transport was assured? The Canyon was the only possible route in and out of Panamint, and in its shadowy depths the knocking off of treasure coaches would be almost beneath the professional dignity of such talent as was on hand.

And so one day it befell that the lordly brown beard and senatorial silk hat of William M. Stewart cast their shadows across the threshold of Wells Fargo as that august personage waited on the pleasure and convenience of Wells Fargo's General Superintendent Valentine. In due course the Senator hung his glossy tile on the Superintendent's deer-antler hatrack, spread the broadcloth tails of his ample frock coat around a banjo chair upholstered in crimson damask and proceeded to the matter in hand.

Panamint needed Wells Fargo and Wells Fargo needed Panamint. He, Stewart, who spoke, sometime counsel for Wells Fargo and now advocate of Panamint, would go on record that it would be mutually advantageous. When would Wells Fargo's treasure coaches start rolling up Surprise Canyon?

The answer he got rocked him on the heels of his elastic-sided congress gaiters. Wells Fargo was not coming to Panamint. The answer was no; an unequivocal, final and irrevocable no. He, Valentine, would like in most ways to accommodate the Senator, but a study of conditions around Death Valley in general and Panamint in particular had convinced the management of Wells Fargo that its best interests lay as far as possible from the precincts of Surprise Canyon.*

Thus, for the first and, as far as is commonly recorded, the last time Wells Fargo declined with thanks the opportunity of matching its Winchesters with the knights of the road. Panamint might take what solace it could from the circumstance that it was unique in this respect, and there is every reason to believe that Panamint did. The Bad Man from Bodie — pooh! In Naegle's Oriental Saloon he was accounted the veriest sissy of sissydom from that day forward.

There is reason to believe that, during the years of its nineteenth-century expansion, the conduct of Wells Fargo's affairs, both in the fields of banking and express, was often on a scale of magnificent and happy disregard for the standards of prudence and conservatism which have later come to prevail in almost all businesses of such heroic proportions. Banditry, embezzlements and sharp practices of all sorts made almost continuous inroads upon its financial resources, and seem, in many cases, to have been regarded with huge indifference by the management, much as the proprietor of a gambling resort regards the heavy winnings of a spectacular player as good advertising for the house. The West lived grandly, wealth was in constant and almost overpowering emergence and circulated freely. Wells Fargo was able to look upon the most substantial losses with amused tolerance. True, a large organization of detectives, guards and law officers was at all times maintained, and functioned with more efficiency and precision than did parallel public agencies, but shooting and looting was part of a routine and seems to have aroused little real indignation in the firm.

In the case of outright robbery, Mr. Hume's department was sometimes willing to settle for recovery of the loot, with little concern for the apprehension of the miscreants even though the theft may have included murder

---

* Superintendent Valentine's emphatic reluctance to enter Panamint in the capacity of express messenger found no counterpart in his business partners Lloyd Tevis and James Ben Ali Haggin, the one president and the other a director of Wells Fargo, who invested in Panamint as individual speculators. For their account and to their eventual distress, George Hearst, while on tour of inspection at Panamint, had purchased the Christmas Gift mine.

of Wells Fargo employees. Risk was part of the business. Loss by administrative misadventure and incompetence only infrequently raised executive blood pressure.

It was not its accustomed function as banker or expressman which brought Wells Fargo to Panamint for its single experience in that outrageous community.

It appears that a careless Wells Fargo messenger had been murdered during the course of a holdup in Eureka County, across the line in Nevada, and the bandits were reported to have invested the $4,500 proceeds of the skirmish in Panamint. There was a reward of $2,000 on the head of each of the two gunmen who, by this time, had become warm men in the Panamint diggings and Senator Stewart was of no mind to have them removed from the community and roughly treated by the law once they had been returned to the scene of the crime. If they were hanged, as seemed certain, their mining properties would be held to satisfy their creditors, work in them would be suspended and Panamint would be the loser. This contretemps Stewart undertook to resolve. For the sum of $12,000 he purchased the mine owned by the fugitive capitalists; the $4,500 was refunded to Wells Fargo by the bandits, the balance was used to clear up their debts and satisfy their grubstaker and the matter of the dead messenger was forgotten by all concerned. All Wells Fargo cared about was the return of its treasure; the bandits escaped the noose and everyone was satisfied.

Denied the protection of Wells Fargo's shotgun messengers, Jones and Stewart solved the problem of transshipping their bullion out of Panamint by the expedient of casting it in 700-pound cannon balls and sending it out, unguarded, in an open express wagon. Not even the most eminent practitioners of banditry were able to cope with such a problem in seizure, transportation and subsequent disposal, and until the day of its downfall Panamint almost literally rolled its treasure down Surprise Canyon and to the mint at Carson in the shape of cannon ammunition.

In the end, Superintendent Valentine's judgment was admirably vindicated, for after three tumultuous years during which time the smoke of burning black powder was scarcely ever entirely absent from view in Main Street, Panamint crashed with the Comstock. With the closing of the Bank of California and the death of the brilliant Ralston, the entire West Coast became engulfed in panic. In Los Angeles, where Senator Jones had hoped to raise most of his capital to finance the Los Angeles and Independence RR and the Panamint mines, the leading bank of Temple and Workman closed its doors with a resounding crash which found an echo when Workman did deadly hurt to himself with a large-caliber revolver. More than $90,000,000 worth of securities based on Panamint's mines, stamp mills and allied ventures went begging in the market. Virginia City added to the general dismay by burning up again, this time on a really catastrophic scale, and Nevada and California mining enthusiasm suffered a setback from which it was not to recover until the last great bonanza of Goldfield after the turn of the century.

No. 2½

956    52¼

53

Dated Tuscarora Nov 11

To S D Brastow

Rec'd at SAN FRANCISCO, March 14 188

Div Supt W F & Co &

Stage from Elko was robbed last night at half past eight one mile from Tuscarora by two men — Robbers two Silver watches & one Pistol only Six fifty in box which robbers overlooked think we know the robbe have no proof yet — Send me a treasr box will write today

Mart Smith agt

WELLS FARGO

J. M. PHILLIPS COLLECTION

NEVADA HISTOR SOCIETY

J. M. PHILLIPS COLLECTION

## THE LIFE AND TIMES OF TUSCARORA

Wells Fargo came to Tuscarora in the early eighties and its former agency there burned down only in 1948. In its heyday, Tuscarora, one of the few important mining camps north of the Central Pacific main line and largely populated with unreconstructed characters from the days of the railroad's construction, was the center of a mining district that produced upwards of $40,000,000 in silver and was second to none in toughness. The picture above shows the town in its noisy noontide while below only the Masonic Hall remains of its former greatness. On the page opposite is the telegraphic lament of one of Wells Fargo's servants in the matter of scoundrelly doings on the Elko-Tuscarora stage run in the eighties. Below is the pillaged stage drawn up before the structure which conveniently sheltered both Wells Fargo and the Bullion Saloon, while at the extreme bottom of the page is one of the town's statelier characters, William J. ("Daddy") Plumb in the act of setting up a glass for Wells Fargo's driver of a somewhat later date, Charlie Doyle. Mr. Detheridge is presiding behind the mahogany of what is believed to be the Idaho Bar.

CHARLES CLEGG

What fire did for Virginia City, flood did for Panamint. The elements, taking a clue from other hostile circumstances, leagued together in the autumn of 1878 to produce a cloudburst and ensuing flash flood which took over where the stockjobbers had left off, and Panamint was carried in wet and noisy chaos down Surprise Canyon to the arid expanse of Panamint Sink, where the timbers of its mine shafts and the sills of its abodes whitened for years in the desert sun. No road at all remained to the town and until the recent evolution of the jeep the scene of Panamint's desolation could be achieved only by patient progress afoot or on muleback.

All in all, it is a pity that Wells Fargo was disinclined to venture into Senator Jones's Panamint kingdom and that its roaring and hurrah are, therefore, not properly the concern of this chronicle. There is much hilarious matter in the story of the rough-and-ready mining camp in the shadow of Telescope Peak. The searcher may find in Neill C. Wilson's *Silver Stampede* the tale of Panamint's first ball at the house of Miss Delia Donoghue, the phenomenal effects of the great comet which roared through the Death Valley skies, and the arrival around the Horn and by mule team to the very swinging doors of Yager's Dexter Saloon of the biggest mirror west of the Ohio River and the fate it met but ten feet from its place of intended enthronement.

Back in the seventies, Panamint had been exceptionally available to stock rigging. It was far from available to the inspection of potential investors; its fame was universal and it was planned by a number of thoughtful men to sell Panamint in a big way to the public of the British Isles, apparently very gullible where mining shares were concerned. Alas, but a few years before Stewart and Trenor Park, a Panamint associate, had been involved in a lamentable venture in Utah known as the Little Emma, whose shares had been fobbed off on the English market with promises of eighty per cent dividends within the year and other considerations which would have evoked snorts from even the most naïve American sucker. There had been a whacking big scandal and a $5,000,000 lawsuit as a result, and even the supposedly immaculate reputation and fair name of the financial editor of the London *Times* had been involved. The day did not seem propitious to float Panamint shares in the City of London. That, of course, didn't prevent their being thrown upon the American market in stunning denominations — a grand total of $42,000,000 shares being on the books — but even the *San Francisco Bulletin*, normally hysterical with enthusiasm at the merest mention of silver, was politely skeptical.

Seventy-five years later Panamint figured briefly in the financial columns when a posse of specialists in such practices undertook to kite the value of Panamint shares in the New York Stock Market where the very name had long since been forgotten. The road up Surprise Canyon was graded sufficiently to allow the passage of a single secondhand Army truck, a score of character actors from Hollywood with miner's tools and a couple of photographers, and a busy day was spent by the cameramen snapping scenes of presumably lucrative activity around the long-abandoned shafts. When the pictures, cunningly placed where they would do the most good in the public prints, came to the attention of the District Attorney of New York County, it took that gentleman's assistant no very long time to convince the promoters of "Consolidated Panamint Silver Mining" that times had somewhat changed since the seventies and Panamint returned to its sleep. Once more ancient tranquillity reigns over the most sepulchral and loneliest of all Death Valley's ghost towns.

## IV: CANDELARIA CHRONICLE

**N**EXT to Bodie and Panamint, perhaps the shootingest mining town in the southern diggings was Candelaria, seven miles by a dirt road off the main highway from Tonopah Junction to the south.

The tense for Candelaria is strictly past, for although it was mined at recurrent periods as recently as the thirties and in its early days produced a cool $50,000,000, Candelaria today is as ghostly as they come and, in the Nevada desert, that is very ghostly indeed. It disappeared from the Wells Fargo roster of agencies in 1904, but until that time the bank and expressing business was brisk and lucrative and, considering the freedom with which powder was burned in private feuds, tolerably immune from armed molestation.

Candelaria was originally a Mexican town, named for one of the festival days of the Catholic Church, and its mines bore such agreeable names as Sanco Pansa, Refugio, Encarnacion and Juana Ordones. Even after the Yankees took over and rechristened them Bully Boy, Home Ticket and Northern Belle, Spanish survived in the speech of the community to a degree unknown elsewhere in Nevada. The Northern Belle was in fact one of the greatest producers in the history of Nevada mining, having established something of a record by paying forty-seven dividends in succession and never having levied an assessment. People liked that sort of mine and Wells Fargo admired to ship out its bullion over the branch of the Carson and Colorado which circled into town from the west where the main iron headed for Mount Montgomery Pass.

The files of Candelaria's two newspapers, *The True Fissure* and *The Chloride Belt,* which are preserved in admirable condition and completeness in the Nevada State Library at Carson City, reveal in their columns the vitality and life which pulsed through this almost forgotten community in its hell-and-high-water heyday. Between shootings, when the streets were tolerably safe for pedestrians if they were alert enough to avoid the brightly painted wheels of the Southern Esmeralda Staging Co.'s vehicles bound, with Wells Fargo aboard, for Columbus, Lida Valley and Gold Mountain, sociable and thirsty Candelarians might choose between the fascinations of the Bon Ton Restaurant, the Star Chop House, the Elite, the Pacific and the Bank Exchange Saloon, which, with admirable restraint, advertised that "a reasonable share of the public patronage was solicited by the management, noted for its courtesy."

Between dogfights, street duels and quick ones in McKissick's, a visitor might be shaved at the Shaving Parlors (Two First Class Chairs) of Eichborn and Gericke and then wend his way down Main Street to the Nevada Hotel which reassuringly deposed that "whisky by the gallon is a specialty." He might then dodge whatever slugs were being exchanged by embittered citizens in the public square, avoid death or mutilation beneath the wheels of Keyser and Elrod's stages for Carson and Tahoe and pour further libations to the continued success of the Northern Belle or Bullwhacker in the Chloride Saloon which made a specialty of the champagne of Louis Roederer & Cie. of Rheims, and occupied "the only brick building in town, truly elegant." On emerging from these premises he would have to be careful not to fall in front of Gilmer and Salisbury's thrice-a-week coaches for Luning and Grantsville or the equally impetuously driven Concords of the United States Stage Line for Bodie, Aurora and Silver Peak.

Add to this tally of oases and travel facilities an almost endless galaxy of truly splendid saloons of minor importance and the twice-a-day trains of the Carson and Colorado and it will be seen that folk moved in and out of Candelaria in considerable numbers and that while there they were offered a variety of earnest and urban entertainment. In Wells Drury's time in Candelaria, where he was called to edit *The True Fissure* while its proprietor went on a prolonged prospecting trip over Mono County way, the fashionable drinking premises of the moment was the Roaring Gimlet Saloon on the south side of Maine Street, and Pickhandle Gulch was the town's tenderloin where no fewer than ten madams solicited, on a twenty-four-hour-a-day basis, the trade of the miners off duty. The cheering and stamping in the fandango houses never ceased for an instant. In addition to the ten madams there were, of course, the unorganized or nonunion fair but frail whose number are not appraised in any surviving estimate.

It is clear that on week ends when there were tourists on the town from neighboring but less favored camps, such as Belleville and Columbus, there was nothing in hell quite equal to Candelaria. Particularly venturesome sightseers even overflowed down to Sodaville to seek amusement in the Chinese opium dens which lent a sophistication to that community and were, indeed, at one time its principal industry. Whether or not Wells Fargo brought in the essence of the poppy in its function of impartial expressman is not available to the record, but it is not improbable.

In its early days Candelaria freighted its ore out to Wadsworth, but with

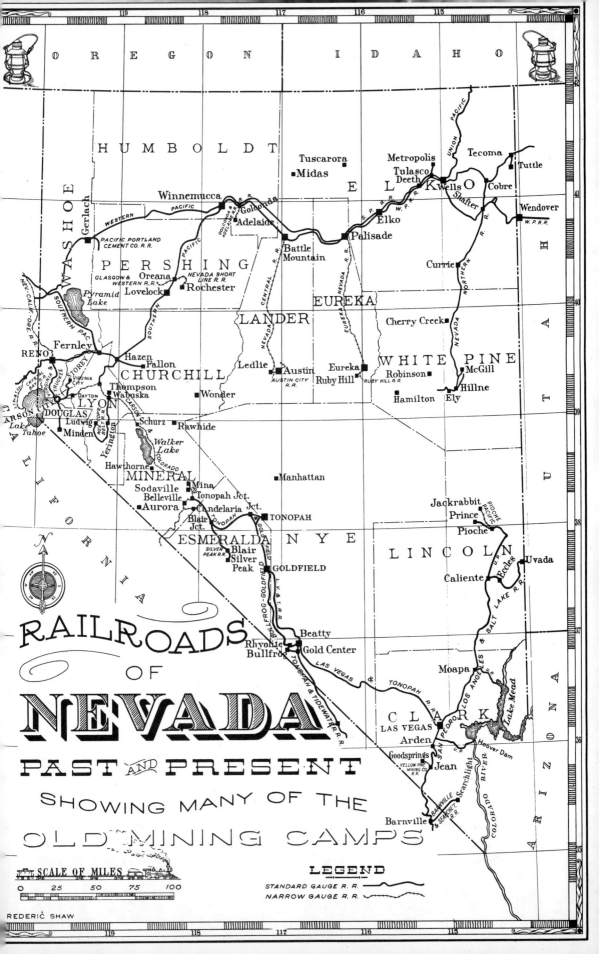

# RAILROADS OF NEVADA

## PAST AND PRESENT

## SHOWING MANY OF THE

## OLD MINING CAMPS

**SCALE OF MILES**

0    25    50    75    100

**LEGEND**

STANDARD GAUGE R.R.

NARROW GAUGE R.R.

REDERIC SHAW

the construction of the Carson and Colorado's three-foot iron which reached Candelaria in 1882 it contributed heavily to the traffic of one of the most romantic railroads in the history of the West. The C & C was built with capital advanced by Darius Ogden Mills although not with his complete approval, and his remark upon its completion is quoted elsewhere in this volume. But whether or not its owner liked it, the C & C has become an integral part of the Nevada legend and to have ridden over its thirty-five-pound rails, some of them rolled in Holland in 1860, in its diminutive coaches and combines, must have been an enchantment which today can be recreated only in the imagination.

A part of the C & C exists to this day in the seventy miles of track between Keeler and Laws, across the line in California, which constitute the only narrow-gage division of the Southern Pacific RR, but passenger service in the Owens Valley has been discontinued for many years. The rails and right of way give some hint of the pastoral wonderments of its youth and there is still in service as a caboose a combine built at the Carson City shops of the Virginia and Truckee.

Originally the C & C was planned to run from Mound House near Carson City where it joined the V & T to the Colorado River, deriving its freight and passenger traffic from the way points of Bodie, Aurora, Benton, Hawthorne, Pizen Switch, Candelaria and the great Cerro Gordo mine in the mountains above Owens Lake. Pizen Switch is today known as Yerington but went by the more picturesque appellation until its citizens threatened anyone using the older name with instant lynching. Bodie was to be connected with the C & C at Benton through the agency of the Bodie and Benton RR, but this road never quite got to the junction. During most of its lifetime the C & C was a railroad of similar disappointments.

Wells Fargo rode the C & C for many years and had a very uneventful time of it, too. It is related that, when there were no passengers on the mixed train of the C & C, its crew would pause at Walker Lake, whose margin the little railroad skirted for many miles, and take a refreshing swim. The Wells Fargo messenger on duty in the wooden combine invariably joined them with a feeling of complete safety, so desolate and lonely was the terrain and so immune from molestation had the trains always been. An hour's delay in schedule on the C & C, a railroad on which all members of the crew carried firearms and shot game from the windows, was nothing. So accustomed were all concerned to these highly informal interludes that one day they overlooked a lone passenger, a schoolmarm of severe philosophy who was by no means accustomed to the spectacle of four or five grown and bearded men disrobing entirely by the right of way and disporting themselves in the water like schoolboys. When she poured out her maidenly complaint to the superintendent there were no more swimming parties.

The six-mile Candelaria branch of the C & C was discontinued in 1906, although the rails were not removed, and was resumed again in 1908 when new capital was brought into the district in the hope of reworking the exten-

## "OUT, OUT, BRIEF CANDLE!"

Out of Candelaria in 1876 (above) Wells Fargo carried over its Nevada lines millions in bullion from the Home Ticket and Bully Boy mines and the armed guards aboard the Hawthorne and Bellville stages were the most alert in the business. A few years later Candelaria had a railroad and a Yosemite Hotel, and its Pickhandle Gulch and Chloride Saloon were famed for their toughness throughout the West. These two photographs, taken almost seventy-five years apart, tell the story of a mining town that flickered into oblivion like the flame of the candles for which it was named.

### BRIGHT HOUR OF THE NARROW GAGE

There is no suggestion in the refuse-filled cellars which today mark the site of Candelaria in the Nevada desert that once the community had a railroad. The narrow-gage Carson and Colorado, however, ran a branch line to Candelaria and here is the daily mixed train in the depot in the year 1898. Wells Fargo's treasure shipments from Candelaria by stage were the object of frequent pillage, but its guards and messengers on the C & C run were never, so far as the record shows, molested.

sive tailings of former operations. In 1932, the Philben-Candelaria branch was abandoned and the track dismantled several years later.

By 1949 Candelaria was completely abandoned to the rattlesnakes which had inhabited it for several thousand years before the coming of the Spaniards. No human being appeared and the most recent date on copies of the *Nevada State Journal*, rotting in a corner, was a decade previous.

In the upper town where once had been the homes of miners rising in terraces there are only weeds and trailing electric wires suspended in disheveled catenaries from shattered insulators. The iron shutters of the Wells Fargo Building retain the last pretensions to paint in all Candelaria, protected by the very solidity of their construction against the elements. Miraculously they still function on their hinges and their edges still meet in perfect alignment, so carefully calculated is their workmanship and installation.

Like so many of the abandoned workings of Nevada mines, the properties of Candelaria high in the hillside above what once was Pickhandle Gulch, in contrast to the state of the town itself, look as though they were only waiting for the next shift of workers to take over their hoists and ore-handling facilities. The tremendous tailings and ore dumps look as though they had been evolved only yesterday, which indeed they were, and there is still litigation in the Esmeralda courts over the rights to take ores from properties in a disputed state of abandonment. It is interesting to know that the files of mining-camp newspapers are often admitted as legal evidence in the Nevada courts in the absence of any other formal record of operational details long since vanished from company files or the memories of men. In a Candelaria litigation as recently as 1948 the Nevada State Librarian was called as a witness and required to produce files of *The True Fissure* as a matter of evidence.

*The True Fissure's* editor, John Dormer, who once on a dull day led his paper during the town's decline with a story beginning: "Dog fights are very numerous for a town of this size," would never have imagined that in the imponderable future the "Mining Notes" of his journal would serve to determine the right to many million dollars' worth of unworked tailings.

Every ghost town has its characteristic, indeed personal sounds which must be associated with its name and aspect in the human memory forever. At Bodie it is the noise of innumerable prairie dogs in midnight converse throughout the seemingly illimitable moonlit plateau stretching away to the south of its ruins, sepulchral in the midnight watches. In Aurora it is the idiot slapping of a door to a long-disused privy high on the embankment behind the Mazda Saloon. In Candelaria it is the harsh scraping of a tin ventilator dangling from a single rusted guy wire and swinging back and forth in the damp wind against a high brick wall. It is depressing past all description. So is the rest of Candelaria, even the inevitable trash heaps and kitchen middens of rusted tin cans and shattered whisky flasks are melancholy beyond the usual.

# CHAPTER VII

## *Vignettes of Violence*

THE year was 1868.

Aaron Yerx Ross, born at Oldtown, Maine, in 1830, six feet four inches tall, black-bearded and a valiant to whom a quart of frontier whisky before breakfast was the equivalent of today's small noggin of orange juice, was a hell of a man. He admired the people he worked for, a quality entirely undiscoverable in a later generation; he never lost a treasure chest or an encounter on behalf of his employers. He took a dim view of crime and low life generally and Indians in particular. In fact he displayed an attitude toward the "noble red man" which would have discouraged the sophomoric humanitarians of his own or any other time. In 1916 he dictated some of his recollections to a court stenographer. The manuscript is in the California State Library and some quotations from it would seem illuminating.

I went to work for Wells Fargo & Co., in October, 1868, at Fort Benton, Montana, driving stage [deposed Ross]. The Injuns drove the drivers off the road and the stage laid at Fort Benton thirteen days before I got there. I drove there four years and had some little trouble with the Indians. The Injuns met me on the road and I stood them off, and they told me they were "good Injuns" and wanted to find out where the Peg Anne [an Indian tribe living on the Teton River] were camped. I told them this was my first trip on the road and didn't know but would find out for them. The next day when I came down they came up and met me. I told them where the Peg Anne were camped and that night they went up and ran off a lot of the Injun's horses and went over the mountains with them. Then they killed two night herders on the prairie and came into town and told what they had done. Some of the men, cowboys and others, had one Injun named Crowtaw in jail but couldn't get hold of him as he had a big knife and stood them off; so they came down to the stable and wanted me to come up and get him. I went up and went into the jail and he came at me with a knife, and I took hold of him, ketched him by the hand and took the knife away and throwed him and held him until the rest got hold of him and then I let go. They took him out and hung him and then we went around town and caught two more and somebody shot them and killed them. Then the soldiers made a fuss and said we'd have to bury them. We put a rope on them and dragged them down to the river and throwed them in and let them go. Made good Injuns out of them.

Dick Gillespie recommended me as guard. They thought a man coming from the State of Maine would not make a fight, and Dick told me he would recommend me. He told Mr. Brastow [Wells Fargo division superintendent] that if he thought there were any better than me for them to take me out with some money and try and take it away from me. Gillespie said they needn't be afraid because I was "the hardest son of a bitch that ever struck the road."

In those days a lot of gold dust and bars were shipped from Helena to Corinne [a station on the Central Pacific main line] and there were a good many holdups. In November 1869 the stage was held up by two road agents who got away with a great deal of dust and bars: about $60,000 and a posse went after them, but all of them quit except Curly Dan Robbins and a man named Blackburn. They overtook the road agents and killed one and wounded the other in the leg. Curly Dan, a division agent for the line, was shot through the belly, but recovered. A doctor was sent from Promontory, Utah, by order of J. M. Seibert, then agent there, to attend him and Mr. Valentine, then general manager, authorized payment of $1,000 to the doctor for attending Curly Dan for a few days. The doctor also cut off the robber's leg so, as he said, "he would never be a road agent again." He said it wasn't really necessary to cut off the leg, but that he felt rather proud of the job.

In those days the company's standing reward was a certain percentage of the amount recovered and Blackburn's share of what was recovered in this holdup amounted to $1,800. I took the money up to him in Marsh Valley where he lived. He was a Morman but had left the church; had two wives and was supposed to be a hard man, which he was: a hard man to fool with. He signed the voucher and I told him I would count the money for him. He said: no it was all right. He said: "Sally, it pays better to kill a man for Wells Fargo than it ever did to kill a man for Brigham Young." Later the company gave Curly Dan a fine gold watch for his gallant service on that and other occasions.

Johnny Brent and I killed a man on the Marsh Valley road. He rode in to stop the leaders, got in between them. We were riding on the top of the stage and shot him and the mule. We supposed he was a holdup.

Later, in 1870, Mike Toby and I were on the stage and we come to Robber's Roost in Pontneuff Canyon, and the stock tenders told us we were going to have a holdup; said there were two men there who had enquired about what time the stage came along and if there were any guards on it. He told them he didn't know, so they stayed around and, after it got dark, took an ax and went toward the fork in the road. We had a four horse team, four big bays, and were guarding about $250,000 in currency, and when we left the station Phelps, the driver, wanted to know which way we had better go, over the grade or down the canyon and we told him to go any way he had a mind to. He said he would go over the grade.

I was riding along side of him and Toby was riding up behind on what is called the "dickey seat" and they shot from both sides of the road at me and Toby — missed me and hit the driver. The team started to run, so I ketched the horses, got the team held up, and took him into the coach. He died just as we got to the station. The last word he said was "Whoa" to the horses. The next morning Mike got an Injun and started on the trail after the road agents. And he went onto them over near Evanston where they had left the road, and killed both of them. We asked if Mike had got the agents, but the Injun wouldn't say he had killed them, just said: "Road agent, he no come back more." Long afterward, when I was at Ross' Fork, the Injun was looking around the station and I asked him what he was looking for. He said he was looking for Mike and I told him Mike was dead. He said: "Too bad Mike dead. Mike heap good shot."

Pause, therefore, in fancy, O traveler amidst the damask and chromium of the *City of San Francisco* as you pass Union Pacific's milepost 914, for the transcontinental flyer scarcely abates its speed for Evanston, and in the mind's eye recapture the Utah of Aaron Yerx Ross. Change has been abroad and it is eminently unlikely that the slugs of road agents will rip through your carpet-bag or Gladstone. Change is there, and there are filling stations at Evanston and uniformed State Troopers on motorcycles and the complete pattern of safety and mediocrity. Perhaps there is even progress, but it is doubtful if Aaron Ross would think so.

The year was 1870.

The great reformation of Wells Fargo and its transition from New York to San Francisco in its corporate entirety was in process. The stages had disappeared from the overland routes and were gradually being withdrawn from even the feeder lines, as railroads such as the Virginia and Truckee were being completed to connect the mines with the main lines of the Central Pacific. Dick Fellows, the hilarious horseman, and an obvious victim of technological unemployment, was safely in San Quentin.

The rails were turning up in the most surprising places. In the by now positively Byzantine metropolis of San Francisco the management of Woodward's Gardens had inaugurated, over the Sutter Street Railroad, a "Street Palace Car" for ladies only, "elegant of design, luxuriously fitted with a velvet carpet and sofas extending the length of the car upholstered in embroidered tapestry costing sixteen dollars a yard."

In such a world of change and extravagance, was it any wonder that, for the first time in the West, armed robbery should extend even to the plush and mahogany interiors of the transcontinental steamcars?

On the night of November 4th the Central Pacific's *Train No. 1*, the eastbound predecessor of today's *Overland Limited,* was drifting down the eastern slopes of the Sierra under a brightly starlit sky. Against this and the outlines of the conifers the trailing exhaust of its brightly painted eight-wheeler was clearly outlined. The locomotive, built at the company's shops at Sacramento, was working no steam on the downgrade. Now and then, however, a shower of wood sparks evaded the spark arrester in its well-proportioned diamond stack as the fireman tossed a length of spruce into the firebox and, occasionally, redglowing cinders were wafted lazily backward in the slip stream from the chimneys of the cannon-ball stoves which were warming the interiors of its baggage and express car, coaches and solitary sleeper trailing at the rear. It must have been a pretty little varnish train clattering gently downgrade through the Nevada night while the reflections from the great storm lantern mounted on the engine smokebox, and surmounted by a pair of ornamental deer's horns, shone on the curving steel as the rails twisted above the Truckee River.

Below Cisco **No. 1** had been delayed by a double-headed westbound freight which had pulled a drawbar and a dozen of whose high cars had gone into the ditch when the shattered draft gear got under the trucks. At Truckee the engineer was letting his train out pretty freely to make up for the delay and the coal-oil lamps on the depot platform flashed but for the briefest moment over the yellow varnish with its neat green trim of the express coach and its bright red painted lettering reading: Wells Fargo & Co., Express, Baggage. The lithographers of the Messrs. Currier & Ives at the corner of Spruce and Nassau Streets, New York, might have taken it as prototype for one of their universally popular engravings.

In his compartment in the express car, Wells Fargo's true and trusty messenger, whose name was Marshall, was dozing in one of those wire-braced wooden chairs which have always been a property of all properly managed mail, express and baggage cars. Thirty-five miles, or an hour's run down the grade to Reno, and he would have from Nels Hammond, the Reno agent for Wells Fargo, a receipt for the valuable shipment of gold and bar silver which even now reposed in the strongbox close to hand.

It now appears that at Verdi, a scant eleven miles out of Reno, a group of seven men boarded the car platform as the engineer slowed for a passing track switch. Two of them armed with handguns confronted Conductor Mitchell on a car platform and convinced him that he was happier and warmer inside. The rest went forward, subdued the engineer and fireman, cut off the motive power and the head-end revenue cars, which of course included the express, and drove down the tracks half a mile. There at their leisure they impressed Messenger Marshall that interference would be folly and, with a hand axe, broke open the treasure chest and retreated into the Nevada night with upwards of $41,000 in hard gold money and bars, leaving as the merest dross $8,000 worth of bar silver and a lot of essentially worthless bank paper.

It was all accomplished with dispatch and a commendable absence of murder or even wanton discharge of weapons of precision. It also was the first armed train robbery in the Far West, another first for Wells Fargo which would gladly have foregone the distinction, and whose various alarmed and discomforted servants at Reno would have been even more vexed had they known that their firm was going to be credited with a second place within a very few hours.

For, nearly 400 miles down the line at Independence, Nevada, a stop no longer mentioned on even the fine-print schedules of the Southern Pacific, **No. 1** was again held up that same day. Here Wells Fargo's true and trusty messenger contrived to shove $10,000 worth of minted gold behind a rack of providentially handy lanterns and signal flares before the miscreants got to him and the net loss to the company in the second haul was a mere $4,000.

Wells Fargo and the State of Nevada were unanimous in agreeing that this sort of thing could not go on and, together with the officials of Storey County, where the first outrage had been perpetrated, and the Central Pacific, rewards of almost $40,000 were posted.

Because of the substantial rewards involved, the novel and sensational nature of the crime and the unrivaled opportunity afforded to play cops and robbers, several large and well-organized posses at once set about tracking down the gang which became known throughout the nation as "the Verdi car robbers." Wells Fargo's detectives soon arrived from San Francisco and, under a variety of circumstances involving no little skill in police work, the entire gang was apprehended within four days of the outrage. Its members included John Squiers, an old hand at stage robbery, E. B. Parsons, notable Virginia City gambler, and Jack Davis, a businessman hitherto unsuspected of anything but civic rectitude and respectability. All but Davis were sentenced to long terms in the penitentiary after a trial which reverberated in the legal annals of the state for years.

Amateurs of frontier Americana living in a later generation occasionally express wonder at the ease with which train robbers overcame the resistance of the head-end crews located in the cabs of locomotives. The cab of a main-line Mallet of today, whose deck alone rides eight feet above the rails and whose steel bulkheads and narrow gangways suggest the invulnerability of an armored truck, might well prove a source of bafflement to men armed with anything less than machine guns and a vast determination.

This was not the case with locomotives in the seventies and eighties. Their wooden cabs, often brightly painted, with wide tall windows, were almost available to gunsight on the part of a tall man without elevating the angle of his weapon. To climb across the diminutive tenders from behind and take the train crew in the rear was not the matter of mountain uplands it would be in a tender of today carrying, say, 30,000 gallons of water fuel alone. A brief scramble over a pile of kindling and the fort was taken. And, finally, the speeds of trains in the nineteenth century, especially where grades were concerned or mountain passes were being negotiated, made boarding them in motion almost as simple a feat as mounting the running board of a Powell Street cable car.

There are even later records of desperadoes of Annie Oakley qualifications who, when their command to stop a moving train was discourteously ignored, drew a bead on the air-line connection between two passing cars or brought the train to a halt by knocking off an angle cock.

It will be seen that under these casual and intimate circumstances and even though an engineer and a fireman might be armed, as they very frequently were on Western runs, they were more available to persuasion than are a hogger and his tallowpot today riding eighty miles an hour around the

## HERE THE CAR ROBBERS WAITED FOR *No. 1*

Little did this track-laying gang of "Crocker's pets," engaged in stringing the advancing iron of the Central Pacific down Truckee Canyon, realize that only a year or two after this photograph was taken the section of track on which they were working would be the scene of the "great Verdi car robbery" which was to electrify the entire West. Here beside the banks of the Truckee a few miles west of Reno, where today the giant cab-first Mallets of the Southern Pacific roll a mile of redball freight up the grade, *Train No. 1,* eastbound, was held up on the night of November 4, 1870, in the first recorded armed robbery of any train in the Far West and Wells Fargo's first experience with car robbers anywhere.

shrewdest curve in a steel-girdled turret high above the roadbed. This was emphatically the case on the occasion of the very Currier and Ives affair in the canyon of the Truckee. The entire railroad was but a few months completed, the ballast was new and soft where it existed at all and it may fairly be estimated that, guided by the uncertain light on its smokebox, the midnight locomotive that exceeded ten miles an hour was achieving a record for this stretch of track.

At the trial of the Verdi robbers, who were by now receiving nationwide publicity as something new and remarkable in the calling of desperado, it was freely admitted by them that they had practically been forced into train robbery, *faute de mieux,* by the steps taken by Wells Fargo to protect its Nevada stages. For some six months past all stages between Carson and Reno and Carson and Sacrameno via Strawberry had been guarded not by one, but by two shotgun messengers mounted atop the Concord, and by two heavily armed outriders who followed the coaches on horseback at a distance of fifty yards. Under such unfavorable circumstances, Parsons and Squiers attested, they had been forced into new channels of enterprise.

After serving his time in Carson jail Davis again reverted to his love, stage robbery, and was promptly decapitated by a well-directed charge of buckshot from the gun of Eugene Blair, a Wells Fargo messenger in White Pine County. More than a decade later a short dispatch in the *Bodie Free Press* for Nov. 16, 1881, announced: "E. B. Parsons, one of the Verdi car robbers, has been pardoned and restored to citizenship." And so passed into history the great Verdi train robbery which was to set a pattern for armed violence along the high iron for many decades to come.

The Independence robbers were apprehended after an even more fantastic pursuit across the desert to the foot of Great Salt Lake which involved posses with special Central Pacific trains and a troop of United States cavalry from Fort Halleck who followed a sort of Ariadne's trail of gold double eagles, rolls of silver dollars and packs of greenbacks thrown from the saddlebags of the pursued. The scoundrels had been rank amateurs, deserters from Fort Halleck who were wanted on any number of counts by several sources of authority, and who lived to regret it.

It was from this not altogether modest beginning that the business of robbing the Wells Fargo express cars while in passage over the railroads of the West had its inception. While the opportunities for this special type of enterprise would reasonably seem to decline with the general perfecting of methods of protection and the rising speed and consequent inaccessibility of trains in motion, it is interesting to note that the graph of armed robbery of Wells Fargo railroad messengers rises steadily from the early seventies until it reaches its apex no longer ago than 1895 in which year there were no fewer than forty-nine successful attempts against the treasure-bearing express cars and that in the decade from 1890 to 1900 the record shows an average of more than twenty a year. In 1887, Mr. Hume made bold to assert in the public prints that the armed robbery of stages was "a thing of the past" and that the net loss

Candelaria, Nevada, Dec. 11–82

he Stage bound from _Candelaria_
_Columbus_ ............................................ was robbed
9 o'clock A.M., _Dec 6th_, 188_2_. _3_ miles from
_Columbus_ .... in .... _Esmeralda_ .... County,
n. by _1_ man, armed with _Rifle_
.................... and disguised with _Sack_
_head and feet_ —
e of driver _Samuel S. Fannon_
_not_ taken and ....................................
, Fargo & Co.'s loss _Nothing_
int recovered ....................................
es. residences, and losses of passengers: ....................................

.......... No passengers.

E B Cushman
Agent W F & Co
Candelaria Nev,

(OVER.)

WELLS FARGO BANK

MILTON SHARP

MIKE TOVEY

## WELLS FARGO WAS PREPARED

Milton Sharp neither smoked, swore, gambled nor chewed tobacco and only drank in moderation, but he held up Wells Fargo's treasure shipments in California and Nevada five times in the summer of 1880. On the sixth attempt his partner in crime was killed by Wells Fargo's indomitable Mike Tovey on the Bodie-Carson run, and shortly thereafter Sharp was arrested in San Francisco. He was brought to Aurora jail and his escape therefrom and subsequent recapture behind McKissick's saloon in Candelaria provided the greatest excitement in the history of the Esmeralda. So frequent were holdups then, that Wells Fargo supplied its agents with a standard form for their reports. The one shown above records a minor skirmish near Candelaria while Sharp was serving twenty years in during the previous year from this form of robbery had been less than $300. What he did not add was. that at this period the holding up of railroad trains was wildly on the increase and that bandits were getting their teeth into their work to the extent of as much as $50,000 and $75,000 in a single haul.

The year was 1873.

The files of Wells Fargo over the years when its bullion and other treasure were still carried by horse coach contain thousands and thousands of records of robberies attempted, robberies thwarted and robberies consummated and their records would tire the most indefatigable amateur of armed crime in the Old West. The one that is here briefly rehearsed is selected because it is almost typical of the bandit technique of its times, devoid of violence to the persons of passengers and stage crew, and devoid too of the florid gallantries and overtones of chivalrous humor with which many such accounts were invested both by participants and newspaper reporters.

Late in the sixties the rails of the ever-lengthening Central Pacific had arrived at Colfax on the eastern slopes of the Sierra and, although the great car robbery at Verdi was still a topic of local conversation, little had since happened to excite the populace. The stages from Nevada City and Grass Valley met the trains once a day at Colfax.

Nevada City's diggings, still carried simply as Nevada on Wells Fargo's roster as late as 1871, although the State of Nevada had long since taken over the name for itself, was another of those places which came into being through the fiat of domestic animals. Back in 1849 the oxen of an early wagon train over the Donner had escaped in the night and when they were at length recovered they were found grazing in a lush upland meadow in the Sierra through the midst of which flowed a clear stream fairly brimming with flaked gold. All thought of continuing deeper into California was then and there abandoned by the pioneers and inside of a fortnight two sawmills were carving out lumber for a town which was first called Deer Creek Dry Diggings.

By the late sixties Grass Valley and Nevada City were two of the oldest, most respectable and richest mining towns in the entire West. Wells Fargo maintained a branch office in each of them, administered by S. P. Dorsey and A. D. Towner respectively, and gold from the fabulously profitable Coleman's Idaho Mine·and other local bonanzas was shipped out of town on daily coaches maintained by local entrepreneurs but each equipped with a Wells Fargo safe securely bolted to the floor. It was the custom of Bob Scott, who drove the Grass Valley stage, to wait till Matt Dailey braked to a stop at Stoke's Exchange Hotel and then proceed together for mutual comfort and encouragement to Colfax.

A widely published photograph from the files of the Southern Pacific RR shows the stages drawn up at the depot at Colfax and very dashing of appearance are their drivers, sporting white linen dust coats, glossy silk hats or bowlers and light-colored gloves as they handle the ribbons.

So peaceful had the run been over the years that nobody was accustomed to go armed and after the unfortunate occurrence here detailed it was found that the only weapon of even approximate precision available among those present had been a small pearl-handled derringer, the property, as its bearer deposed, of a lady friend.

One tranquil summer evening in the early seventies, as the stages, bound back toward Grass Valley from meeting a Central Pacific train at Colfax where they had received $7,500 in the newly minted gold of Carson, had barely achieved Morrison's Station and were toiling up a heavy grade on the other side, the peaceful record of Grass Valley staging was rudely shattered. The miscreants were four, their armament sufficiently heavy to make resistance folly and their disguise what appeared to be axle grease on their faces and gunny sacks around their feet. The *Nevada Daily Transcript*, in a red-hot extra which shortly appeared on the streets, described the facial disguise as "Kuklux" with a blue muslin mask on one of the party.

The Wells Fargo safe in these stages was built in under the rear seat and there was no chance, therefore, of carrying it off and blowing it at leisure. Giant powder was produced. There was afterward a witness who suggested that the explosive was powerful enough to have been nitroglycerin, but the lingering odor of giant black powder familiar enough to miners' noses, discredited this melodramatic suggestion, and the safe was well and truly "bursted" as the *Transcript* had it, in jig time.

Just before the coach was detonated, the robbers were asked by the driver to remove a Saratoga trunk from the roof, there being no need to damage passengers' property, and this the robbers did. "But they failed to replace it after the explosion," chronicled the reporter for the *Transcript* with the suggestion that the bandits were certainly no gentlemen.

The affair caused a great stir. Wells Fargo promptly offered a reward of $2,500. The *Transcript* printed verbatim accounts of the survivors. Sheriffs' offices, even in those days of comparatively simple facilities for the investigation of crime, were plastered with likenesses of suspects, and in less than a fortnight Wells Fargo detectives and local officers had rounded up the entire gang and locked them up in the county jail.

The most telling aspect of this encounter with crime was that it was seized upon instanter as a highly persuasive argument for a railroad into Grass Valley, an agitation which shortly led to the financing of the celebrated Nevada County Narrow Gage of gentle memory. After 1876 the treasure of the region went in and out of Grass Valley and Nevada City in the express compartment of this charming little railroad where no grease-painted highwayman in "Kuklux" attire molested its going.

Gilbert Kneiss records that gold bars and bricks traveled in a small sheet-

# $2500 REWARD

On Sunday night, 27th inst., the Stage from Colfax to Grass Valley was stopped by four highwaymen and our treasure box robbed of following amounts:

## $7,000 IN COIN.

In a leather pouch, and three packages of coin containing respectively $50, $18 and $10. We will pay the above

## REWARD OF $2500

in Gold Coin for the capture of the robbers and the recovery of the Coin; or

## $1250 FOR THE CAPTURE

of the Robbers, and

## $1250 FOR THE RECOVERY

Of the Coin.

## L. F. ROWELL,

Ass't. Supt. of Wells, Fargo & Co.

iron safe in the baggage compartment and that bags of double eagles were returned from the Carson Mint stacked casually in the corner beside the cannon-ball stove with no formal protection at all.

The year was 1875.

In the first week of May there were commotions at home and abroad to occupy the hand-set columns of agate and brevier type in the mining-town newspapers of Nevada. One of its periodical "great fires" had ravaged Virginia City and thousands of miners were sleeping in tents or warehouses as a result; there was a rash of bogus twenty-cent pieces, or double dimes as they were known in Sacramento; a bold robbery had been committed on the person of the tollgate keeper on the Cerro Gordo road; the unsinkable Senator Jones had purchased a patent for making artificial ice and was looking forward to a quarter-million-dollar profit from it annually; a letter to the *Reese River Reveille* reported that bold robbers had held up the office of Wells Fargo in Panamint, a canard which fooled nobody as it was notorious that Wells Fargo would have no part of Panamint; the first passenger train ran through the Hoosac Tunnel in far-off Massachusetts; a Virginia and Truckee section foreman at Franktown was murdered for $6,000, which he was carrying on his person, and people remarked that everyone connected with the V & T seemed to be made of money; oil was reportedly discovered north of Los Angeles; but the big news of the day was the death of Jack Harris, archfoe of Wells Fargo and a scoundrel who had added notably to the gray hairs of a score of peace officers in Nevada and the adjacent marches of California. In the *Reese River Reveille* and the *Carson Appeal,* in the *Borax Miner* of Columbia and the *Eureka Standard* his obituary led the paper for the day or week. He was known well and unfavorably to all of them.

Jack Harris was, perhaps, the archetype of bad man with whom Wells Fargo had to contend in the argentine years of the Nevada mines. Uneducated, vicious, continually being taken *in particeps criminis,* he was much more representative of the ruffler and gun fighter of the frontier than were, say, Black Bart or Dick Fellows, who, in their way, were specialists, almost character actors.

His obituary, as printed in the *Borax Miner* for May 6, 1875, in its literal transcription, is probably more adequate to the depiction of the man than any amount of rewriting could be.

Jack Harris, who died in Pioche on Sunday last, was a well known character in this state, having directly and indirectly been identified with many of the scenes of violence of the early days. He was a native of Massachusetts, and in

WELLS FARGO BANK

## THE SHELLEY OF THE SHOTGUNS

The dressy old gentleman in a curly-brimmed bow
and satin-faced Chesterfield is the elusive and
commonly mild-mannered highwayman who, in
seventies and eighties, delighted newspaper read
with his sardonic verses signed "Black Bart
PO8" and caused the blood pressure of Wells Farg
Chief of Detectives Hume to alarm his physic:
Black Bart's technique combined larceny in the gra
manner with the accomplishments of a character ac
His stage holdups in the Mother Lode country :
elsewhere on the highroads of California were inv
ably accomplished in a disguise which suggested
"Kuklux" costume of the Grass Valley robbers in
its most arresting item was a flour sack with eyeh
worn over what was unmistakably a derby hat. B:
first holdup was productive of a thumping big W
Fargo treasure consignment ravished from the Son:
Milton stage. Upon occasion he left verses at the s
of his well-planned crimes, the most celebrated
which read:

> I've labored long and hard for bread,
> For honor and for riches,
> But on my toes too long you've tred,
> You fine haired sons of bitches.

Such genteel sentiments enchanted newspaper rej
ers and readers alike and for eight years and twe
eight holdups Bart's accomplishments were favor
compared with those of Matthew Arnold and Al
Tennyson, then much in the literary limelight. W
he was at last captured by Hume, through the ag
of a laundry-marked handkerchief, he was tried
but one holdup and gossip had it that he had n
a dicker with Wells Fargo in the matter of recove
some of their treasure. It was also whispered afte
release from durance that Wells Fargo paid h:
handsome pension not to molest their stages. Jo
Henry Jackson disinclines to this belief. Evelyn \
Podesta is pleased to believe it true. Wells Farg
no record of any such arrangement, but there v
good deal in Wells Fargo's conduct of busine
those years which never got on the ledgers. Rea
having paid their money, may take their choice i
legend.

188

his early manhood he followed the sea for a livelihood. At the breaking out of the California gold excitement he went to that State, and resided for many years at Marysville and vicinity, where he was known as a desparate character, and suspected of being implicated in various highway robberies. In 1859 or 1860 he came to Washoe, as the region of the Comstock was then called, residing principally in Carson City where he married. For several years he kept a saloon in Carson, during which time his reputation was similar to that borne by him in California.

In 1865 the Pioneer Stage running between Virginia City and Placerville, was stopped just below Silver City, one morning, by three men, and Baldy Green politely requested to "hand out the box." Baldy's accommodating spirit in matters of this kind was proverbial; he never took a second look down the barrel of a double-barrel shot-gun which was shoved under his nose; but simply said: "Certainly, gentlemen," and handed out Wells, Fargo & Co.'s treasure box as soon as he could get it out of the front boot. The box on this occasion contained a large amount of money and valuables, and immediately on the announcement of the robbery, W. F. & Co. offered a large reward for the arrest and conviction of the robbers. The entire police machinery of the State was at once set to work, and in a short time Harris and two others were arrested, charged with the commission of the robbery. Harris and one of his accomplices were arrested in Austin. The party arrested with Harris has since become a respectable citizen so we shall not mention his name in this connection. The other man was Al Waterman, who was arrested in Sierra Valley. The robbery was committed in Lyon county, and the three arrested men were incarcerated in the Lyon county jail, at Dayton. The party whose name we do not mention turned State's evidence, and showed the officers where a portion of the spoils were secreted, but though there was evidently a clear case against Waterman and Harris, there seemed to be an indisposition on the part of Wells, Fargo & Co., to prosecute them. As a matter of form, however, they were tried. We forget the exact result of the case of Harris; but at any rate he left the country shortly after the trial, and Waterman was convicted and sentenced to thirteen years in the State Prison.

Harris went to Washington, where for a short time he served on the detective police force of that city, but soon turned back to the Pacific Coast, remaining several months on the Isthmus. In 1867 he opened a saloon in Austin, in partnership with Nicanor, a notorious cattle thief and highwayman, who recently escaped from the Lincoln county jail. In the winter of this year he had a quarrel with Charley Brooks, one of Waterman's bondsmen, in which knives and pistols were drawn, but which ended without bloodshed.

When the White Pine excitement broke out he removed to that district and opened a saloon in Hamilton, in 1869, removing thence to Eureka. Eureka was then a small camp and offered a small field for his genius, and he returned to White Pine. On the day of the Hamilton City election of 1870 he engaged in a street duel with Charles McIntyre, in which he received a shot through the right hand, which permanently disabled that member.

In 1871 he went to Pioche, where he was more or less mixed up in the lot and mine jumping troubles, and where he had several altercations, on one occasion clipping a lock of hair from the side of the head of Major O'Keefe, the jumper, with a bullet from a "Whistler." Years ago it was prophesied that Jack Harris would die with his boots on and the prophecy would have been fulfilled in the cases of ninety-nine men out of every one hundred who had followed a similar course of life: but his death-bed was cheered with the grim satisfaction of knowing that these prognostications as to the manner of his death were unfulfilled. Waterman, however, did die with his boots on, being killed in Virginia City by Miles Goodman, under circumstances which fully justified that gentleman.

In the above we have given but a brief sketch of a career by no means uncommon on the Pacific Coast, led by a man who was type of a class now becoming extinct. We may have made some errors in the matter of dates, but the facts are substantially as stated, and the lack of space prevents our giving them more in detail.

It is of more than passing interest that this obituary, written for a mining-town newspaper nearly three quarters of a century ago, conforms in all but the most minute stylistic details to an obit of similar importance as it would be written today for such paradigms of contemporary journalism as the *New York Times* or *Herald Tribune*. Jack Harris got a very stylish send-off indeed.

The year was 1876.

In the seemingly illimitable distances and among the snowy peaks of Northern California where the six dancing horses of the California and Oregon Stage Co.'s ponies drove tirelessly from Redding to Yreka and from Yreka north across the borders of Oregon, staging was encountering obstacles quite on a scale with the wind and sky of the countryside. Not even the imperial coach of King Holladay was immune from molestation and delay.

The old grandfather of the staging business had caused to be built for his personal and expeditious transportation a special private carriage which was, from contemporary accounts, a forerunner of the private palace cars which an only slightly later generation of railroad satraps was to design in such an image of luxury and elegance that the world is still impressed with their mention. Ben's coming anywhere west of the Missouri was heralded by advance riders who galloped, in the king's name, to alert stationmasters, hostelers and drivers alike to his impending progress, to impress the best horseflesh available and generally to see to it that there should be no delay at the division points. Only the general manager of a great railroad is so anticipated on his rounds today.

Ben's coach was equipped with whatever could contribute to its owners comfort, convenience and the expedition of his going. There were built-in food lockers to eliminate stops at eating places. A rack of silver-topped decanters eliminated the possibility of his having to sample any of the tarantula juice which passed for beverage in outland places. A cunningly adjusted coal-oil lamp with shielded reflector made it possible for him to peruse documents of state or other reading matter during the night watches when, in any event, sleep was problematical. In this splendid conveyance Holladay traveled literally posthaste, scattering gold double eagles for the least attention from roadhouse attendants along the way, and once he covered the distance from California to the Missouri in the record-breaking time of twelve days, ruining several teams of valuable horses in the achievement. Time, when the King traveled, was extremely of the essence.

It was on the first Friday of November, 1876, that three ill-mannered fellows, either uninformed of who was on the road or lacking in all respect for majesty, stepped from behind a clump of trees three miles south of Redding and bade the driver stand and deliver. Aboard were Holladay and Mrs. Holladay, W. L. Smith, division agent of the road, and an unidentified lady. On the box was Charlie McConnell, crack driver of the run, and under his feet in the boot were the mails and the Wells Fargo box, for no matter what his haste, the old King never neglected an opportunity to take aboard and expedite what in modern railroad parlance is known as head-end revenue. The speed with which such freight reached its destination was good promotion and its tariff was also a source of satisfaction.

The gunmen got $1,100 from the box and about $700 from the mails, and the stage was hastened on its way, according to the account a week later in the *Yreka Union*, without molestation to its occupants. This was not the case when Holladay figured in another stoppage of the imperial coach and was forced to hold his hands high above his head on the roadside. While in this predicament his nose began to itch and he asked the nearest bandit for permission to scratch it. To save him the trouble the fellow did it for him with the foresight of a howitzer-size cavalry pistol. The bald-headed, spade-bearded old coaching king, who was afraid of nothing in the cosmos except delay, was outraged at the moment but later told the story with something approaching satisfaction.

This unfortunate happening giving King Holladay some insight into the strenuous way of life as it was lived by his own viceroys and intendants in the north California marches was only one of a series of stage robberies in and around Reading and Yreka. About this time the *Yreka Union* was able to run the following brief account of recurrent contretemps on the Siskiyou highroads:

## AND STILL ANOTHER STAGE STOPPED

We learn that the Shasta and Redding stage was stopped on Thursday morning near Shasta by highwaymen and compelled to give up the Wells Fargo & Co's Express. As on the stoppage on Monday they got nothing but letters as far as is now known. This makes the third time within a week that highwaymen have stopped a stage within Shasta County and the fourth time within two weeks. This is getting somewhat monotonous for the people of Shasta County and we expect to hear, about the next thing, that some highwaymen have been seriously hurt. The $600 standing reward for the arrest and conviction of each and every highwayman within the state ought to be some inducement.

If the robberies of the mail and express between Yreka and Redding continue, Wells Fargo & Co may draw off the route, as it is a losing business to them, having barely made expenses last year and liable to lose money this year if any more raids are made upon their treasure box. . . . If the mail is continually molested every other trip the contractors might call on the military authorities for a cavalry escort which the Government is bound to furnish.

Wells Fargo did not, however, "draw off the route," and two years later we find it mobilizing all its resources, Superintendent Valentine and Chief of Detectives Hume in their proper persons, sheriffs, deputies and guides, rewards, informers and the facilities of the magnetic telegraph in an all-out campaign against the knights of the road around Redding with a variety of gratifying results and a positive vertigo of newspaper accounts, excursions and public tumults.

One Saturday early in September of 1878, at the improbable hour of 3:30 in the morning, the down stage from Yreka to Redding with Charlie Williams on the box and John Reynolds carrying Wells Fargo's well-advertised ten-gage beside him and a valuable treasure in the ironbound chest in the boot was slowly breasting the grade a few hundred yards from the summit of Scott Mountain. Out of the darkness of the roadside stepped three men, one with the conventional or Black Bart flour sack over his head and what was unmistakably a Colt's dragoon revolver in his business hand. Williams raised his right hand to signify that he was unarmed while keeping a firm grip on his team with the left and at the moment when it would do the most good Reynolds let go with both barrels at the almost irresistible target the flour sack offered across the near lead horse. There was a returning volley of assorted calibers as flour sack disappeared into the ditch and the team started off at a gallop which it maintained until the near wheel horse went down in the traces as dead as any horse might well be.

While Reynolds and the only male passenger aboard, a valiant and unafraid gentleman of Portuguese descent, undertook to cut free the dead horse and reharness the team, Williams descended from the box and walked back alone into the darkness to the scene of the holdup, thus anticipating the effrontery of Mike Tovey in the face of deadly danger in the affair of the Bodie stage several years later. At any moment he might have been assassinated by the two surviving bandits from their place of concealment, and yet for twenty minutes Williams performed sentry duty in the middle of the highway while his allies up front wrestled with one dead and five skittish live horses. At the end of this period the stage was in readiness, its crew and passenger climbed aboard and off it rolled to the New York House at the foot of Scott Mountain grade. It is difficult, at this remote point, to imagine what salary within the gift of Wells Fargo could adequately compensate a man for making himself so conspicuously a target on the Reading road at what must by this time have been almost four o'clock in the morning.

From the New York House the wires fairly smoked to the office door of Wells Fargo's Agent R. G. Dunn at Reading. Dunn informed Division Superintendent W. L. Smith at Trinity Center who promptly set off for the scene of the outrage where he found flour sack as dead as mutton and somewhat less attractive due to the wholesale manner of his taking off at the muzzle of Reynolds' ten-bore. He was identified as a Copper City shoemaker with ideas beyond his capacity for their execution. From San Francisco General Superintendent Valentine wired Dunn to pay instanter to the proper party the $300 gold coin of the Republic which was the standing offer maintained by Wells Fargo for all and any dead highwaymen.

Two days later the Shasta scene was enlivened by the arrival of no less a sleuth and dignitary than Chief of Detectives Hume who took personal charge of the man hunt for the surviving bandits.

Meanwhile two strangers of something less than imposing appearance had arrived for breakfast at the Picayune Creek cabin of Dennis Donovan, honest and hornyhanded son of local soil. There was a venison ham handy for the asking and, although honest Dennis didn't like their looks, he hesitated not to give them freedom of his larder. It was there that the two unsavory strangers discovered and set upon a full bottle of whisky. The record does not say what size the full bottle measured or whether its contents were the pure rye of the frontier or the aristocratic spirits from Bourbon County, Kentucky. It was whisky and that sufficed. It sufficed to move one of the heavily armed strangers to remark that they had just held up the Reading stage and the other to boast that he had contrived the taking off of the near wheel horse in retaliation for the shooting and doing to death of a damned fool of a partner in crime who had exposed his person in a manner at once foolhardy and fatal.

After their departure into the dawn, honest Dennis, spoiled of his whisky and himself spoiling with big news, lost no time in hastening down canyon in the direction of Callahan's. There he found in process of formation a posse which included Deputy Sheriff T. K. Cummings, George Murray, the local blacksmith, and a celebrated Indian hunter known as Sisson Jim. It gave an attentive ear to his tidings and within the hour was on the trail of the by this time fuddled and noisy fugitives. As the Reading *Independent* subsequently remarked in an outburst of editorial generosity: "Who can say that whisky cannot be put to some good purpose when it will make the guilty convict themselves?" Twenty-four hours later, tracked by the Indian and their own uncertain progress through the countryside, the highwaymen were apprehended slumbering beneath the mountain pines, "dreaming perhaps of happy days when they were innocent of crime and respected by all who knew them."

It was upon this occasion that Chief of Detectives Hume, for the first time in the available record, used a primitive sort of ballistics in the identification of criminals. The buckshot charges found in the possession of one of the prisoners, purchased a few days earlier at Callahan's, was of a special and easily identifiable manufacture and corresponded perfectly to the buckshot found in the dead stage horse. The case was considered watertight from this point on and States Prison was just the place for stage robbers to sober up in.

The year was 1881.

The story of Wells Fargo in Arizona in general and Tombstone in particular is the story of Wyatt Earp, the most colorful of all the many frontier marshals whose six guns flashed and banged their way to American immortality. Secondarily, to be sure, it concerns itself with his brothers, Virgil and Morgan Earp, and with Doc Holliday, the enigmatic molar and bicuspid artist whose nickel-plated Colt's equalizer came more readily to hand than the accustomed instruments of dental surgery.

Wyatt Earp had first come onto the Wells Fargo pay role in the hills of Deadwood, South Dakota, in 1877. In this northland desolation he was already one of the ranking peace officers of the old frontier, his exploits in Wichita, Abilene, Dodge City and the other tough cattle towns of Kansas having invested him with a reputation which lasted until his death well into the twentieth century. Earp and his brother, Morgan, had been prospecting, hauling fuel, teaming and otherwise engaging in unexciting but remunerative occupations in Deadwood at a time when the stages were being held up and Wells Fargo's boxes removed with distressing regularity.

Wyatt was anxious to be quit of Deadwood and when he applied one day in April, 1877, for passage on the outward-bound coach for Cheyenne the Wells Fargo agent in Deadwood saw a great light.

"I'll give you free passage and fifty dollars gold to boot," he told Earp, "if you'll ride shotgun for me on the stage tomorrow."

An hour later a crudely lettered sign appeared on Wells Fargo's offices to the effect that the spring cleanup would go out on the Monday stage, "Wyatt Earp of Dodge City, Kansas, riding shotgun." The spring roundup was more than $200,000 in gold which had accumulated during the winter months in Wells Fargo's cast-iron safe and the agent was, in his own way, anxious to be well shut of this uneasy treasure.

Earp, who was unmolested on the road to Cheyenne although the countryside was crawling with gunmen who would have gladly made safari against any stage with an ordinary guard, afterward said it was the easiest fifty

## WATCHDOGS OF WELLS FARGO'S TREASURE AND TRANSPORT

Wells Fargo in the Black Hills of South Dakota bore a close resemblance to Wells Fargo wherever bullion demanded transport and the chaperonage of armed men. Here, in 1890, is the Deadwood treasure shipment loaded, according to the caption in the Wells Fargo Bank's files in San Francisco, with $250,000 of gold bullion from the Homestake Mine bound, presumably, for the bank account of Mrs. Phoebe Hearst, wife of the senator and mother of William Randolph. Wyatt Earp had long since departed Deadwood to serve as peace officer in Tombstone, but had the need arisen, Wells Fargo's Chief of Detectives James B. Hume (below) would have supplemented his agents in the Dakotas with his own presence.

dollars he ever earned, but it was the beginning of a long and favorable understanding between Wyatt Earp and Wells Fargo.

Now, in Tombstone, Arizona, the year being 1880, Earp was again on Hume's pay role and this time in a much more perilous capacity, for Tombstone at the feverish moment was what Stuart Lake, classic biographer of Earp, calls "the howling wonder of the Western world" and Wells Fargo was having as tough a time of it as ever it had experienced in Bodie, Candelaria or Hamilton in the most spacious days of those extremely spacious communities.

The Wells Fargo setup in Tombstone was unusual in that it entailed not only the services of well-identified agents and messengers but also a brace of secret agents whose business was to report in confidence directly to John Valentine and the police department of the Southern Pacific back in San Francisco. These two men were J. B. Ayers and Fred Dodge, ostensibly proprietor of a wide-open faro game which was conducted in Hafford's saloon in Tombstone. In his capacity as dealer and part proprietor of such a gathering place for law-abiding citizens and shady characters alike, he was able to pick up much information of great value to Hume and Valentine when it was relayed to Wells Fargo's offices. According to Stuart Lake, not even Marshall Williams, Wells Fargo's chief agent at Tombstone, knew Dodge's true occupation in the service of his own employers, although, of course, he was quite aware of the identity of John Thacker and Hume when they visited Tough Nut Street.

Chief of Detectives Hume had special grounds for vexation over the situation in Arizona and around Tombstone. The Tombstone-Benson stage on which he had taken passage had been held up one frosty dawn near Contention and Hume had been awakened by two swaggering and unmasked miscreants whom he recognized as Pony Deal and Curly Bill Brocius, followers of the outlaw banner of N. H. Clanton, the "Old Man Clanton" of many a border saga of pistols and pillage. With comments detrimental to the dignity of Wells Fargo's head sleuth, they had joyfully relieved Hume of a matched pair of ivory-handled, gold-inlaid six guns that were his accustomed armament and which he carried in shoulder holsters under his immaculate and inevitable long-skirted black morning coat. Hume had a grudge fight with all and any Arizona bad men from that day on.

Before the Earps became peace officers at Tombstone, "Old Man Clanton," as he was widely known, had prospered for years in the capacity of leader of a band of cattle rustlers, but as the products of southern Arizona mines increased throughout the seventies, the Clanton gang gave more and more of their time to Wells Fargo as represented by the treasure chests on outgoing stages. Nor were the incoming stages laden with currency for payrolls neglected, and Hume, grieved by the loss of his ornate weapons and concerned for Wells Fargo s treasure, bethought himself of the Earps' former services. Wyatt was retained to ride the stages between Tombstone and Tucson and it was this which directly precipitated the most celebrated single gun battle in the record of the Southwest. Its only real parallel in border legend was the bank robbery at Northfield, Minnesota, which in effect put an end to the James boys.

The Clanton gang made no affectation of innocence around Tombstone. After Wyatt Earp was retained as a Wells Fargo special officer there were two holdups of stages on the Bisbee run involving Wells Fargo treasure, in one of which the stage driver and a passenger were killed. Although Earp knew well who had committed the crimes, he urged Valentine, back in San Francisco, to circulate all of Arizona with posters offering a reward of $2,000 apiece for the gunmen, alive or dead. When potential informers questioned Wells Fargo's *bona fides* in the matter of the corpse reward, L. F. Rowell, Valentine's assistant, wired the marshal's office in Tombstone that the inanimate clay was just as much esteemed by Wells Fargo as the live article, perhaps more so.

The feud between Wyatt Earp and Ike Clanton was highly personal as well as professional. It was obvious to all Tombstone that an epic battle impended with Wells Fargo and the law-abiding element of the community ranged on one side and the Clanton followers and Tombstone's criminal populace on the other.

The pay-off was the epic powder burning at the O. K. Corral.

The build-up to this battle is of no consequence in this brief chronicle. It can be found in minute historic detail in Stuart Lake's *Wyatt Earp, Frontier Marshal.*

The participants were Ike Clanton and his son, Billy, Frank and Tom McLowery, a brace of uninhibited gangsters, and Billy Claiborne, a frontier character who insisted on being addressed as "Billy the Kid," being under the impression that he had fallen heir to the murderous mantle of this over-touted New Mexican punk. Arrayed against them were the three Earps, Wyatt, Virgil and Morgan, and their strange ally, Doc Holliday, the enigmatic fang puller. All were armed with the conventional brace of six-shot revolvers of varying makes and patterns except the eccentric Holliday who carried a walking stick under one arm and a double-barreled Wells Fargo shotgun in the other hand.

Witnesses to the meeting of the two factions that summer afternoon in 1881 at the O. K. Corral in Tombstone's Fremont Street varied in their testimony as to the time it occupied. Spectators not factually involved estimated that the gunfire lasted between fifteen and twenty seconds. Wyatt Earp afterward said half a minute would cover it adequately. All agreed that since Manassas it was improbable there had been so much dust, powder, smoke, noise and carnage. Thirty-four cartridges were, in actual fact, exploded but what with the black powder of the times and the limited space involved, the commotion had been extremely concentrated.

Billy Clanton, Tom McLowery and Frank McLowery were dead in and around Fremont Street, their bodies mutilated to an alarming degree by a number of heavy slugs fired at nearly muzzle range. Doc Holliday had contributed his bit by exploding both barrels of his scatter-gun loaded with buckshot into Tom McLowery's stomach and when McLowery had wavered a minute before falling dead, had smashed his head open with the gun butt under the impression he had somehow missed. Ike Clanton had fled the scene without firing a shot. Claiborne, who had killed three men for laughing at his self-assumed role of "Billy the Kid," had done the same.

Two of the Earps, Virgil and Morgan, were wounded, neither fatally, and Doc Holliday had been mauled by a slug in ricochet. It was not the end of outlawry in Arizona and there were holdups involving Wells Fargo shipments afterward, but the shooting at the O. K. Corral was among the briskest in the history of Wells Fargo's agents and has been an epic of the Southwest from that day to this.

The year was 1901.

The hazards of serving as Wells Fargo's shotgun messenger were not confined to gunfire and the hostile attentions of bandits. In the middle of December of 1901 there was a bad wreck involving the Southern Pacific's train *No. 10* on the Coast Line at Uplands. The head-end revenue cars, including a bullion car of Wells Fargo carrying a huge shipment of Mexican silver pesos consigned to the Orient, were all badly smashed and immediately caught fire from the Baker heater in one of them. Nobody will ever know just what happened to Owen Thurber, Wells Fargo's messenger in the bullion car, but it was supposed that one of the chests of silver fell upon him either killing or rendering him unconscious. When the fire was extinguished there was no trace of his whereabouts or fate except the twin barrels of a ten-gage shotgun which protruded from a vast mass of coin that had been melted down in the flames with the mortal remains of Thurber in its core. Being entombed in silver was a new sort of accident in the records of the express company.

# CHAPTER VIII

## Affairs of the Nabobs

NINETEENTH-CENTURY California was to produce a generation of the lords of creation which has become legendary. The saga of their acquisition of wealth, the fame of their estates and tangible possessions, the parade of their wives and their descendants, and their influence on the destinies of the entire world have been rehearsed in a thousand histories ranging from the agreeable "reading notices" of Hubert Howe Bancroft to the abuse of rancid little men consumed with envy.

They erected monstrous mansions on the hills of San Francisco and in London's Mayfair. They married into the noble houses of France, England, and Italy, and they indulged in internecine warfare among themselves and, dying, endowed universities, museums, libraries and a profusion of florid good works and public monuments. And they left a tradition of spaciousness and an imperial way of life without parallel in the modern world.

Generally speaking, the upper tendom of California's satraps in broadcloth fall into four groups according to the source of their power and wealth. There are the railroad monarchs: Hopkins, Huntington, Stanford, Crocker and the less exploited David Colton. There are the viceroys of the mighty Bank of California: Mills, Sharon and Ralston. A third category is that of the bonanza kings, their wealth deriving largely from the Comstock but most of them in essence and fact San Franciscans: Flood, Fair, Mackay, O'Brien, George Hearst, Adolph Sutro, Marcus Daly, John P. Jones, Alvinza Heyward and Lucky Baldwin.

And the fourth group is the succession of Wells Fargo's emirs of the express business: Ben Holladay, the brothers Barney, D. N. and A. H., John J. Valentine, James Ben Ali Haggin, Lloyd Tevis, Louis McLane, Homer S. King and a multiplicity of Fargos.

All of these groups were to a very great extent interlocking as was only natural in the structure of California's finance and industry. The destinies of the mines, railroads, banks and transport were interdependent and extremely involved. Most of these men were members of interlocking directorates and owned substantial properties in ventures other than those with which they were most closely identified. And the princes of Wells Fargo were as richly endowed with color and vitality as any Californians of their generation, which was considerable.

## POVERTY ROW, JUST OFF EASY STREET

During the sixties speculation in Comstock properties in San Francisco transcended any similar hysteria in the financial annals of the United States. Tipsters, stockjobbers and high-pressure investment salesmen, in cahoots with operators in Virginia City, caused fluctuations which made paper millionaires and factual paupers in a matter of minutes. Great ladies and serving maids, manual laborers and otherwise responsible men of affairs, riffraff and aristocrats, all were in the market in a speculative debauch compared to which the market operations of 1929 were decorous to the point of insipidness. The symbols of the era were the gold brick and the bogus stock certificate. Here stock sharpers ply their trade in Montgomery Street within a stone's throw of the offices of Wells Fargo, backing their sales talks with high-grade ore samples and grandiose prospectuses.

By the beginning of the sixties Wells Fargo was fast becoming a world name. In 1863, it maintained agencies in 156 towns in California, Idaho, Oregon and Utah and with the opening of new bonanzas towns in Nevada and Arizona were added to the roster almost overnight. With the discontinuance of Freeman's Mexican Coast Express it had established Spanish-American agencies at Cape St. Lucas, Guyamas, Mazatlán, Acapulco and La Paz. It was shipping treasure in sums in the millions out of British Columbia and forwarding them to London. As much as 3,000 pounds of gold dust, nuggets and bullion were daily passing through its San Francisco express offices. It had branches in Australia and Honolulu, in London, Southampton, Paris and Le Havre. In a few more years, through its railway connections and affiliates, it was to have branches in every large city of the East and South in the United States and, eventually, when gold was discovered in the Klondike, in Alaska.

Throughout the fifties, when Wells Fargo was transporting as much as $58,000,000 in gold on its California lines alone, it was paying dividends to the tune of ten per cent every year. In 1860, it paid an extra dividend of eight per cent on 6,000 shares of its stock, making a total for its holders of a neat eighteen per cent annually on their investment. In 1862, there were four quarterly dividends of three per cent each on all the company's stock, while the following year a stock dividend of forty-two per cent was paid on some classes of stock in addition to the regular year's dividend of twelve per cent on its entire capitalization.

Until 1860, when it came into possession of the Pioneer Stage Co. serving the fabulous Comstock, Wells Fargo had never made a practice of owning the stage lines over which its treasure and mails were carried, preferring instead to pay the heavy charges for the carriage of its cargoes and messengers in other people's vehicles. It pursued, too, its inflexible policy of making good on the barrelhead to its patrons any losses incurred in shipment from whatever source, highway robbery, fire, loss at sea or any other natural or man-made catastrophe. Its expenses were extremely heavy, especially in the express department, and the fact that it was able to pay such princely dividends is testimonial to the amount of business the firm was doing and the measure of its gross profits.

Wells Fargo's experience with the Pony Express and Russell, Majors & Waddell, not to mention the close interlocking of their affairs with John Butterfield both in the East and the West in the middle sixties, prompted the firm to a step not altogether dictated either by prudence or foresight. Since 1852, Wells Fargo had been in direct competition with the Post Office of the Federal Government, advertising and maintaining an overland letter service between California and the East. The service was somewhat better than that of the United States Postal Department and, because of its superior speed in delivery as well as the added convenience of daily lists of letter recipients posted in its offices, people were glad to pay the extra fee.

Four years later, Wells Fargo began to interest itself in the affairs of Ben Holladay's Overland Mail and Express Co. running east from Salt Lake. Holladay also controlled a former Butterfield property, the Overland Dispatch, which gave him entry to Denver by way of Topeka and Leavenworth.

But Holladay was in trouble. He had overextended himself; the Indians were causing him severe losses and he, at least, foresaw what Wells Fargo refused to see: the eventual completion of the Pacific Railroad. He therefore announced that his entire staging concerns between the Missouri River and California were for sale and Wells Fargo purchased them for a reported price of $1,500,000 in cash and $300,000 worth of Wells Fargo stock. By this move Wells Fargo, possessed since 1860 of a monopoly of all important staging routes in California, now acquired control of practically the entire business of passenger and express forwarding of every sort and description in the Western United States.

WELLS FARGO BANK

## EMPIRE'S END

When, on August 26, 1875, the Ba[nk of]
California closed its doors the tita[ns of]
finance of the western world had f[ailed.]
The next evening, while swimmin[g, as]
was his daily custom, in San Fran[cisco]
Bay, the brilliant and imperial W[illiam]
Ralston, the bank's president, [was]
drowned in circumstances of my[stery]
unsolved to this day. Wells Fargo, [hap-]
pily, was unaffected by the epic col[lapse,]
but when, as successor to the Ba[nk of]
California's prestige and authority[, the]
Nevada Bank was incorporated, i[t was]
eventually absorbed by Wells F[argo.]
Here an artist for *Leslie's Weekly* s[hows]
the terrible run on the Bank of Cali[fornia]
and, next evening the newsboys o[f San]
Francisco faring forth on horseback[ with]
the equally terrible news of Ral[ston's]
death.

WELLS FARGO BANK

In New York, Fargo, Butterfield and Wells were the ranking officers in the American Express Co., originally organized back in 1850, as the antecedent company in the East. The new capitalization was for $1,000,000. Twenty years later the business was to be valued at just twenty times this sum.

The years 1869 and 1870 were nothing less than a vertigo of tumults and excitements for Wells Fargo whether it was among the bonanzas of Nevada, in the countinghouses of San Francisco or along the multitudinous routes and via-structures which connected these points or lay adjacent in outlying communities on branch lines and less traveled highways.

The year 1869 saw at Promontory the progress toward fulfillment of the affairs and the first iron of the Central Pacific RR. It saw, too, the beginnings of the Virginia and Truckee, a railroad with whose destinies those of Wells Fargo in the Comstock were inevitably interlocked. It saw the death of old John Butterfield and Wells Fargo's withdrawal on a sweeping scale from the staging business in Montana. It saw the decline of the first bonanza at Virginia City and the great Crown Point underground fire and, in prophetic mood, it witnessed the royal decree by the Emperor Norton that Oakland become the terminal of the Pacific Railroad and that a bridge be built between Oakland and San Francisco. The first of these commands went into effect almost immediately while the other was delayed for a time by the parliamentary processes of relative democracy even though it functioned under monarchist auspices.

The completion in May of the Pacific Railroad had an obvious and far-reaching impact upon the operations of Wells Fargo's express business, but it brought with it an even more profound revolution in the financial economy and internal structure of the company and one which was later to be characterized by historian Wilson as "the biggest hold-up of all."

Wells Fargo had always taken a dim view of the Pacific Railroad. It had opposed it legislatively, ridiculed it editorially and worst of all, it had, from the dim canyons of New York's financial district, underestimated its potentialities, even discounting the probability of its completion. The stagecoach had made Wells Fargo dominant in the West and Wells Fargo would stand or fall by the stagecoach and, anyway, it wasn't possible to finish a railroad from the North Platte to the Golden Gate within the foreseeable future. The business was chimerical.

In Sacramento and in San Francisco, however, there were certain parties who thought otherwise and were willing to back their poetry with blue chips. The express business on their projected railroad was comparatively a small-time operation, but the Messrs. Hopkins, Crocker, Huntington and Stanford were not the sort of players to overlook any bet at all, and their front men, Darius Ogden Mills and Lloyd Tevis, had never been accused of being slow fellows where a million or so dollars was concerned. Back in 1867 they had organized a rival, the Pacific Union Express, whose races with Wells Fargo's messengers in the traffic between Reno and Virginia City are described

## BIG WHISKY DOINGS AT PROMONTORY

The dramatic and consequential meeting at Promontory, Utah, on May 10, 1869, of the locomotives *Jupiter* and *119* of the Central and Union Pacific railroads was to have a profound effect on the destinies of Wells Fargo. It was also to be read into the record in as spurious and mendacious a manner as any event in the American legend. Later-day representations in motion pictures, pageants and idealized art have come to invest Promontory with a quasi-religious respectability and stateliness of preposterous proportions. Historians of the cambric-tea school are pleased to depict the completion of the railroad as a symbolic and fraternal meeting of the East and West in the cause of progress and good works. But the record, both from the photographic evidence and the accounts of what few coherent witnesses were present attest that Promontory was a thunderous drunk whose convulsions included almost everyone present and lasted several days. The classic photograph made on a wet plate by Colonel Charles R. Savage of Salt Lake, official photographer for the railroads, does not so much depict the "pilots touching head to head" as it does what appears to be two section hands in amiable dispute over an outsize bottle. In idealized recreations of this scene the flagon of red eye is now and then amazingly changed to a small American flag. When it came time for Vice-President Durant of the U.P. to smite the ceremonial spike, such was his state of exhilaration that the ceremonial maul failed to connect and the job was finally accomplished by a less august mechanic. Other photographs show a grateful multiplicity of bottles in evidence and newspaper correspondents were to a man enthusiastic over the sideboard resources of President Stanford's business car.

204

## TUMULT IN MONTGOMERY STREET

Ever a parade-conscious town, San Francisco beat the bell in celebrating the Golden Spike ceremony at Promontory by a full two days. This photograph was taken on May 8, 1869, while the big doings in Utah didn't take place until two days later. San Franciscans, apprised of the premature nature of their rejoicings, simply turned it into a three-day celebration during which every business house in town locked its doors and the saloons of Kearny Street never closed. Here part of the parade has just passed the office of the *Dramatic Chronicle*, the forerunner of today's *San Francisco Chronicle*. Only Wells Fargo inclined to take a dim view of the general jubilation.

elsewhere, and whose agencies were appearing at strategic points in the West with a crescent frequency which would have alarmed any but the complacent Wells Fargo management.

There were other straws in the wind that would have been a tip-off to a more prudent administration. As the two ends of track were approaching Promontory, Wells Fargo quotations on the New York Stock Exchange declined from a tidy $100 a share to $13 and at Wells Fargo's offices the notion might have gained credence that somebody was driving down the value of its shares with an eye to purchasing them at fire-sale prices. Somebody was.

After Promontory,* in the spring of 1869, Wells Fargo metaphorically shrugged its shoulders and, at the direction of the New York offices, prepared to retire its stages from the Overland service and reassign them in feeder service, and at the same time took steps to open negotiations with the management of the Central Pacific for the carriage of its express business just as it had done with other newly completed railroads such as the Sacramento Valley in 1856 and the San Francisco and San Jose nearly a decade later.

This was the moment for which the Big Four of the Central Pacific had been waiting, and Wells Fargo was politely but firmly given to know that, through a contractual agreement which had been made back in 1867, the Pacific Union Express Co. had the exclusive right to shipment of express over the Central Pacific and had affiliated rights over the rails of the Union Pacific between Ogden and Council Bluffs. Thus, through the front of Mills and Tevis's Pacific Union Express, the Central Pacific kings had acquired a complete monopoly of passengers, merchandise and express over their railroad and its connections and, if any further persuasion were needed to convince the directors of Wells Fargo that they had fallen into a monstrous bear trap, Mills and Tevis were in almost complete control of Wells Fargo's stock, purchased at depreciated prices in the New York market.

At a meeting of the high contracting parties, hurriedly called at Omaha, the entire corporate structure of Wells Fargo was revised in favor of the victors of this bold and predatory coup. The company's capitalization was increased from $10,000,000 to $15,000,000, the Pacific Union Express, which had by now accomplished its purpose, being bought out with the additional $5,000,000. A new executive board, in which the name of Wells did not appear, was drawn up, and in 1872 Lloyd Tevis of San Francisco became president, a position which he held for two full decades. The main offices of the company were removed bodily from New York to San Francisco and Wells Fargo became the predominantly Western institution it has remained

---

* It is humorous to note that historians who chronicled these gaudy doings during the lifetime of those concerned were extremely hesitant about characterizing this unabashed brigandage by its right name. It is impossible, for example, for the reader to discover in Stimson's *History of the Express Business,* published in 1881, any suggestion that "the biggest hold-up of all" was anything but a routine transaction accomplished with courtliness and good will on the part of all concerned. The cynical may believe that the reason for this dainty handling of the record is to be found in the back of Stimson's volume where, among the advance subscribers, are listed: Lloyd Tevis and J. J. Valentine of Wells Fargo and William G. Fargo, J. C. Fargo and Charles Fargo of the American Express Co.

ever since. In one of the most adroitly consummated financial maneuvers ever evolved even in an era of grandiose corporate strategy, the old bearded kings of Montgomery Street took over, lock, stock and treasure chest, not only the tangible assets of a multimillion-dollar going concern, but the inestimable prestige and good name of Wells Fargo. Wall Street had been sent to the cleaners.

With the end of Wells Fargo's supremacy in the field of overland staging and express came the end of the golden age of horses and the Concord coach. True, they were to function as feeders to the railroads and on remote and inaccessible routes not available to the ever-widening empire of the steel rail, and the last Wells Fargo treasure box to be tossed down from a Concord's boot was at the end of the first decade of the twentieth century at Rawhide, Nevada. But the glory was gone from the Overland run and with it out of the life of Wells Fargo went its president, Louis McLane, whose faith in horses had been a religion. It was McLane who had secured for Wells Fargo its near monopoly in the Comstock by the purchase of the Pioneer line, but it was also McLane whose scorn of the Pacific Railroad had ended an entire succession of officers and directors of Wells Fargo.

The fall of McLane meant the rise of a new group of Wells Fargo executives, who were to dominate the express scene as they dominated the financial and economic life of San Francisco for many years to come, and the most fabled name in this category is that of Lloyd Tevis. Tevis came to Wells Fargo as Vice-President and a member of the Board of Directors after the debacle of 1869 at the same time that directorates were occupied by Darius Ogden Mills, President of the Bank of California, Leland Stanford, former Governor of the State, and Collis P. Huntington of the Central Pacific. Here was an interlocking directorate of wealth and authority to stagger the imagination.

The reign of Lloyd Tevis and, through their business partnership which owned an impressive quantity of Wells Fargo stock, of James Ben Ali Haggin is still memorable in the annals of San Francisco where, throughout its history, both before and after The Fire, grandeur has been a native commodity.

Tevis was a Kentuckian of formal education and some previous association with the law who had come to California in the spring of 1849 via the Overland trail and had worked for a time in the exciting surroundings of the Mother Lode diggings.

His luck at the long toms was not, however, of a piece with his subsequent fortune in the world of affairs, and in the following year he set up a legal partnership with another Kentuckian and friend, Haggin, a partnership which was to last for forty-nine years until Tevis' death. The two future nabobs married sisters and their association was destined to be one of fantastic success and productivity, more as a business partnership than a law office although their legal background was never anything but an asset.

Before his entry upon the Wells Fargo scene, Tevis and, of course, Haggin— for their partnership was close and absolute in all ventures — had been interested in transport and communications. They were connected with the

# AMERICAN
# Speaking Telephone Company

### OFFICES

| | | |
|---|---|---|
| 222 SANSOME STREET | 211 KEARNY STREET | 833 SUTTER STREET |
| 965 MISSION STREET | TWENTIETH and MISSION | HAYES and LAGUNA |
| CALIFORNIA and FILLMORE | POWELL and UNION | BUTCHERTOWN |

## TELEPHONES RENTED AND LINES CONSTRUCTED

## LIST OF SUBSCRIBERS JUNE 1, 1878

Names preceded by stars are connected with the **CENTRAL OFFICE SYSTEM**, and can be switched into private connection with each other.

* Anderton & Stratton, Tanners Butchertown
* Anthony G W & Co, Brokers 102 Krny
* Anthony G W & Co, Brokers 240 Krny
* Abrams & Carroll, Druggists 345 Front
* "Arion Hall," Henry Grimm Sutter & Krny
* Bank Wells Fargo & Co, Bankers Cal & Sansome
* Bank French Savings, Bankers 411 Bush
* Board of Education, Gen Ofc Old City Hall
* Board of Education, Col J A Laven 30 Sac
* Board of Education, J W Taylor 501 Mkt
* Baldwin Pharmacy, H B Slaven Mkt & Powell
* Bradbury W B, Centennial Planing Mills 556-572 Brannan
* Baker & Hamilton, Hdwe 7-19 Front
* Baker & Hamilton, Hdwe 2d & Townsend
* Barnes W H L, Atty 426 Cal
  Bulger Martin, Supt P M S S Co Mail Dock
  Bulger Martin, Supt P M S S Co 31 Russ
* Blake Geo M, Oils 123 Cal
* Blake Geo M, Oils 1601 Van Ness
* Brandenstein & Co, Butchers 339 Krny
* Brandenstein & Co, Butchers Butchertown
  Buckingham & Hecht, Boots & Shoes 528 Mkt
  Buckingham & Hecht, Boots&Shoes Haight&Gough
* Ball & Julian, Occidental Wool Depot Townsend bet 5th & 6th
* Bernard Chas, Coffee & Spice 707 Sansome
* Boyson Dr Thomas, Physician 112 Krny
  Crittenden C S, Club Stables Taylor St
  Crittenden O S, Dexter Stables 221 Bush
* City Hall, Secy's Ofc Mkt St
* Chief of Police, City Hall Krny St
* Cal Furniture Co, Furn 222 Bush
* Cal Furniture Co, Furn 649 Mkt
* Crocker H S & Co, Statnry Sansome & Sac
* Crane & Brigham, Druggists 520 Mkt
* Christy & Wise, Wool 607 Front
* Cal Wool Depot, Jno F Knox Townsd bet 5th&6th
* Cal Cracker Co, Bakers 203 Sac
* Cal Cracker Co, Bakers Battery & Bway
* Cutting & Co, Pkg & Canning 17 Main
"Code Efelt & Co, Pkg & Canning 314 Wash
* Code Elfelt & Co, Pkg & Canning 125 Davis
* Cal Paint Co, Paints 329 Mkt
* Cal Paint Co, Paints 27 Stevenson
* Centennial Planing Mills, W B Bradbury 556-572 Brannan
* Cassimer J, "The Fountain" Sutter & Krny
  Chy Lung & Co, Chinese Mchts 521 Krny
  Chy Lung & Co, Chinese Mchts 640 Sac
  Club Stables, Livery Taylor St
* Coffin Sanderson & Cook, Brokers 312 Pine
* Cal Electrical Wks, Electricians 134 Sutter
* Day Thos, Gasfitter 122 Sutter
  Dexter Stables, Livery 221 Bush
* Deming Palmer & Co, Flour Mills 202 Davis
* Dewey & Co, Publishers 202 Sansome
* Dewey & Co, Publishers 414 Clay
* Dunphy & Hildreth, Butchers 533 Krny
* Dunphy & Hildreth, Butchers Butchertown
  Dry Dock Co, Dry Docks Hunters Point
* Engine House, Fire Dept Post & Webster
* Eureka Warehouse, A J Gove Mtgy & Chestnut
  Eldridge Oliver, Pres Dry Dock Co 318 Cal
* "Fountain The," Saloon Sutter & Krny
* Fashion Stables, Livery Sutter St
* Field Stephen D, Electrician 2319 Cal
* Gallagher Thos J, Atty 602 Coml
* Gilbert & Moore, Furn 219 Bush
* Gladding McBean & Co, Drain&SewerPipe 213 Mkt
* Gladding McBean & Co, Drain&SewerPipe1312Mkt
* Ghirardelli & Danzel, Coffee & Spice 415 Jackson
* Guittard E & Co, Coffee & Spice 405 Sansome
* Guittard E & Co, Coffee & Spice 205 Front
* Grangers' Business Assn, Produce 106 Davis
  Grun & Vogelsang, Saloon 215—3d
  Grun & Vogelsang, Saloon 142—4th
* Grand Opera House, Theatre Mission St
* Gamble James, W U Tel Co 300 Pine
* Gove A J, Eureka Whse Chestnut & Mtg
* Hunt D D, Druggist 5th & Folsom
* Howes E K & Co, Woodenware 122 Front
* Howes E K & Co, Woodenware 37 Main
* Hochkofler R, Mdse Broker 205 Front
* Journal of Commerce, Publishers Clay & Sansome
* Kiel F C, Druggist 4th & Mkt
* Knox Jno F, Cal Wool Depot Townsd bet 5th & 6th
* Langley Chas & Co, Druggists Front & Pine

* Lipnitz & Co, Druggists 236 Sutter
* Liebenbaum & Co, Grocers 529 Krny
* Liebenbaum & Co, Grocers 1303 Polk
  Lane Dr L C, Physician 652 Mission
  Lane Dr L C, Physician Clay & Buchanan
* Ladd Geo S, Pres G & S Tel Co 222 Sansome
* Ladd Geo S, Pres G & S Tel Co 515 Van Ness
* Macondray & Co, Shipping & Comm 204 Sansome
* McCord & Malone, Fashion Stables 16 Sutter
* McKinlay Jas, Pac Commercial Co 28 Sac
* Mining & Scientific Press, Dewey & Co 202 Sans
* McCall J G, Ry Agt 15 New Mtgy
* McCall J G, Ry Agt 614 Wash
* Murphy Horn & Byrne, Butchers 533 Krny
* Murphy Horn & Byrne, Butchers Butchertown
* McMenomy J H, Butcher Cal Mkt
* Michelsen Brown & Co, Butchers 308 Front
* Michelsen Brown & Co, Butchers Butchertown
* Miller & Lux, Butchers 533 Krny
* Miller & Lux, Butchers Butchertown
* Mayhew Earnest & Co, Grain 302 Davis
* Mills D O, Capitalist Over London & S F Bank
* McDonald M J, Broker 215 Sansome
* McDonald M J, Broker 1096 Post
* Mahe Gustave, Banker 411 Bush
* Maxwell Dr B T, Physician 135 Krny
* Newton Bros & Co, Grocers 204 Cal
* Newman Carlton, Prop Glass Wks 1585 Folsom
* Oriental Bonded Warehouse, Pool & Harris Bryant & 1st
* Odd Fellows Assn, Odd Fellows Bldg 325 Mtgy
* Odd Fellows Cemetery, Cemetery
* Palace Stables, Hacks & Coupes 615 Howard
* Police Office, Chief of Police City Hall
* Postoffice, Wash & Battery
* Postoffice, Station C Mission & 20th
  Poheim J, Tailor 202 Mtgy
  Poheim J, Tailor 103—3d
* Pacific Commercial Co, Coal 28 Sac
* Pacific Commercial Co, Coal Geary & Mason
* Pacific Commercial Co, Coal Sutter & Larkin
  Pacific M S S Co, Transportation Mail Dock
* Painter Emlen, Druggist Clay & Krny
* Painter Emlen, Druggist 11th & Mission
* Poly Heilbron & Co, Butchers 339 Krny
* Poly Heilbron & Co, Butchers Butchertown
* Pool & Harris, Oriental Whse Bryant & 1st
  Quong Lee, Chinese Mcht 828 Dupont
  Quong Lee, Chinese Mcht 408 Mcht
  Quong Lee, Chinese Mcht 410 Krny
* Redington & Co, Druggists 529 Mkt
* Richards C F & Co, Druggists Clay & Sansome
* S F & Pac Glass Wks, C Newman King St
* Sage L P, Warehouse Battery & Union
* Slaven H B, Druggist Mkt & Powell
* Selig M, Butcher 331 Krny
* Selig M, Butcher Butchertown
* Stallard Dr J H, Physician 37 Post
  Sabin Jno I, Supt G & S Tel Co 1812 Pierce
* Sturm Victor H, S Cassimer&Co 25th & S Jose Av
* Taylor John & Co, Druggists'Glassware 512 Wash
  Taylor Jno W, 'Gutta Percha 501 Mkt
* Tevis Lloyd, Capitalist Bank of W F & Co
* Trumpour J P, Dentist 2021 Mission
  Trumpour J P, Dentist 401½ Hayes
* Tay Geo H & Co, Stoves & Tinware 614 Battery
* Underwriters' Fire Patrol, Ecker & Stevenson
* United Carriage Co, Hacks & Coupes Palace Hotel
* United Carriage Co, Hacks & Coupes Sutter&Lwth
  United Workingmen, Boot & Shoe Co 410 Mkt
  United Workingmen, Boot&Shoe Co 25th&Bartlett
* Verdenal D F, Mining Secy 327 Pine
* Verdenal D F, Mining Secy 1525 Sutter
  Vermeil & Wellington, Hay & Grain 608—4th
  Vermeil & Wellington, Hay & Grain 4th & Berry
* Western Union Tel Co, Pine & Mtgy
  White Capt Russell, Fire Patrol Stevenson St
  White Capt Russell, 627½ Howard
  West Coast Furniture Co, Furniture 4th & Bryant
* Wingate J C, Oakland Express 6 Sac
* Williams Blanchard & Co,Agts P M SS Co 218 Cal
* Wellman Peck & Co, Grocers 416 Front
* Whitney & Webster, Wool Whse King St
* Waldstein A, Lithographer Sac & Sansome
* Waldstein A, Lithographer King nr 3d
* Wangenheim Sol, Pkg & Canning 120 Davis
* Wells Fargo & Co's Bank, Bankers Cal & Sansome
* Willard G H, Broker Safe Deposit Bldg
  Wilson J Y & Co, Prov Packers 508 Mkt

## ITEMS OF CALIFORNIANA

The express Building on the east side of Montgomery Street was completed in January, 1854, and occupied by Wells Fargo shortly thereafter. Masonic Hall and Armory Hall, the adjacent buildings, were erected the year previous. On the page opposite is the first telephone directory to appear on the Pacific coast. Wells Fargo is listed twice, but had only one telephone set, located in a corridor for anyone to answer who was handy, for several years thereafter. The same phone is listed as the one of Lloyd Tevis, "capitalist," while Darius-Ogden Mills, "Capitalist, Over London & S F Bank," had one all to himself. Wells Fargo's nabobs, generally speaking, did not approve too much of the "speaking telephone" and continued right into the twentieth century to convey messages, as God intended, by note of hand.

California Dry Dock and California Market in San Francisco, had speculated briefly in the affairs of the State Telegraph Co., and Tevis had served as President of the Southern Pacific, not yet the vast organization it was soon to become, and was President of the Pacific Ice Co. Already his interests and ventures were on a scale to compete in variety with those of William Ralston, the golden boy of the moment in California finance.

Four years after Tevis assumed office, Wells Fargo's old quarters in the structure built for Adams & Co. by John Parrott became inadequate to its needs. The banking department moved into the former quarters of the National Gold Bank and Trust Co. at the corner of Sansome and California Streets, "considered the finest banking rooms in the city." The Gold Bank was an institution which had been hard hit in the panic of 1875 and Wells Fargo moved in with general rejoicing and a splendid banquet at the then brand-new Palace over in Market Street.

The sign over the Sansome Street office portal read "Wells Fargo & Co.'s Bank," and although it was still an integral part of Wells Fargo & Co., the banking department was henceforward to conduct its affairs in almost complete independence. Homer S. King, who had built the beautiful Victorian mansion on the sides of Sun Mountain in Virginia City, was Treasurer and Tevis was President both of the bank and the express company, with offices in the Sansome Street address. John J. Valentine ran the express business from its new quarters in the Halleck Building, at the corner of Halleck and Sansome.

A pleasant picture of the life, at once stately and opulent, in Wells Fargo's offices during the seventies has been painted by an old-time employee and remains in the Wells Fargo files in Montgomery Street, available after three quarters of a century to the interested reader.

"Mr. James Heron was secretary and cashier when I first went to work at Wells Fargo," wrote Eric Francis, "and Charles Banks was the assistant. Mr. Banks was later the sensational absconder. Mr. Heron was a charming gentleman who had been connected with the United States Embassy at Paris and spoke French like a native Parisian.

"In those days the office was the visiting place in San Francisco for all the celebrities who were either interested in Wells Fargo or else friends of Mr. Tevis, Mr. Haggin, Governor Stanford, Mr. Huntington, Mr. Crocker or Mr. Valentine. Among our visitors was the celebrated Colonel Mosby of Mosby's Raiders in Civil War times. I can see him now with his one eye, rattan cane, and fierce manner. Many other Kentuckians came in. Henry George who wrote "Progress and Poverty" was a frequent visitor. He was the brother-in-law of John J. Valentine, who was the Superintendent of Wells Fargo. Then came Commodore Jefferson Maury of the Pacific Mail, who lost the steamer 'City of Tokyo.' This was the vessel that in 1879 brought General U. S. Grant home to S. F. from his celebrated trip around the world.

"The Commodore was a frequent visitor; he was a tall handsome man with a white beard as I recall. General Mariano Guadalupe Vallejo with his handsome face and charming manner, also Governor Romualdo Pacheco, whose daughter Mabel married young Will Tevis, son of Lloyd Tevis, also came in quite frequently. He was a handsome courtly gentleman of the Old Californian type.

"We had also many fine Mexican gentleman friends of Mr. Heron visit the office. I used to pass around the dollar cigars at the request of our urbane secretary. Then we had the famous Bill Hamilton of Stage Coach fame, bald as a billiard ball and most profane; also John Allman, a saturnine, dark gentleman, who looked like Jacob McCloskey, the villain in Boucicault's great play of 'The Octaroon.' Mr. Banks used to call him 'Little Satan,' and he certainly looked the part. He was one tough hombre in the early days, and was (they whispered it) said to have killed a man with a Bowie knife at one time, in the early days up north. We also had lady callers on the secretary, Mrs. Jane Stanford, Mrs. Phoebe A. Hearst and Mrs. James G. Fair. Mrs. Fair would come down from Nob Hill in her carriage with coachman and footmen in livery. The gold plated harness shining resplendently on the pair of beautiful horses that drew the stately equipage.

"We used to have the old Pony Express Riders, and P. G. Hodgkins, otherwise known as Chips, with his gold earrings. Wm. A. Pridham and many other old stage drivers. Bill Barnard, whose father used to have the stage line between San Quentin and San Rafael. The Ferry from San Francisco used to land at San Quentin then. Bill was a character who used to work for his father on the Stage Line. He once drove the circus wagons for the famous John Wilson's Circus, a wagon show of the early days in San Francisco. I also met many other men who were the pioneers who made the stage routes possible. Bill Barnard was driving a big two horse wagon for 'Fargo' when I knew him first.

"Among the Division Superintendents was Solomon D. Brastow, at one time treasurer of the Bohemian Club. He was a fine, gruff fearless man and highly respected by all who came in contact with him. He had the Northern Division and Leonard F. Rowell, smooth diplomatic and at that time very profane, had the Southern Division which included Los Angeles, Arizona and the Southwest. Mr. Rowell 'got religion' and gave up his profanity, much to the astonishment of his many friends. He often used to come in our office and chat with Mr. Heron and Banks.

"Then we had T. P. Carroll, the auditor, a fine gentleman from England, and an efficient auditor. He often came in at the end of the day to read the bulletin and was mildly chaffed by Mr. Banks, who had a subtle wit.

"Mr. Heron was very easy going. He loved to dine at the fine French Boarding Houses, which flourished then on Geary Street. He would generally go out at 11 A.M. to 3 P.M. for lunch.

"When we had directors meetings I had to take unsealed written notices of such meetings and deliver them personally to the directors' homes on Nob Hill. There were no type-writers then, and Mr. Heron wrote like copper plate. Who can now? The art of fine penmanship seems to be nearly extinct.

WELLS FARGO BANK

## AN OLD FRIEND OF WELLS FARGO

Best known of San Francisco's eccentrics who flourished in rich and gaudy profusion during Wells Fargo's spacious years was Norton I, Emperor of the United States and Protector of Mexico. A once well-to-do merchant whose repeated bankruptcies as a result of grain speculations had gently clouded his mind, the Emperor, carrying a court sword and wearing a cockaded silk hat and military epaulets, was for more than twenty years a familiar figure in the town's public life. His edicts and manifestoes were almost invariably accorded generous space by newspaper editors; his person was gravely saluted by all comers and when he needed funds his modest drafts against "the imperial treasury" were honored by all but churls. Wells Fargo's cashiers had strict orders to accept his scrip in reasonable sums at face value and his presence was regarded as a distinction by saloonkeepers when he dined at their free-lunch counters. Norton's decrees, generally fanciful and grandly conceived, were sometimes prophetic, as when he commanded the Central Pacific RR to set up its western terminal at Oakland Mole and ordered that there be built a suspension bridge from Oakland Point to Yerba Buena. When the good old gentleman died in 1880 all San Francisco unaffectedly mourned his passing, and in 1934 a group of prominent citizens erected a shaft to his memory at Woodlawn Memorial Park. On the page opposite is an example of the Emperor's scrip and below it a document marking one of the few times when he was at odds with Wells Fargo. Usually he was on the best of terms with Lloyd Tevis and Superintendent Valentine and he was allowed to hold informal courts and levees in the California Street office when there were not too many customers around. Once, when the Emperor felt that Wells Fargo was a party to sedition, public denunciation resulted, well calculated to bring the firm to its senses.

The Imperial Government of NORTON I.

UNITED STATES

Promises to pay the holder hereof, the sum of Fifty Cents in the year 1880, with interest at 6 per cent. per annum from date, the principal and interest to be convertible, at the option of the holder, at maturity, into 20 years' 5 per cent. Bonds, or payable in Gold Coin.

Given under our Royal hand and seal, this 12 day of June 1878.

# PROCLAMATION.

WHEREAS, Certain parties having assumed prerogatives, pertaining only to my Royal self; AND WHEREAS, in the furtherance of such assumption, they have printed and circulated treasonable and rebellious documents, circulars, sermons and proclamations, calculated to distract and divide the allegiance of my subjects; AND WHEREAS, it has come to my knowledge that a certain seditious proclamation and command has been distributed amongst the most faithful of my agents and subjects, of which the following is a copy, to-wit:

"OFFICE WELLS, FARGO & CO.

"SAN FRANCISCO, JULY 4TH, 1868

"TO OUR AGENTS·

"C. Averill, formerly Forwarding Clerk, and late Messenger to our Mexican Coast Offices, has left our employ and gone with the Pacific Union Express Company.

"You will treat him as any other employee of an opposition Express Co.

"CHARLES E. McLANE,

"Gen'l Agent."

NOW, THEREFORE, I, EMPEROR NORTON the First, do hereby command that no notice shall be paid to proclamations issued by Pretenders to my authority, ability, and Regal position

AND IT IS FURTHER COMMANDED, that any violation of this command shall be reported to me, in order that I may banish the offender from my Kingdom.

NORTON, EMPEROR THE FIRST.

After work I would go up on Nob Hill. First to Governor Stanford's home. The butler would ask 'who shall I say?'

"And I would answer 'A messenger from the secretary's office.' Governor Stanford would receive me in the dining room. He was a great eater, and it is said he could eat two chickens at a meal besides wine in proportion. He would read the notice and say 'Present my compliments to Mr. Heron and tell him it will give me pleasure to attend the meeting next Wednesday afternoon at 2 P.M. Have a glass of wine my boy?' Which I being on company business politely declined. He knew that as well as I did, but he was a gentleman and a fine man. Then in turn to the Crocker home and the others in town.

"On the day of the meeting, I would go into the vault and give each director a $10 piece for attendance fee. I would then go out in the street and walk around till the meeting was over. I would sit down at my little desk near the door. Often Mr. Crocker, Stanford, and C. P. Huntington would pat me on the head and give me a dollar. I remember the first time this occurred I said afterward to Mr. Heron that 'I do not like to be tipped as my father has a good job.' He said cryptically, 'If you refuse it, you will only get me into trouble as well as yourself. Buy your girl a box of candy and forget it.'"

"Banks the absconder," to whom these reminiscences refer, was in fact one of the nabobs himself and caused great consternation in Wells Fargo in the middle eighties by looting the company of a vast sum of money and making a dazzling disappearance with it. When discovered he was beyond the reach of Mr. Hume's most expert agents, and the notion will suggest itself that when, upon occasion, Wells Fargo harbored a viper in its corporate bosom it was a viper of uncommon personality and distinction.

From the very inception of the venture the company's executives, its functionaries in Sansome Street, its armed messengers, guards and detectives, its agents and other responsible servants included a remarkable average of men of determined character. Even Wells Fargo's staff embezzlers and peculators, as well as the men who, like Black Bart and Milton Sharp, achieved national reputations by arraying themselves against Wells Fargo's armed might, were persons of quality in their particular field of endeavor and activity. Little that was mediocre seemed to evidence itself in the Wells Fargo record.

Perhaps the most celebrated of all Wells Fargo's embezzlers — and a character, on the other side of the fence to be sure, but still of a magnificence worthy of rank with Tevis, Hume and Valentine — was Banks, who was one of the relatively few malefactors over the decades and whose obituary could not be written in the classic words: "Wells Fargo Never Forgets."

It is, of course, possible over the years to invest almost any nineteenth-century scoundrel with a certain degree of romance. The manners, the period costumes, even the beards of the time, lend a picaresque quality to embezzlements and abscondings, holdups and crimes of genteel violence which would be altogether lacking in a twentieth-century till rifler attired in a ready-made business suit and chewing gum.

One of the most elegant of such legends is that of Banks, and it embraces almost all the properties which later came to be essential to the aristocratic economy of an E. Phillips Oppenheim shocker. It involved yachts, mistresses, royalty, ace detective operatives, large sums of money and a protagonist of more or less romantic qualifications. Its settings were the eminently financial precincts of San Francisco's banking district and the dreamy lagoons of South Sea Islands. What Sunday-supplement editor could ask for more?

Charles Wells Banks was a fine figure of a man when, in 1886, San Francisco knew him as a member of the Union and Bohemian Clubs, of the San Francisco Microscopical Society and as cashier of the Express department of Wells Fargo's Sansome Street office. He was full-bearded, fond of costly if conservative attire as suited his station, married and devoid of any visible vices which might have been looked upon by his principals with alarm. He had been wounded, as a sergeant in the Union Army, at Pleasant Hill and later served as a United States Customs officer in New York harbor. More than a little his speech resembled that of a cultivated Englishman and, aside from the activities of the Microscopical Society, he indulged a taste for yachting on a modest scale.

"I never met a man anywhere else of Banks' all-round ability," Eric Francis wrote of him many years later. "He could add up three columns of figures and write about fifteen different hands, being a wonderful penman. He could do anything four times as quickly and efficiently as you could.

"Banks used to lend me his horse and buggy to drive in the Park every Saturday and Sunday, being the soul of generosity. The horse was also fine for the saddle and many a fine ride I have had to the old Cliff House in the 80's. I can truthfully say that in all these years I have never seen a man who set me a better example of the Dr. Jekyll side of his character which was the only one with which I was acquainted and I often recall him for his kindness and instructive conversation."

From every evidence of his associates both in the Sansome Street counting house and in the meetings of the Microscopical Society at Irving and Mercantile Library Halls, Banks' was a model of propriety, probity and temperance.

It was, therefore, with alarm tempered with incredulity, that the senior officers at Wells Fargo one fine morning in 1887 came to the unavoidable conclusion that during the night their paragon of cashiers had, to put it crudely, taken it on the lam. When Banks had failed to show up for work at the usual hour, other members of the staff privy to the combination of the great safe had spun the knobs, produced flat brass keys from their gold Albert watch chains and remained frozen around the cashbox in Prince Albert coats and Mother Hubbard attitudes. The cupboard was bare. The customary notice, posted over Mr. Hume's signature, mentioned $1,000 reward and the missing sum as being in excess of $20,000. Banks' subsequent manner of life would indicate that this was an understatement.

Investigation revealed that, late the previous afternoon, the courtly cashier had ordered his little yacht anchored at the foot of Mission Street, at about five o'clock had sent for two members of the crew to assist him to remove three bulging carpetbags from his private office and had gone on board. In a later generation it seems probable that carrying aboard a seagoing yacht a quantity of afterhours baggage from a banking office, would occasion the raising of eyebrows if not the watch. But San Francisco in the eighties was different and, besides, Banks' splendid whiskers, silk hat and assured manner did not encourage impertinent inquiry from anyone.

Bemused Wells Fargo officials going over his books in the ensuing interval were not particularly surprised when Mr. Hume's operatives brought in the report that, in addition to his lawful and ever-loving wife, the object of their most assiduous attentions had maintained no fewer than three mistresses at strategic points around town and that, prior to his departure and with a nice eye to the conventions, he had given each of them fifty dollars while handing his wife a hundred. His taste in such matters was generally recognized as flawless.

Wells Fargo and Mr. Hume had little enough to go on. The world was full of bearded sirs and small yachts were no great rarity. One uncommon clue only could Mr. Hume discover by which to advertise and perhaps, eventually, identify his quarry. Banks, despite a full set of false teeth, had a consuming passion for French gumdrops. He had carried a store of them, similar to the store of pemmican cherished by Arctic explorers, aboard his yacht, and for months bearded men eating gumdrops in public places up and down the Pacific coast were subject to outrageous questioning from determined-looking men in bowler hats.

When traces of the elusive Banks eventually materialized, however, they were far from Los Angeles or even Seattle. Wells Fargo operatives had by this time been placed aboard every outbound steamer for Australia, the Asiatic ports and the South Seas. Their ratcatcher traveling suits and sportive side whiskers were discernible in a score of climes and latitudes playing shuffleboard with the passengers, dining elaborately at the captain's table and combing water-front resorts in tourist attitudes, all on company expense money. In Sydney, Saïgon, Singapore and Auckland their concern for gumdrops provoked the rumor that a group of San Francisco financiers were out to corner the market, and French gumdrops were soon selling at a premium in the bazaars from Nome to Rarotonga.

It was in Rarotonga that the company's operatives struck pay dirt. Yes, there was a white American there with a beard and a hanker for strange foreign sweets which island traders were now and then able to pick up for him at considerable profit. He was married to a native woman named Ngakapu and, although possessed of unquestioned private means, he was employed by A. J. Moss, advisor to the British native government of the islands, in the capacity of chief secretary and expert accountant. He kept a small yacht

staffed by white men, was an exquisite penman and cherished a consuming passion for what answered the description of French gumdrops.

Wells Fargo agents converged by every steamer upon Rarotonga and it was apparent that the due processes of law were about to function with all the austere grandeur for which they were noted. It was to be the pinch of the century.

Their final arrangements made, at dusk one evening no fewer than half a dozen special operatives descended upon the compound of the merry embezzler, but not to discover the beachcomber gone native as they had anticipated. On the strength of his record in San Francisco the detectives may be excused for having envisioned him pillowed in native and voluptuous luxury surrounded by at least a score of wives and probably far gone in the vices which, in the islands, proverbially laid hold upon the white man.

Banks seemed to have resisted the fabled allurements of the tropics. To be sure his compound did appear to be unusually populous with native spearmen of menacing appearance and threatening armament. The more vivid imaginations fancied they saw human heads ornamenting the ceremonial spears of the attendant warriors and one or two of the operatives were willing later to swear that some of the heads wore bowler hats and wing collars, bearing a disturbing resemblance to the appearance of Wells Fargo detectives. It was a long way from Sansome Street.

The amiable absconder received them at what was apparently the conclusion of dinner. He was attired not in the native costume in which his pursuers had envisioned him nor did he appear overwhelmed with the voluptuous devisings of Oriental vice. He wore immaculate European evening attire of white linen and was smoking a cheroot which the more sensitive Wells Fargo noses present were able to identify as clear Havana, probably costing four bits on Nob Hill. A magnum of champagne was in a cooler at his elbow and a brown-skinned native butler supported by a corps of house servants was at hand. What could Mr. Banks do for his guests?

There are moments to which only the detectives of fiction could do justice and Mr. Hume's operatives, whatever their other qualifications, were not up to the apprehension of a man who, to all appearances, was an Oriental potentate. Besides, there were those spears in the outside compound and the native retainers seemed restless, even eager for some signal from their overlord. Perhaps it would be better to retire and consider strategy. Their hard hats with fashionably curly brims, the latest thing from Roos Brothers' gentlemen's emporium, would look better on the ornamental rack back at the Barrel House on Third Street than on even the most elevated pike in the Cook Islands.

The truth of the matter was that Banks, a fellow of genial and persuasive personality, had a distinctly favorable "in" with Rarotonga's two-hundred-pound Queen Makea and that she alone could sanction the service of extradition papers on anyone within her realm. This she was disinclined to do and Mr. Hume's minions were in the paradoxical position of being able to lay instant hands on their long-sought quarry and at the same time quite unable to do so. In the end they retired, impotent and discomforted, and Banks was left to the enjoyment of his stolen wealth, a conspicuous example to other potential embezzlers. When, after some years in the easy service of the British intendant, he became blind, he was given a handsome pension and lived out his days in affluent retirement. He died in 1915 and was buried in the churchyard of the London Missionary Society in Avarua in an atmosphere of almost sanctimonious respectability. His was a success story which gave no satisfaction to Wells Fargo.

There is one last happy detail associated with the saga of Charlie Banks and his elegantly larcenous progress. A feature article in the *Portland Evening Telegram* for July 31, 1897, chronicled the story of Banks, his successful technique and joyous immunity at some length. In the precisely adjacent column appeared an advertisement for Studebaker's rubber-tired carriages and up-to-date vehicles of all descriptions. It was headed: "Would You Too Like to Live on Easy Street?"

Throughout such commotions and excitements Tevis and his partner Haggin were interesting themselves in a variety of ventures quite aside from

Wells Fargo, although there were often overlapping interests between the different companies. The Spring Valley Water Co. was one. Another was the Risdon Iron Works, and a third the great tunnel Adolph Sutro was building against the opposition of almost everybody in the Comstock. Tevis and Haggin owned the California Street Railway, some 1,300 miles of stage lines in parts of California where they didn't compete with the ever-growing Southern Pacific, herds of sheep and blooded cattle and thousands of acres of grazing land.

Tevis also had vast and comprehensive mining interests in the gold and silver bonanzas of Nevada, Utah, Idaho, South Dakota and the state of his adoption and residence. He, Haggin, George Hearst and Marcus Daly were co-owners of the Great Anaconda Copper holdings in Montana and the legendary Homesteak Mine in the Black Hills. When, in 1889, Tevis sold out to a syndicate organized by John D. Rockefeller, it was reported that his share in these isolated mining properties alone was in excess of $8,000,000.

As recounted elsewhere in this chronicle, Wells Fargo was too conservative to have anything to do, in an expressing or banking capacity, with the tumultuous camp at Panamint in the Death Valley region of California. Tevis and Haggin, in their private capacities as the coast's most aggressive capitalists, were conditioned by no such inhibitions, and among their other far-flung possessions was Panamint's Christmas Gift mine, purchased after a personal inspection of its possibilities by their associate, George Hearst.

But not even the sum of these remarkable interests could outweigh with Tevis the fascination of being President of Wells Fargo, and some idea of the growth of the company during the term of his office may be derived from the fact that in 1892 the number of Wells Fargo offices and branches throughout the world was 2,830. And, of course, the home citadel of all this far-flung dynasty of money and transportation was still San Francisco.

It is generally believed that, over the period of years when it used horses and horse-drawn conveyances, Wells Fargo maintained the greatest non-military resources of mounts and draft animals in history. In San Francisco its horses and equipages were the finest to be seen in the streets, rivaling in harness, grooming and general maintenance even the splendid stables of the nabobs who affected gold-plated harness and liveried footmen on their boxes. Old-time San Francisco can still remember the Wells Fargo painted mailboxes which were placed, usually alongside those of the United States Post Office, at vantage points throughout the city and from which collections were made at frequent intervals throughout the day.

Downstairs from the express department in Sansome Street was Wells Fargo's famous letter department where thirty-five or forty ponies were kept tethered and saddled at all times with riders handy. For two bits a merchant could have an urgent message delivered on horseback anywhere within the city limits and many men well known in later life — Walter Stanhouse, Paxton Wright, Joe Drury and Clarence Lawrence, for example — as boys rode the galloping ponies of the cobblestones. A hook-nosed old Quaker, Zacharias

Birdsall, was stable superintendent and popularly reputed to be the shrewdest horse swapper west of the Mississippi. During a widespread epidemic of epizootic in the seventies, Wells Fargo's heavy teams were drawn throughout San Francisco by oxen. Most of the firm's wagons were built to order at Graves' carriage factory in Pacific Street.

The disappearance of coaches and staging on a grand transcontinental pattern coinciding with the disappearance from the Wells Fargo scene of Louis McLane, the equine champion, set the stage for a new era in Wells Fargo's epic of transport: the age of railroads. Wells Fargo had already experienced the advantages in rail shipments over the little Sacramento Valley between Sacramento and Folsom, and, beginning with the completion of the Pacific Railroad, it was to find itself increasingly involved with steam and steel. Its expansion both in territory and in the technique of expressing by way of the iron highroad was to continue almost without interruption down to the dissolution of the individual express companies by Woodrow Wilson's son-in-law, William Gibbs McAdoo, during his ruinous railroad administration in the first World War.

This transition was, of course, primarily shaped and dictated by the changing times in which Wells Fargo found itself operating. It was forwarded by Tevis, who had been a railroad president before he became president of Wells Fargo, and by the new directors of the company, many of whom were members of interlocking railroad directorates and all of whom were in some way or other connected with or interested in railroads. The iron horse supplanted his flesh-and-blood prototype in an economic revolution which swept the galloping ponies of pioneer times forever from the main-line communications of the nation.

There can be no question that, in the mind of the American public, the visible symbol of Wells Fargo will always be the classic Concord stage with its proper complement of six prancing ponies and shotgun messenger atop beside the bearded jehu. It might, however, with equal validity be the beautiful little railroad trains of the seventies and eighties with their diamond-stack, eight-wheel locomotives and gaily painted coaches on which Wells Fargo rode to wealthy destinies undreamed of by the stage masters and division superintendents of Louis McLane's generation.

Wells Fargo had always been interested in the carriage of perishables and fine foodstuffs, ever since the day, so long ago, when Henry Wells had delivered the oysters fresh from Long Island's Great South Bay in time for the dinner at Laidley's in Buffalo. It had shipped the first ice to Los Angeles, had rushed table delicacies over the Sierra to luxurious Virginia City. Wells Fargo had brought fresh creamery butter from Vermont across the Isthmus of Panama to the Mother Lode towns of California in the sixties. Now a new era in gastronomy was to be opened for the American people by the genius of Wells Fargo for conquering time and distance.

During the nineties, after Wells Fargo had succeeded in gaining access to Chicago, Philadelphia, Washington and New York over the Santa Fe, the

# Wells, Fargo & Company,

## Express and Banking,

*San Francisco,*                    April 10, 1894

Managers, Superintendents,
   Asst. Supt's, Route Agents, etc.,
      WELLS, FARGO & CO'S EXPRESS.

Dear Sirs:

We have re-issued, with approval, a circular letter of the American Express Co. of January 24, 1894, commenting upon the evils of drinking and gambling, and of official laxity in regard to them, a copy of which we wish placed in the hands of every employe of this Company, and I now particularly call your attention to the same. The amount of money squandered by persons indulging the drinking habit, not only uselessly but disastrously, and the resultant suffering and sorrow in countless ways to themselves and to innocent families have been a burning question from time immemorial, but some recent addresses by an eloquent speaker of this State calling attention to the innumerable mischiefs, evils and woes, suggest to me the propriety of directing the attention of employes of this Co. to the subject, and of asking them to ponder seriously not merely the importance to each of them of an earnest consideration and observance of the suggestions contained in the Circular referred to, but of the immense advantage that would accrue in the aggregate to the 6,000 employes of this Company in economy of time, saving of money, health, nerves and character by abstinence from the use of liquor in any form.

Yours truly,

*[signature]* President

Baltimore and Ohio and the Erie railroads, a new wrinkle or, as it would be termed today, a new angle was developed in the express business. Some years before, a Wells Fargo superintendent named Dudley Mervine had experimented with some success with a Santa Fe baggage car rebuilt as a refrigerator car which could, by reason of its high-speed wheels, safety trucks and regular passenger draft and running gear, be run in fast passenger trains. At first Wells Fargo considered the shipment by such fast express, and at consequent high cost, of only the most expensive perishables and out-of-season delicacies of garden produce: the first strawberries from Texas, fresh figs from California and similar table matters at seasons when their prices justified the special handling.

In the nineties, however, it became apparent that the success of this business would warrant its very considerable expansion and Wells Fargo had built a fleet of special refrigerator cars designed to run in passenger service on railroads all over the country where it had connections and at all times of the year instead of only out of season. The California citrus industry and its possibilities of marketing were quadrupled almost overnight. Fresh fish from the Great Lakes rode into the cities of the East as head-end revenue freight in the consist of the *Erie Limited* and the *Royal Blue*. Salmon from Alaskan waters began appearing on dinner tables in Boston and New York, usually, to be sure, nominated on the menu as "Kennebec" to conform to local prejudice. Fresh shad from the Delaware, hitherto beyond the range even of the princes of Chicago's Gold Coast, was listed on the bill of fare at the Palmer House. Garden truck from the Imperial Valley rolled over the Raton and into Kansas City ahead of the mailcars on the Santa Fe's *California Limited*. Out-of-season table matters from distant points and widely divergent climates, hitherto available only at the fanciest prices, became commonplace in the most modest kitchens. The first green peas of the season were no longer the pride of New England dinner tables on the seventeenth of June as tradition had for decades decreed. They rolled up in January from Old Mexico in the varnish trains of a score of Wells Fargo railroads with the same speed as the first-class mails.

Wells Fargo was coining money out of green groceries and seafood once more.

Historians of Wells Fargo will look in vain for any record of the precise conduct of the company's internal affairs during the last several decades of the nineteenth century. It was a very closed corporation and what its right hand, represented by Wells Fargo Banking did, was generally unknown, except among the highest echelon of executives and directors, to its left hand, represented by Wells Fargo Express. From 1872, however, until 1902 the company never paid less than six per cent annually, and most of the time it was eight per cent.

This was the golden age of the nabobs in broadcloth. Stockholders had better manners in those days and it wasn't until the turn of the century that Wells Fargo's shareholders were rude enough to suggest that possibly there

## "PUNCH, BRETHREN, PUNCH WITH CARE,

Wells Fargo directors, Stanford, Tevis, Mills and a number of other "warm men" in the San Francisco seventies, were heavily interested in the spectacular and well-financed California Street RR, one of whose two-unit trams is shown here in 1882, its "cars in full motion, from an instantaneous photograph." While not operated over the tracks of the California Street system, Casebolt's "balloon car" amused San Francisco during the seventies and became a humorous institution. Its carriage work was built on a swivel so that, at the end of the run, a turntable was eliminated and the driver merely reversed the direction of his team while the trucks remained stationary on the track.

was more due them than met the eye. The carriages of the nabobs gleamed with gold trim on their harnesses as they rattled across the cobblestones between the tracks of the California Street RR, and if they were slightly jolted in the process they were able to reflect that it was all in a good cause. Didn't the California Street Cable RR belong to Governor Stanford whom at that very moment they were joining for a Pisco Punch at Duncan Nicol's Bank Exchange or for a few splits of Louis Roederer at the bar at the Palace? What was a little jolting between friends?

Only slightly less important, in the annals of San Francisco's regal decades, than Barry & Patten's and the Palace, was the Bank Exchange. This was an establishment of almost parochial propriety and Chesterfieldian manners although it was a favorite with "the Washoe crowd" who were never, elsewhere, noted for the decorum of their conduct or abatement of their naturally expansive temperament. Here John Valentine and Homer King delighted to "have a smile" with Jim Flood or George Hearst and the "smile" was almost invariably a Pisco Punch made from Peruvian brandy with austere elegance by Duncan, the proprietor. Piscos were an arrangement of quintessential refinement which laid gradual and seductive hold upon the senses, so that the consumers moved dreamily through Duncan's splendid premises where the oils on the walls were distinctly *not* barroom nudes and the handles of the beer pumps were beautiful things of real Wedgwood china.

Here the executives of Wells Fargo often lifted a genteel glass to each other and congratulated themselves on possessing the largest cash assets of any commercial firm upon the Pacific coast.

Some evidence of the degree with which the Coast regarded the activities of the nabobs may be found in the record of an investigation by the Federal Government in 1879 into the activities of Wells Fargo as a carrier of the mails. The investigating commission ascertained that its express was endeavoring to establish a monopoly of the mail-carrying business in the Far West, that it was hiring postmasters as its own express agents, that it was carrying free of charge the mails of such allied enterprises as the Central Pacific RR and was otherwise acting in a manner to cause Postal authorities to frown with a great frowning.

But was the Post Office able to do anything which might even for a moment embarrass Wells Fargo or cause it inconvenience in its strictly unlawful occasions? Indeed not! Businessmen on the Coast, accustomed to the excellences of Wells Fargo and knowing all too well the sort of service that might be expected from any agency of the Federal Government, raised such an outcry and brought so much influence to bear that Washington dropped its charges and permitted Wells Fargo to continue without molestation in the private post-office business.

The nabobs in Duncan Nichol's cocked an eye at the austere proprietor as a signal for another round of Piscos.

# CHAPTER IX

## *Such as a King Should Build*

S ING, O Muse of History and Bounce, of San Francisco in the middle 1870's! Of San Francisco two decades and more after the dolorous failure of Page, Bacon & Co. and the Bank of Adams & Co. Of San Francisco a decade after the conclusion of the War between the States when the cascade of treasure flowing across the Sierra from the mine shafts of the Comstock and the stamping mills of the Carson was of proportions to confound Golconda and to render pale by comparison the legends of Montezuma and the wealth of the Incas. The Big Bonanza, its fabulous secret so long locked in the depths of Mount Davidson and more recently in the office vaults of the Bonanza Kings, was a functioning reality, raising the value of two mines alone from $40,000 to an almost unimaginable $160,000,000. The Pacific Railroad was an accomplished agency of communication with the East, to the momentary discomfiture of Wells Fargo to be sure, but eventually identified with it by gilt-edged bonds of incorporation. The dazzlements and splendors of the Palace in New Montgomery Street were one of any number of testimonials to the inexhaustible resources of Mount Davidson. Steamer Day had, unhappily, passed into legend, but there were multiple other excitements and diversions in a city where tranquillity did not exist.

By 1875, Wells Fargo was opening new agencies and offices throughout Nevada with such overnight urgency that at times Lloyd Tevis himself couldn't rightly tell how many it supported or where they all were. Not only had the Big Bonanza inundated the West with a tidal wave of sudden wealth and wealthy expectations, but over in the White Pine and along the Reese, in Eureka and Austin, new bonanzas were coming in in such unpredictable abundance that their own little railroads were being built to take care of their ores and the word borrasca had disappeared from the general vocabulary.

Wells Fargo was everywhere, by coach and aboard the steamcars, its agents the universal proconsuls of an imperial network of treasure transport, remittances and authority, but its heart and soul, the core of its being, were irrevocably and indissolubly in San Francisco.

San Francisco, the most splendid, flashing, richest and altogether the most gratifying, most satisfactory town in all the star-spangled United States. Paris might be the place where good Americans went when they died, but

San Francisco was where good Americans went when they were most vitally alive! It ate and drank heroically at no fewer than 350 restaurants of every type and nationality, with every degree of heartiness and refinement to suit the taste of a cosmopolitan and well-heeled citizenry. It had four or five different sorts of weather every day, sometimes several of them at once. Its hotels were of staggering splendor: the Palace, the Lick, Russ, Baldwin's, the Grand, Occidental and Cosmopolitan. It had more saloons than a sailor's dream, gambling premises that would have popped monocles at Monte Carlo, a spa not yet made famous by a twentieth-century music-hall ballad. It had grand opera, it had the Cliff House, Lotta Crabtree, the Poodle Dog, Pisco Punches and the amazing mansions of the Railroad Kings dominating the city from the splendid eminence of Nob Hill. It had a Stock Exchange and Exchange Board which in no aspect of its conduct resembled parallel institutions in Wall or State Streets. It had the *Alta California*, whose pages would comfortably serve as sheets in a double bed, and it even had, in the precipitous slopes of Nob Hill, an ingenious tram pulled on a cable and peopled with stately sirs in top hats and fearful arrangements of whiskers. Oh, San Francisco was a fine and elegant town and getting more so every day!

Today when the management of San Francisco's peerless and world-famous hotel, the Palace, situated in New Montgomery Street directly across Market from the offices of the Wells Fargo Bank and Union Trust Company, are confronted with a state dinner for royalty or a smaller entertainment for very important personages, they send the steward, the venerable Adolph Bach and an armed guard across the street to Wells Fargo's vaults for the priceless gold dinner service. The Palace owns one of the half dozen such services in the United States and its storage between banquets with Wells Fargo is symbolic as well as a convenience.

For with the possible exception of Barry & Patten's saloon, handily adjacent to the first business premises of the firm, no other single similar institution in San Francisco has so many and such warm associations for Wells Fargo as has the Palace. To be sure the Palace came into being just two decades after Wells Fargo, but from the first opening of its doors Wells Fargo has arranged state dinners and business conferences there; the weddings of its executives have been solemnized at this historic hostelry, it has entertained visiting notables in the Palace's sumptuous suites and many generations of Wells Fargo personnel have gloried and drunk deep in the endless succession of bars and taprooms, men's grills and other oases that have been part of the gastronomic economy of the noblest hotel of the Western World.

Indeed, at one time, when secrets concerning the movement of treasure were being smuggled out of Wells Fargo's more formal business premises with disturbing regularity and accuracy, Wells Fargo maintained a secret hideaway in one of the upper floors of the Palace from which a pool of trusted messengers were dispatched on missions of great weight and moment without the details of their routing being available to the rest of the staff.

The affinity between the Palace and Wells Fargo had its beginning almost from the moment the doors of the hotel were first opened in 1875. Wells Fargo had freighted down the wealth of the Comstock which had underwritten the construction of the Palace. Its resources of hospitality and entertainment were handy to the Sansome Street countinghouse of the company, just as they are even handier today when separated only by the width of Market Street, and from the start it was obvious that men of the position and importance of Wells Fargo's executives could hardly afford not to be seen frequently and conspicuously in the city's hotel of ranking importance and prestige.

When the Palace came into being it was quite literally palatial. For its construction William Ralston, in whose fertile brain the hotel was conceived, built and put into operation a brick factory. To furnish it he started a furniture factory. To decorate it W. & J. Sloane of New York opened a San Francisco branch which is in business to this day. To lay its floors a forest of oak trees was purchased in the High Sierra. An army of artisans worked for three years to finish the structure whose upper floors were to shelter 1,200 guests in 755 rooms in a degree of luxury generally believed to have been unparalleled since the time of Nero.

When in 1875 the first Palace was opened with a stupefying state banquet attended by the directors of Wells Fargo en masse, the whole world marveled at the ingenuity of its contriving and the splendor of its furnishings. There were electric call buttons, the first ever installed, in every room and telegraphic communications between floor pantries in the kitchen. There were electric clocks, also the first ever seen in public, in each apartment, and electric signal stations for checking on the night watchmen. There were five miles of fire-control standpipes and four miles of hose and even a primitive air-conditioning system. Five hydraulic elevators lifted the guests to the hotel's seven floors and a local newspaper, having fun with the superlatives of the Palace's promoters, remarked: "There are thirty-four elevators in all — four for passengers, ten for baggage and twenty for mixed drinks. Each elevator contains a piano and a bowling alley."

There were for service in its restaurants thousands upon thousands of plates, cups and saucers from the French works of C. F. Haviland. No fewer than 9,000 cuspidors arrived to accommodate the masculine fashion of the times. Carload upon carload of looped and fringed portieres, marquetry tables, cloisonné, ormolu and Turkey carpets rolled over the newly completed Pacific Railroad to furnish its apartments. On the walls of its public rooms there were literally acres of "hand-painted" oil paintings, mostly depicting the Golden Gate at sunset or the Sierra at sunrise. San Francisco was at once stunned and enchanted, and all the world came to see.

Most famous feature of the first Palace was the great court leading off Montgomery Street into which arriving guests were driven in their carriages and deposited in a thicket of potted palms under a vast glass dome. The glory of the hotel's cuisine brought gourmets from the quarters of the globe to dine off the valley quail and mountain trout, California oyster omelets, roulade of sand dabs and oysters Kirkpatrick, named by Chef Ernest Arbo-gast for the hotel's resident manager. When, a quarter of a century later, the elder J. P. Morgan arrived at the Palace with his personal chef, a fellow named Louis Sherry, San Francisco was pleasantly outraged. Morgan also brought his personal steward, cellarman and other members of an imperial entourage in a six-car private train.

For a full generation thereafter, San Francisco's life and being seethed excitingly and opulently through the public rooms and private apartments of the Palace. In 1879, General Grant and his family arrived via a Pacific Mail Liner and was wafted into the Great Court in a chariot drawn by six snow-white steeds amidst bravos and hurrahs from the silk-hatted citizenry. The Grand Duke Boris breakfasted repeatedly in the Grill off oyster omelet and a dry champagne. Henry Ward Beecher and Robert Ingersoll followed one another at close intervals, to gaze up Montgomery Street from its fabled bay windows which admitted a daily maximum of chamber-of-commerce California sunlight; others included Mrs. Stuyvesant Fish, Prince Louis of Savoy, Presidents Hayes, Harrison and McKinley, Prince Albert of Belgium, Ferdinand de Lesseps, Chauncey Depew and Lord and Lady Randolph Churchill. No hotel in the Western Hemisphere could boast a guest list such as the San Francisco newspaper reporters scanned each morning and seldom without profit to their editors.

In his *Golden Gate*, Felix Risenberg, Jr., wrote that at this period "the state of California was run from the Palace bar," a circumstance which is still as true as when it was written, but in the seventies and eighties there were giants in the land and one and all, governors, supreme court judges, Wells Fargo directors, newspaper publishers and bankers, they advanced at noontime and again at dusk in a solid phalanx of boiled shirts, Prince Albert coats and 18-carat watch chains to hoist fraternal Pisco punches at the long mahogany.*
The headgear might vary from the gleaming silk top hat of Ned Greenway to the wide plainsman's sombrero of Joaquin Miller, but their mannered courtesy, their respectful salutations, their passage of the time of day and their monumental thirsts were all cut from a pattern. Willis Polk, "White Hat" McCarthy and Will Crocker rubbed broadcloth shoulders with Gover-nor Stanford, Lloyd Tevis and the elegant James Ben Ali Haggin. Upon occasion even stern, patriarchal old Darius Ogden Mills, chilly and incorrupt-ible, would venture in for a glass of the Palace's Old, Rich, Superior Madeira. Charles F. Crocker, a Wells Fargo director of course, was a regular in the company of Central Pacific's David D. Colton. Of the Central Pacific's "Big Four," for some inscrutable reason, the only nonregular at the Palace bar was Uncle Mark Hopkins. Collis P. Huntington lived upstairs in the Palace, a highly convenient arrangement.

But while the nabobs swaggered grandly among the potted palms and marquetry wonderments of the public rooms of the Palace and admired the use of its bar as their nightly starting point for "seeing the elephant" over

---

* Pisco punches were exclusively Duncan Nicol's creation but were widely counterfeited elsewhere.

San Francisco's world-famous cocktail route, there was one guest at the hotel of whom Wells Fargo would have disapproved most heartily had they known of his presence, even though, paradoxically enough, they were paying his bills for what later appeared to have been a vertiable monsoon of champagne and for an elaborate suite of rooms kitty-corner from that of the august Collis P. Huntington.

The Baron Karl Harmann first swam into the delighted ken of San Francisco's sporting world late in October, 1894. To be sure he never really said he was a baron, but it appeared that his sister had been the late Baroness Harmann of Westphalia and this, and the circumstance that he was undeniably and gratifyingly solvent, Teutonic and aristocratic, established him at once among the habitués at Lucky Baldwin's Hotel and at the Palace bar as a baron of unimpeachable ancestry. The Baron was registered at the Golden West Hotel, but he played the field impartially. His wardrobe was extensive and a bit on the bright side, running to plaids on which games might have been played, diamond studs and what the *Chronicle* later had occasion to describe as "stylish walking sticks," but there was something undeniably patrician about the manner in which he ordered Moet & Chandon's White Seal champagne: always a dozen bottles at a time. While splashing happily around in this tonic Niagara, only a churl would have remarked that now and then he lapsed into a strange argot whose economy included such phrases, odd in a *hochwohlgeboren Herr Baron,* as "dodging the bulls," "riding the beams" and partaking of "mulligan" among "the drifters."

The Baron was middle-aged with graying hair cut *en brosse,* short and thickset with flaring mustaches and a slightly vinous nose. Experts called in to assay his authenticity reported that not only did he speak a fluent German but passable French, Italian, Danish and several other Continental languages as well. His wealth, which was also unquestionable and valid, he explained, he had inherited from his sister, the late Baroness, and that what he spent was merely the interest on his interest. There was plenty more where this came from and — waiter, another dozen of the White Seal on ice!

Such qualifications as these could scarcely go unnoticed even in the San Francisco of the nabobs. At the Ingleside race track, where he frequently greeted Wyatt Earp with glad fraternal hello, he was known as "The Bank." His favorite house in Sporting Row was that presided over by Miss Nina Hayman and after he had made it his headquarters for the evening, the premises fairly erupted in a profusion of new furniture most of it bearing the highly respectable imprimatur of W & J Sloane & Co.

One of the Baron's favorite pavilions of refreshment was Kordt's Saloon in Oregon Street. When Kordt found himself in financial straits, the Baron obligingly loaned him $6,000 in thousand-dollar bills and took in exchange his note, at eight per cent, with a mortgage on the premises as security. He also became enamored of the artistic atmosphere of the Louvre Saloon at No. 8 O'Farrell Street and, when creditors pressed, loaned Hagens, the proprietor, the sum of $800 against his note, also at eight per cent.

His showiest and most enchanting business association was with a casual acquaintance named George Riephof, possessor of the secret for manufacturing a rheumatic bitters warranted to cure anything and also, being a cool eighty per cent alcohol, to fascinate your Aunt Hattie who was a temperance advocate. Nothing would do but Riephof must have a new wagon to deliver his wares and one was accordingly built by Graves in Pacific Street who built Wells Fargo's drays, but nothing like Riephof's was ever ordered for Wells Fargo. It was entirely outlined in electric lights, a sensational novelty for the time, and there were more electric lights outlining the harness of its horse. An unforgettable promotion party costing $300 was held at Zinkand's Wine Rooms to celebrate the inaugural run of this splendid herdic, during the course of which one case of bitters was sold. On the way home to the stable with Riephof at the reins in a silk hat, and with both the wagon and its driver blazing brightly, there was an unfortunate encounter at a grade crossing with a Southern Pacific fast freight. Riephof, his hat in bad order, emerged scatheless from the ruins, but the engineer was shortly afterward retired, unnerved for life. Baron Harmann promptly set his friend up again in the wholesale liquor business at 410 McAllister Street, taking a note on the premises at the usual interest.

It was during this interlude of frenzied finance that the Baron seems to have decided that a captain of industry deserved nothing but the very best things of life. He moved into an expensive suite on the sixth floor, Market Street side, of the Palace and rode up and down with the nabobs on their way to call on Collis Huntington down the corridor. His ratcatcher suits and Tattersall waistcoats didn't altogether endear him to the claw-hammer evening coats in the bar, but the management was inclined to shrug its shoulders resignedly over some of his guests on the sixth, since his currency was good and was forthcoming in snowstorms. One evening on the way to Miss Hayman's love store he rode down in the lift with a lady unaccountably attired in a black rubber fireman's coat and an ornate division chief's fire helmet. He inquired about her and found he was a neighbor of Mrs. Lillie Hitchcock Coit, the lady fire buff, at the moment en route to a 4-11 alarm on the Embarcadero.

It was at the Ingelside track that the Baron first met Miss May de Vaughan, a professional young lady who was then betting on the horses the proceeds from her previous evening's bagnio chores. Later May told the press: "I looked on him as a gold mine. He was a gay old Bohemian and never bought champagne in anything but dozen lots. I thought he must be a wine salesman because he never drank but one brand, White Seal, but he drank that like water. Later he set me up in a dream of a flat at 412 Post Street. He made friends wherever he went."

Shortly after this the Baron unaccountably tired of San Francisco and headed East aboard the *Overland Limited*, "to Germany to look at some of my castles." In Chicago he contrived to spend $400 on his first evening at the Palmer House, and when he recovered, boarded a Michigan Central train for New York. New York, he discovered, was a lonely sort of city even for a genuine baron with a bank roll, and he wired May $1,000 on which to come East and join him. In the meanwhile, while ordering dozens at the Waldorf bar in Fifth Avenue, he contrived to meet George Kessler, American agent for White Seal Champagne, and their mutual admiration expressed itself in a party which is still remembered with wonder and satisfaction by all who, although not invited, seemed to be present.

But letters from the Coast confided that the faithless May had used the $1,000 to set herself and a friend named Harry up as bookmakers at Ingleside and, petulant and disillusioned, the Baron headed back for the lights of O'Farrell Street and the pleasures of the Poodle Dog.

This was a mistake.

With approximately the speed of light the word circulated around the bars — the Lick House, the Cobweb Palace, the Poodle Dog, the Cliff House — that "May's millionaire" was back in circulation again, only that now he was "everybody's millionaire," and the sale of White Seal, always in dozens, at the Palace, Lucky Baldwin's, Solari's, Marchand's and the Tehama boomed to vast proportions.

Then one day, as the Baron stood at the corner of New Montgomery and Market, surveying the world benevolently over a Henry Clay perfecto, two men in bowler hats moved in on either side of him and suggested that the three of them pay a visit to the express offices of Wells Fargo & Co. The Baron expressed polite surprise and doubted if they would serve him a dozen bottles of White Seal there, but he was nevertheless persuaded. His host was Wells Fargo's Chief of Detectives Hume who had been looking for him for almost two years, but not in the right places.

Hume didn't have a warrant for the Baron and didn't bother to get one for several days. He regarded the San Francisco police as a sort of ultimate convenience and nothing to bother with in matters of the first importance. Hume, the Baron and several assistant detectives spent a pleasant and instructive night closeted together at Wells Fargo and then, further to continue their conversations, they moved to a room in the Union Hotel, taking care to avoid the Palace, scene of former triumphs.

When the story broke in the *Chronicle* the Baron was no longer a baron but plain Charlie the Dutchman, a vagrant in good standing in every tramp jungle from Walla Walla to Fort Worth. His wealth had derived, not from his sister the Baroness and her castles, but from a train robbery perpetrated almost two years before on the main line of the Southern Pacific a couple of miles west of Sacramento. The holdup and looting of Wells Fargo's treasure car of $50,000 had not been accomplished by Charlie the Dutchman, but by Jack Brady, a well-known train robber, a member of whose gang had been shot during the holdup. In the haste of making a getaway, Brady had been unable to carry off his loot and had secreted it by the right of way. The entire melodrama had been witnessed by Charlie the Dutchman from a hobo jungle in an adjacent grove of cottonwoods. As soon as the Bradys had taken their leave, Charlie and a companion named August Kohler had scurried forth and made away with $32,000 in gold, by far the greater proportion of which was appropriated instanter by Charlie, leaving his assistant accessory with only enough for a comparatively modest three-day romp in the flea bags of Sacramento. Two days later the Baron Karl Harmann appeared in San Francisco.

Chief of Detectives Hume sent for Charlie's trunks and other luggage and discovered that Wells Fargo was in possession of a startling collection of silk underwear, "stylish walking sticks," costly if orchidaceous suits and overcoats, manicure sets, mustache curlers, scented lotions and toilet waters, champagne openers, two diamond collar buttons, and boxes and boxes of "up-to-date hats." The *Chronicle* reporter's eyes popped at the hats. There were Homburgs in a variety of colors, there were bowlers with curly brims and bowlers with flat brims, there were silk top hats and collapsible evening Gibuses, Tyrolean hats, Panamas and Billy-cock numbers. Boxes and boxes of them.

Mrs. Leonhardt, proprietor of Charlie's apartment house of the moment at 625 Post Street, told the press that the Baron owed her $300 and that he "brought all kinds of people to my house, day and night, and I fired him out." Hume, however, pointed out that the Baron had paid for a quantity of furniture in Mrs. Leonhardt's establishment and that, since it now belonged to Wells Fargo, he was sending up a van to get it.

There were also the notes on the Rheumatic Bitters Company, the Louvre Saloon, the liquor business in McAllister Street, Kordt's Saloon in Oregon Street and a couple of other minor flings in finance in which the Baron had invested. Mercifully, the electrically lit bitters delivery wagon was not in the inventory.

There was also a very small amount of cash.

Wells Fargo had been tipped off by Charlie's mistreated accomplice who, having approached his now-prosperous pal for a handout upon encountering him one day in Sutter Street, had been aristocratically booted into the gutter.

In jail, Charlie's "careless smile, his flippant insouciance, and manner disappeared," according to the *Chronicle*. Just before he was sentenced to three years at Folsom, he told the reporters: "Nobody knows how to spend money with more real enjoyment than I do. I really don't care for money. I just love the things it can buy. My only regret is that I didn't have time to spend every cent of Wells Fargo's money before they caught up with me."

Wells Fargo realized what it could from the assorted oddments it recovered and, for some time afterward, Chief of Detectives Hume was observed to wince painfully at the sight of an opera hat, a diamond collar stud or any extreme example of Grand Rapids furniture design, while other Wells Fargo nabobs averted their gaze as they frequently passed the portals of the Louvre Saloon at No. 8 O'Farrell Street.

As for the Palace, its receptionists and managers kept a copy of the *Almanach de Gotha* ready at hand for months and checked with painstaking

SAN FRANCISCO CALL-BULLETIN

## A RESORT FAVORED BY THE BARON

This simply furnished apartment was the reception room of Tessie Wall's house of mirth in O'Farrell Street, a resort which appealed strongly to the Baron and one where he spent many carefree evenings ordering dozens of White Seal and admiring the objects of art with which Mme. Wall surrounded herself. When the day of reckoning came Chief of Detectives Hume was unable to claim any of her crystal chandeliers or French gilt furniture. Mme. Wall had provided for her guests' comfort out of her own pocket.

double checks on every member of the German aristocracy who registered. You couldn't be too careful!

Outside of the Central Pacific RR, and later the Southern Pacific, there was no institution in the entire Old West with which Wells Fargo was more closely connected than the Palace.

The night of April 17, 1906, was the last night of the old Palace and there are those alive who recall its excitements as from another world, wistful, tearful, vanished forever. San Francisco's opera season was in full swing. After a triumphant appearance as Don José in *Carmen*, Caruso dropped into the Palace bar for a cognac with Alfred Hertz, the director, and then with Sembrich and Eames went up the slope of Nob Hill to the home of James Ben Ali Haggin in Taylor Street for supper. Hertz, who had to conduct the next evening, retired early but Caruso didn't roll out of hack until three o'clock and it was two hours and thirteen minutes later that destiny arrived in the form of the most publicized of all earthquakes.

WELLS FARGO BANK

## BEFORE AND AFTER THE END OF THE WORLD

WELLS FARGO BANK

Here, at the conjunction of Pine and Mont
gomery Streets, in San Francisco's teemin
financial district, were located the offices c
the Wells Fargo Nevada Bank, famed for it
$10,000,000 capitalization, its Comstock over
mantles of rich gold ore, its vast authority i
the monied matters of the West. Many of th
bank's records and all its tangible office prop
erty were destroyed in the fire of 1906, but i
a few days it was doing business again an
its affairs have never since been seriousl
interrupted.

## LAST HOURS OF THE PALACE

This photograph taken at 3.30 in the afternoon of the day of The Fire from the sidewalk in front of what is now the Wells Fargo Bank and Union Trust Company shows The Palace in flames while mounted troopers from The Presidio watch its destruction. Below is Lloyd Tevis, silk hat in hand, on one of the Palace balconies chatting with friends.

Caruso's next public appearance was in the lobby of the Palace wearing a bath towel around his middle and carrying a signed portrait of Theodore Roosevelt under his arm. Plancon, another member of the company, came down immaculately attired in morning coat, boutonniere and silk top hat, but with his beard undyed, and everyone present later agreed that it appeared to be bright green. Caruso was violently ill. "Give me Vesuvius!" he shouted noisily and then got into a fist fight with one of the house servants. The last act at the Palace was among the best on its long bill.

It was not until afternoon that The Fire actually reached the Palace. Charles Caldwell Dobie afterward recalled that at noon he had walked through the lobby of the hotel and that Chinese servants in immaculate white duck were dusting the furniture and emptying ash trays for all the world as though at that very minute the house fire department was not extinguishing small blazes on the roof.

An hour or so later, however, the vast reservoirs beneath the Palm Court were exhausted. At half past two the Monadnock Building, a new structure directly across Annie Street, was a fountain of fire and shortly afterward the Palace itself appeared to be a seething mass of flame simultaneously in every part. "The Palace, for the first time since its building a third of a century earlier, was deserted," wrote Oscar Lewis, "abandoned by all save one last, sinister guest."

236

Forever afterward San Franciscans, remembering the final, almost unbelievably theatrical exit of the scene of their stateliest sarabands, would remark with mingled pride and wistfulness that it was the very most expensive fire of all time and that when the Palace burned only the very best of everything supplied fuel to the flames.

At almost the identical hour in the afternoon, the offices of Wells Fargo Nevada National Bank at the corner of Montgomery Street and Pine, as if reluctant to allow the Palace to steal the show with its final act of immolation, burned to the cellars. Even as the many-colored glass dome of the Great Court was crashing in indescribable ruin, Wells Fargo's mantelpieces of gold quartz, worth a thousand dollars each, were disintegrating under the fiery blast. San Francisco's two most spectacular institutions shared the exit together.

It was several years before the Palace was to rise again in enduring splendor on the identical site of its triumphs and eventual holocaust, but Wells Fargo was open the following Monday — it had been burned out on Thursday — and its *resurgam* was staged in the home of E. S. Heller, a company executive, at 2020 Jackson Street. Although the firm's records were highly incomplete when the vaults were opened, all claims for funds by depositors were honored and, although millions were paid out in this informal manner, the Wells Fargo Nevada National Bank lost less than $200 through fraud or error.

When San Francisco rose in its present magnificence of steel and stone, Wells Fargo rose with it.

# CHAPTER X

## The Last Bonanza

### I: TONOPAH

WHEN the gold and crimson curtain of fortune went up on the last great bonanza the scene it discovered gave no promise of melodrama.

At the turn of the century the once illimitable resources of the Comstock had been exhausted for two decades. The stamping mills on the Carson were idle and falling into ruin. The argentine years of the Mexican and Gould and Curry were only a memory in Washoe and the spacious days a souvenir of wonderment among the graying gaffers of C Street. The state of Nevada had lost a third of its population. From an all-time high of $47,000,000 in 1878 its production of precious metals had dropped by 1900 to a scant $2,000,000. The desert was becoming populous with ghost towns, and alkali and sagebrush were reclaiming their ancient own.

The last great bonanza in precious metals on the American continent in which Wells Fargo was to participate in an expressing capacity was generally known as "the southern mines" of Nevada and lasted almost precisely over the decade from 1900 to 1910. Its two most celebrated and wealthiest sources of gold and silver were at Tonopah and Goldfield, but the bonanza itself included a multiplicity of less spectacular strikes in the Nevada desert at Rhyolite and Bullfrog, at Rawhide, Manhattan and a vast number of lesser satellite camps which briefly flourished in the sagebrush and then utterly disappeared.

Never had a quarter-of-a-billion-dollar bonanza come into being to such an orchestration of monotone, and even when the evidence of its possible resources had made itself apparent, its discoverers were in no great haste to set about the exploitation of the boom at Tonopah and Goldfield in the saline reaches of the desert, below the headwaters of the Reese and a few miles east of the California-Nevada boundary at Mount Montgomery. The feeling was widespread that the great times were over and it took two years from the time of the first assay of the Desert Queen before Tonopah was the most tumultuous bonanza town since Virginia City, and the samples from the Mizpah the gee-whiz news of the century.

Some idea of the low esteem in which reports were held of new mining strikes in Nevada may be gathered from the willingness of the great Darius Ogden Mills, ordinarily considered an astute enough operator where profitable prospects were concerned, to dispose of the Carson and Colorado RR.

The C & C had been built to connect with the Virginia and Truckee at Mound House, near Carson, back in 1880, running to Keeler and the Cerro Gordo Mine in Owens Valley, California, a distance of 293 narrow-gage miles by way of Mount Montgomery Pass. Mills sold the C & C to the Southern Pacific for $2,750,000 in 1900 despite the circumstance that reports of the Tonopah discovery were already in circulation and that the C & C provided the only railroad link with the new fields. When Tonopah became an established reality and, two years later, Goldfield joined the bonanza tide, the narrow gage was deluged with enormously profitable traffic and repaid its purchase price to the Southern Pacific in a single year! People shook their heads sadly at Darius Ogden Mills.

There were, however, grounds for pessimism. A score of lesser bonanzas had come upon lean days in addition to the Comstock: Bodie, the Coeur d'Alene, the Reese River, the Sangre de Christo, Nez Perce, the Bitter Root, the White Pines. Few believed another boom of major proportions was possible and, among conservative investors and mining men, it was felt that Nevada was as played out as the California diggings had been before it. Nevada had better turn to ranching and forget the golden past except for the benefit of the tourist trade.

In 1899, a not too promising strike had been made at Southern Klondike, an uninhabited desert spot known to the Indians as Tonopah, and a prospector named Jim Butler had taken time off from his ranching at Belmont to look into the matter. No true prospector ever retires and, when news of the Southern Klondike came through, Butler packeᴀ a few necessities on a burro and headed south. One morning, after camping in the vicinity of Tonopah (Little Water), Butler's burro strayed and, while waiting the errant animal's return, Butler from force of habit chipped a few samples from an outcropping and made a mental note of its location. The Southern Klondike, when he reached it, was obviously a washout, and Butler returned to his ranch to get in the hay crop. The samples from the outcropping he passed on to a friend, Tasker L. Oddie, with the remark that, to him, they looked promising but that he hadn't the price of an assay to spare and would Oddie know anyone who might do an assay on credit? Oddie did and the samples went forward to the superintendent of schools at Austin, who, like almost everyone else in Nevada at this time, was something of a metallurgist himself.

The school superintendent took his time, but when he got around to conducting a complete and workmanlike assay he took one look at the button of silver that resulted, choked, reached for a reviving slug of whisky and started another assay. Obviously somebody had passed off some high-grade ore onto the prospector from Belmont as a practical joke. It had happened before. But the second assay not only confirmed the first; it exceeded it in richness. There was no chance of having doctored this sample, and the Wells Fargo stage carried off the news to Oddie and Butler with somewhat less delay than had characterized proceedings up till then.

In connection with the foregoing account it should be noted that the Tonopah bonanza was discovered in the classic manner of all the best mining strikes of history: i. e., through the agency of a wandering domestic animal, preferably a prospector's burro, although a cow or pony would do in a pinch. It will be apparent that in the current century, when most prospecting is accomplished by means of the Model T Ford or, latterly, the jeep, there can be scant hope for any major discoveries. In fact the decline of prospecting and the emergence of the automobile are too nicely integrated to be a mere accident of chance, and it will be noted that while the Goldfield bonanza was discovered in the age of burros, the falling off of its revenues from this source began about the time Oldsmobiles and Stanley Steamers became familiar sights in Crook Street and there has never been a bonanza of major proportions since that time.

But to resume. Even the urgency of the assay report could not divert Jim Butler from his haying, but word got around as it always does, and there was a small but spirited rush to the vicinity of Tonopah even though none of the participants knew where to stake their claims. It was not until August, 1900, that Butler's hay was harvested to his satisfaction and, with financial resources totaling $25 and Mrs. Butler for moral support, he started on his leisurely way with mules and wagons. Those already on the scene and awaiting Jim's good convenience are reported almost to have perished, in the meantime, not from any peril of the desert, but from a perfect frenzy of frustration.

History records no other discovery of precious metals whose initial exploitation advanced at such an unhurried pace.

This was immediately accelerated, however, after Butler had staked out the Mizpah and the smelter at Austin had sent back a check for $800 on the first ton of ore laboriously freighted out to Sodaville in a mule team. The rush was on and Tonopah blossomed into its first being, a tent city of terrific excitements and very few comforts or conveniences.

Where shall the historian turn for the true chronicle of the gaudy wonderments of the last great bonanza? Shall he pore over the annual statements of the Combination Fraction, the Goldfield Mohawk Mining Company or the quotations on the Curb Exchanges of New York and San Francisco for the decade between 1904 and 1914? Or shall he turn to the news columns, the sports and society pages of *The Tonopah Miner, The Tonopah Bonanza* and *The Goldfield News?* Or, for perspective, shall he consult the dispatches filed by staff correspondents of *The Deseret News* of Salt Lake and *The Denver Post,* leading gazettes in communities where mining news had a priority of interest over almost everything not concerned with the exploitation of the earth's metallic resources? Then, too, there are the reliable memories of many men still living who knew Nevada at firsthand just after the turn of the century, and there are the merest handful of formal literary records, such as C. B. Glassock's *Gold in Them Hills* and the archives of the Nevada State Historical Society.

Probably the discreet chronicler will draw a little from all of these, for the last great bonanza manifested itself in many ways and the social record is

GOLDFIELD                                    NEVADA HISTORICAL SOCIETY

## CIVILIZATION COMES TO THE NEVADA DESERT

The birth and growth of townships and mining districts in Southern Nevada during the last bonanza were happily available to modern photography. The picture at the top of the page shows the first arrivals at a newly discovered location in the sagebrush unloading from burros the primal essentials of frontier camp life. Below, once the location had proved itself rich, town lots were auctioned off or disposed of by lottery.

ELLENDALE                                    NEVADA HISTORICAL SOCIETY

Finally a township came into being with its gambling resorts, stables, saloons, dance halls and stores. Wells Fargo usually arrived when the first frame dwellings were being run up, but sometimes came in the tent-site stage. The desert town shown at the foot of the page is in no way atypical. Every structure in sight is a saloon. If its mines were successful substantial homes and businesses supplanted the shacks just as the shacks supplanted the tents.

CALIENTE                                     NEVADA HISTORICAL SOCIETY

probably just as important as and a great deal more interesting than the *United States Geological Survey.*

By the spring of 1901, when Tonopah had survived its first desert winter and was a proven camp, the stampede to southern Nevada became the last great roundup of the Old West, the final bivouac at the rainbow's end. Once again the alkaline dust of the Nevada wastelands rose in powder clouds beneath the boots of prospectors — old-timers these, ready for one last skirmish with fortune — who had known Virginia City when there were tents in C Street and before the bar of the International Hotel had gone to the Reese. There were sourdoughs who had followed their burros or ridden the Concords into Candelaria and Hamilton, Deadwood and Yreka on the far-off borders of Oregon, who had burned powder in Tombstone's Tough Nut Street and packed the first specimens out of Coeur d'Alene and the Fraser River. The beards of the old men were stiff with dust from the winding coach roads of the Mother Lode to Volcano and Fiddletown. Even the oldest Sierra hill towns had known them in the days of bonanzas long since in borrasca: Grass Valley and Nevada City before George Hearst ever had made his million, and they had been legendary figures in Aurora and the Cosos.

Here was a confluence of all the heroic pioneers who still survived in a West that was about to vanish forever before the progress of the auto stage, the long-distance telephone and stock promoters in forty-dollar Stetsons. Men who knew their names, lounging at the bar of the Tonopah Club, were stricken with amazement, for some of the figures passing before them in final review returned from beyond the realms of death, or so it seemed, so far had they come down the riding years and so long had been their landfaring over the forgotten highroads of the West.

And, as if mindful of a compulsion a thousand times more powerful than the need for staging out the treasure of Tonopah to the loading platforms of the narrow gage at Sodaville, Wells Fargo came with them to the last of the great bonanzas. It came in six-horse stages with its Winchester express rifles couched in the arms of yellow-mustached messengers and drivers in trousers of unturned buffalo hide, and took over offices two doors down from the Tonopah Club and across the street from Butler's Meat Market, the only building in Tonopah's main street today which survives from the first year of the camp. Wells Fargo was still to have a few short months aboard the rocking Concords in the valiant West of Frederick Remington and Abbot, Downing & Company, before the coming of the Pope Toledos, the Stanhopes, and the first brass-bound, seagoing Stevens-Duryea Motor Carriages. It was a brief moment in transition, epic and irrevocable.

There are several aspects in which the Tonopah-Coldfield boom differed from the Comstock bonanza, not the least of which was that the Comstock had attracted the attention of several first-rate reporters, among them Horace Greeley, Mark Twain and Dan De Quill, all of whom lent it literary luster in varying degrees, while the nearest thing to compare with them in a latter-day Nevada were the sports writers who flooded in for the Gans-Nelson boxfight.

## COMMOTIONAL DOINGS IN BOOMING TONOPAH

This parade of vintage vehicles was organized by Mrs. Key Pittman to convey a number of interested guests and potential investors in Nevada mining properties from Tonopah to Goldfield about 1905 when the thirty miles of desert separating the two camps was a major operational hazard to motorists. The scene is in front of the State Bank Building in Tonopah, kitty-corner from the Mizpah Hotel. Wells Fargo was at this time reluctantly turning from horse-drawn stages on the Tonopah-Goldfield run to Popes, Appersons and Packards. Below is a rare photograph of the first arrivals at Tonopah, Tasker Oddie, Wilson Brougher, who was asked along because he had a wagon, and Jim Butler, in his inevitable pioneer derby, and Mrs. Butler. It was probably taken in October, 1900, when the happy-go-lucky quartet was prospecting what later turned out to be the Desert Queen or the Mizpah.

243

Nor was there present at Tonopah and Goldfield the physical violence and high index of murder and assassination which is in the Virginia City record. There was a great deal of uproar, to be sure, and some of the gunplay inseparable from a raw community where wealth was on every hand and shady characters could be counted on to abound, but the perpetual burning of powder which was characteristic of C Street at all hours of day and night during its first flowering was lacking.

And from the mining angle there was to appear in Tonopah a new technique in the financing of mining operations which had been hitherto unknown. Probably the system of operating under the terms of a lease was the direct outcome of Jim Butler's aversion to physical effort. The best Tonopah ledges were monumented in his name and that of his wife but both the means and the inclination to mine them himself were wholly absent in easygoing Jim, so that when Henry C. Cutting, a Reno entrepreneur with more abundant energy and capital, offered to work the Mizpah under the terms of a lease with one quarter of the gross going to the owner and none of the responsibility for working the claim, Butler jumped at the opportunity.

The lease was to run until December 31, 1901, and before midsummer of that year Butler had leased more than one hundred similar properties without the exchange of a single contract or memorandum of agreement, the entire enormous transaction having been achieved by verbal understanding with its every detail committed only to Butler's memory. One lessor was shortly thereafter to receive from the smelter the almost incredible sum of $575,000 for a single shipment of forty-eight tons of ore, and before the year's end Tonopah was to produce tangible wealth to the extent of four million dollars, thus doubling the output for the entire state of Nevada for the previous year. The evolution of this considerable wealth among a group of men largely unaccustomed to formal business methods produced no single incident of litigation and no disagreement or misunderstanding sufficiently serious to appear in the record.

The first winter in the diggings was accompanied by a highly unpleasant manifestation which came to be known all over the land as "the Tonopah sickness," and from the effects of which there were a number of sudden deaths. Writing later of the business, George Cole in *The Carson Appeal* reported that the retreat northward across the desert as the dread and mysterious malady spread resembled nothing so much as the Battle of Bull Run and that prospectors abandoned tents, firearms and all manner of impedimenta in their haste to leave the scene of the pestilence stalking the noonday. By Thanksgiving there were half a hundred graves in an adjacent canyon and only about four hundred pioneers still on the scene. Medical science later identified "the Tonopah sickness" as a lung congestion induced by silicate content in the diggings, but at the time there was a widespread belief that some pollution of the water supply was responsible.

The water was shortly proved to be of unimpeachable purity, but Tonopah was outraged when a San Francisco paper suggested that the whisky avail-

## THE OLD ORDER CHANGES AT TONOPAH

From the jerk line which controlled the covered-wagon team in Tonopah's main street in 1903 (above) to the air-flow motorcars of 1949 (below) is a long way in terms of mechanical change. But the Nevada hills in the distance are unchanging and Tonopah is still a bold, virile mining town of saloons filled with mining talk and mining men.

CHARLES CLEGG

CHARLES (

NEVADA PHOTO SERVICE, RENO

## SPACIOUS TIMES IN POPULOUS TONOPAH

In the days when Tonopah boasted a formal society, grand opera and millionaires such as George Wingfield and Charles M. Schwab in its public places, the Tonopah and Goldfield RR ran trains of solid overnight Pullmans from San Francisco and maintained its own rolling stock of passenger coaches, ore cars, combines, high cars and even owned a complete wrecking train. The above scene of animation was made at Tonopah depot in 1907. The insert shows the station and yards in 1949, their tracks torn up, the railroad a memory. Below is the great Belmont Mine at Tonopah in its flourishing times, from whose mill originated much of the bullion which Wells Fargo carried out, first in its stages and later aboard the treasure cars of the Tonopah and Goldfield.

NEVADA PHOTO SERVICE, RENO

able there might be responsible for the wave of deaths and sent a reporter out to collect samples for analysis, a type of journalistic enterprise which was later to be revived by newspaper editors everywhere during prohibition. According to Cole's chronicle of the event, the reporter started analyzing his samples on the way out of town and only contrived to last as far as Sodaville where he fell from the stage and could rise no more. His recovery was watched with breathless interest by the community and when, a day or so later, he was in a state of repair which permitted him to continue on his way, it was the general opinion that the whisky was blameless.

When at the end of 1902 the Director of the Mint in his annual government report for the area was able to list the assets of Tonopah as "thirty-two saloons, six faro games, two dance houses, two weekly newspapers, a public school, two stage lines and two churches," the camp was recognized everywhere as being in the stage of development where the prospecting element had justified its claims and was an established economic and social entity. After the prospectors came the claim lessors and after them the big-time mine owners and operators. This is the life cycle of the classic mining boom in precious metals and was followed in the Comstock, in Leadville and Cripple Creek, Tombstone, Bisbee, the Reese, in Panamint, Butte and Rawhide in various degrees of completion depending on the resources of the mines involved, with this exception, that claim leasing was practically a new mining technique at Tonopah and existed only there and in the bonanzas and pseudo-bonanzas which followed it.

The pattern of the last bonanza was, as has been remarked, much the same as those which had gone before it except that the properties which were a part of its atmosphere and background were those of the twentieth century and the frontier West combined in a peculiar and almost unique synthesis. The saloons, fandango houses, the wide-open gambling, the mining stock exchanges, staging system of Wells Fargo, the narrow-gage bonanza railroads, thousand-miler shirts, Winchester express rifles, Colt's patent revolvers, the gold, the girls and the gunfire were what they had been at Virginia City, at Bodie, in Panamint and on the Reese. But in place of the silk top hat and Prince Albert coat of the old nabobs there appear in the photographs of the time the Stetson XXX hat and the corduroy Norfolk jacket. The coach and the mud wagon are in the picture at its inception but before the rush to Tonopah, Goldfield, Rhyolite and Rawhide was over, the Oldsmobile and Hayne-Apperson touring car had made their appearance. There were long-distance telephones across the desert, direct Pullmans to San Francisco, Eastern capital, labor organizers, paved sidewalks and hotels with hot and cold water in multiple bathrooms. The effete devisings of civilization were beginning to crowd the self-sufficient simplicities of the dying frontier.

Tonopah abounded in the individualists and characters attracted by all strikes since the times of Marshall and Sutter. One of the most notable was Fraction Jack Stewart whose microscopic claim bisected the adjacent properties of a bigger company. Thirty thousand dollars was the price he asked when approached in the matter by the big-time superintendent.

"Thirty-thousand dollars, hell!" was the super's reply. "Your property's too small to work and is no good even if you could work it. It's just a nuisance like yourself. I'll give you a thousand dollars to clear out."

"Never let it be said that Jack Stewart allowed a mere twenty-nine thousand dollars to stand in the way of a deal," said Jack. "You're on!"

Tasker L. Oddie and John Hays Hammond organized the Tonopah-Belmont Company. The Tonopah Club, for three decades the leading gambling premises and saloon as well as masculine forgathering place of the community, was started early by Tom Kendall. George Wingfield, later to become the richest man in Nevada, opened a faro game without a limit there, and Sam Dunham, through the agency of his *Tonopah Miner* was informing the world in boxcar headlines that Nevada was once again the coming mining Mecca of the known universe and that early comers could still get in on a good thing. They came.

Although a good deal of powder was burned in the early days of Tonopah and Colt's equalizers banged with satisfactory frequency, the only big-time gunman who came to town was Wyatt Earp, the celebrated peace officer of Tombstone and Dodge City, the latter of which he had ruled with a hand of drop-forged steel in the days when Cyrus K. Holliday's new Santa Fe RR was attracting every cowpoke and gunfighter in the Southwest. Earp, a contemporary of such frontier Olympians as Wild Bill Hickok and Doc Holliday, who was no relative of the top-hatted Cyrus mentioned above, was getting on in years and his mission in Tonopah was a private one as the founder of the fortunes of the Northern saloon. Earp had started it as one of the original thirty-two saloons which were in operation before there was any private dwelling in town more pretentious than a tent. Glassock reports that the mere mention of his name was sufficient to evict a group of claim jumpers from the property of the Tonopah Mining Company, but this is apparently the only time he functioned in even a quasi-legal capacity.

Even earlier in their brief but vivid flowering than most bonanza communities, Tonopah and later Goldfield were dazzlingly aware of the social amenities and the uses of stylish properties. Clerks, junior executives and office managers who arrived with wardrobes largely consisting of fringed buckskin jackets and Mormon hats were soon sending to Roos Brothers in San Francisco for claw-hammer evening coats, starched linen and white glacé gloves in which to attend the seemingly interminable succession of dinners, card parties, balls, first nights and other routs which flourished under the night skies of the desert. For the miners there were thundering banquets at tables seating fifty or sixty handle-bar mustaches each, according to the photographic record, with a foil-topped bottle of champagne at each place and a wealth of patriotic bunting on the walls.

For the elite there were sumptuous dinner parties with Eastern lobster and terrapin, pheasant *en plumage* and other viands which from time immemorial had been the hallmarks of *chic* in the mining communities of the West.

When the Tonopah Opera House opened in May, 1903, in a stunning explosion of red plush and starched shirt bosoms, the community was scandalous with pride. The boxes bulged grandly with miners in uncomfortable attire but fully conscious of the *ton* of the occasion and that the intermissions would be of sufficient duration to assure getting to Butler's Saloon down the street to stay themselves with flagons before the curtain rose again. The grand opening was reported next day by the *Tonopah Miner* in glowing terms: "Some of the artists who appeared were Evans and Lindsley, horizontal performers who are unexcelled in their particular line of work; Mr. and Mrs. Jack McGee who as laughsmiths stand preeminent in their class; and Dora Pelletier, the Tyrolean warbler from the Sunny Alps who puts the nightingale in the shade for sweetness of voice. . . ."

Forty-five years later almost to a day, Dora Pelletier was at the bar of Sammy's Bowery Follies in New York where she was billed no longer as the "Tyrolean Warbler" but the "Queen of the Bowery."

DURABLE TROUBADOUR

Dora Pelletier, "the Tyrolean warbler," who charmed Tonopah when its Opera House opened, as she appeared nearly half a century later in a music hall in New York's Bowery.

"Tonopah was a hell of a town in those days," deposes Miss Pelletier, who had, in fact, been born just off Montgomery Street in San Francisco at a date she refused to nominate but which might be generally identified as in the era of the first Poodle Dog Cafe. "There was hurrahing and hollering and a good time in those places all night long. A girl could have a good time there. I did have a good time. Champagne and quail for supper and champagne and pork chops for breakfast. You may quote me as saying Tonopah was a hell of a town. I would like to go back to Tonopah. Do you think it is just the same?"

The news was gently broken to the Queen of the Bowery that the bloom had been off Tonopah and Goldfield for over thirty years.

"Well, anyway, as I was telling you, there was so much money around there in those days you'd never imagine you could be broke again," continued Miss Pelletier. "I lost $1,500 in the goddam Tonopah Mining Company, but I was making $200 a week then and didn't care. If this is for publication you had better say $300. It sounds classier. That was a lot of chips for yodelling and warbling in those days. I used to wear a princess gown and a little hat like Paris, always classy, and do you know what rocked them right back on their heels? It was when I yodelled 'Sleep, Baby, Sleep.' That used to fetch me a shower of big silver dollars and I always saved it till the last of my act so they could ring the curtain down while we picked up all the dollars. It wouldn't have looked so classy to have everyone see us poking around the stage for money and down on our hands and knees under the sets most likely."

Miss Pelletier, who is a mine of slightly disordered information about boom towns, can also be induced to remember things about Cripple Creek's Julian Street and San Francisco before the fire, although these fascinations have no part in this chronicle. It is interesting, however, to note that, having left San Francisco in 1905 and having never returned to the scene of her first triumphs, she was unaware of the holocaust which followed so closely on her departure.

"I don't read the papers much any more," she explains, "but you tell me there has been a fire and no Poodle Dog now? My, my, San Francisco must have changed."

Ore assays were not the only thing to run high in Tonopah before the emergence and florid rise of Goldfield. The indexes of mortality, the poker stakes at the Tonopah Club and the ratio of fun to laborious sobriety were also high. In a twelve-hour session at the Tonopah Club with the goddess of chance through the medium of a roulette layout, a casual newcomer named Charley Taylor contrived to drop the sum of $34,000, the first big money ever seen in town, and with what chips remained in his pocket bought champagne for everyone present. That would be considerable money today but in the hard currency of the turn of the century and in a mining camp as yet to achieve the big time, it was stupendous.

Water was scarce. A single barbershop for a time provided the community with its only baths through the agency of a punctured kerosine tin suspended from a framework and filled by a handpump. When, therefore, two citizens digging within the town limits in search, not of specimen ores, but water, were finally rewarded with a stream of bright green, sticky fluid from some subterranean source they were in no way abashed. In the Butler Saloon, where they repaired to celebrate, they reported triumphantly that they "had struck a *crème de menthe* mine, but rich!"

Nobody in Nevada, a determinedly silver state ever since the report of the first assays from the Comstock had been brought back across the Sierra from Nevada City to the slopes of Mount Davidson, was impressed by the possibility of "gold in them thar hills," in the vicinity of Tonopah. A *crème de menthe* outcropping, yes and certainly. But when a few old-time prospectors in search of a grubstake mentioned gold, C. B. Glassock, ranking and almost only historian of the southern Nevada strikes, remarked it was practically an affront to civic pride. Until, that is, it was discovered in startling quantities to the south in Marsh and Stimler's Sandstorm Mine at Goldfield.

Unlike the other Nevada mining communities which followed Tonopah in the first decade of the century, Goldfield, Rhyolite, Manhattan, Bullfrog, Greenwater and Rawhide, Tonopah is still a city with some pretensions to animation. It is the distributing center for a number of smaller camps for supplies: oil, gasoline, dynamite, mining machinery and ordinary necessities of life. Its Mizpah Hotel is the only reputable hostelry on the long desert drive between Reno and Las Vegas. The Tonopah Club is still a seemingly monstrous gaming parlors and bar, and the weekly editions of *The Tonopah Times-Bonanza* are still optimistic with news of mining grosses, assays and the location of new desert properties.

## II: GOLDFIELD

THE thirty-five miles of north and south road between Tonopah and Goldfield today is as lonely and desolate a stretch of highway running along the escarpment of a low-lying range of barren Nevada hillsides as can be found anywhere north of the Funeral Mountains. In December, 1902, there was no road at all and the journey, which can now be made comfortably in well under an hour, took Harry Stimler and Billy Marsh two days in a buckboard loaded with enough grub, staked by Tom Kendall and Jim Butler, for a week. Stimler was twenty, Marsh a decade older and they both felt that Tonopah was getting a little too citified. Several of the saloons by this time had plank floors and the Crystal Water Company had actually laid in a pipe line to supplant the water cart that had served the community for its first year. It was time to be moving on.

Goldfield wasn't Goldfield at all, but merely Columbia Mountain until Stimler and Marsh staked out the Sandstorm, assaying a little better than sixty dollars, but sixty dollars in gold, not silver, and that was news in Nevada. For no particular reason they decided to call the place Grandpa. Later Grandpa was to become Goldfield and was to prove a locality of singular interest to such then unsuspecting characters as Charlie Schwab, Bernard Baruch, Frank Lowden, onetime governor of Illinois, John S. Reynolds of the Pullman Company, Senator William A. Clark, August Heinze, George Nixon and George Wingfield. Some of them were even going to make money out of it.

None of the old Bonanza Kings of the Washoe, however, were to be in on the Goldfield strike, for John W. Mackay, last of the imperial dynasty of Virginia, had died at Carlton House Terrace the July previous, and new names dominated the imagination of the world and the boards of its mining exchanges.

By indirection at least, the destinies of Wells Fargo were implemented and conditioned by a variety of animal life other than that embraced by the conventional six horses of the Concord or even the many spans of mules which, on less de luxe hauls, served the mud wagons and heavy freight teams. There is hardly a notable bonanza in the history of the entire West, with its consequent enlargement of Wells Fargo, whose discovery did not somehow involve either wild life or domestic beasts.

In Tuolumne County, according to the legend, a miner shot a grizzly in the early fifties and when the wounded beast toppled over a hillcrest he landed on

## GOLDFIELD OR BUST

Before the coming of the Tonopah and Goldfield RR everything necessary for life and commerce was shipped into these Nevada boom towns in enormous wagon trains like this. One Goldfield housewife of the period recalls that when she arrived there in 1903 she brought with her one rocker and two wooden kitchen chairs and it was a year and a half before she was able to purchase another rocker. Most freight space was devoted to mining machinery, and household goods were at a great premium. Also shown is Mrs. Key Pittman, wife of the silver senator and an energetic Nevada pioneer in her own person. She was a daring motorist of the early chain-drive era, a photographer of note, and here she is showing the way to Goldfield before there was any road in the desert south of Tonopah.

the site of the richest sort of Placer diggings. A strayed cayuse belonging to Wells Fargo is generally credited with leading Pony Bob Haslam to the rich specimens whose indentification started the rush to the Reese River district. Far to the south in Arizona, Harry Wickenburg shot a vulture on the wing and where it fell on the banks of the Hassayampa he discovered the Vulture Mine which produced so mightily that by 1879 the eighty stamp mills he erected there were producing bullion worth $21,000 a week.

And there are other redactions of the legend involving tarantulas, rattlesnakes, coyotes, timber wolves and assorted birds of the air, indeed almost every form of life native or imported to California and Nevada except, possibly, the Bactrian camel. A claim was hardly respectable unless its establishment had somehow involved the beasts of the field.

Goldfield's discovery and initial exploration cannot be attributed to anything as conventional as Jim Butler's wandering burro, which became a symbol of Tonopah's emergence and which, with its owner, was paraded upon every civic occasion, but Goldfields birth had equine overtones, nevertheless. Al Myers, Billy Marsh and Harry Stimler had returned to Tonopah for the appropriate celebration of the Fourth of July, leaving Grandpa, which by this time boasted four tents, in the safekeeping of L. L. Patrick and J. D. Hubbard, the second-comers to the scene. Patrick and Hubbard spent one of the liveliest Nights Before the Fourth on record, not detonating fireworks or even elevating the patriotic flagon, but defending their camp from hundreds and hundreds of wild horses who made repeated attempts to stampede their picketed animals. More than 500 of these animals were counted racing around the borders of the encampment during the short Nevada night raising equine hell, an indication of how desolate and uninhabited was a section of the desert which in a few months was to blossom with steel and stone hotels, motorcars and New York financiers.

Tonopah and Goldfield both had the benefit of the most respectable sort of animal chapters in their early lives.

The subsequent months in Goldfield's history were a record of the sort of frenzied finance that would have amazed even Thomas Lawson, a later day expert in the Get-Rich-Quick-Wallingford-Blackie-Daw school of underwriting. There was a boom in town lots. There was a boom in mining properties. There was an all-over boom in Nevada. Town lots in Goldfield changed hands so rapidly that no registrar of deeds could be found to record the transactions. There is the record of a $45,000 profit on a $500 real-estate deal. The most famous of all leases, that of Hayes and Monette on the Mohawk, produced an all-time record of $5,000,000 in 106 days. The fame of the Mohawk, Jumbo, Red Top, January, Combination, Sandstorm and Kendall was bruited abroad in Threadneedle Street and on the Paris Bourse, and Wells Fargo increased its schedule of stages from three trips a week between Tonopah and Goldfield to three a day and the fortune hunters rode in clinging to the axles and outrigging.* The telephone came into Goldfield while Wells Fargo was still maintaining its clattering stagecoaches and a cycle was fulfilled. The company that had supplied communication by the Overland Stage and by Pony Express and finally by the all-conquering railroad, was still driving its oldest form of conveyance alongside the looping catenaries of the Bell system.

Then, as now, the glass insulators on the crossarms carrying the whispering wires were irresistible as targets for highway marksmen and the telephone company's maintenance department begged the stage drivers to discourage their outside passengers from target practice en route, but without perceptible effect.

Not all Wells Fargo's traffickings into Goldfield were concerned with the romantic excitements of precious metals and prospecting passengers. Upon one occasion a mining lease was in prospect to J. P. Loftus with a limited term during which ore could be removed from a certain property. Machinery for the operation of the shaft was necessary in haste, once the lease was obtained, but traffic over the one-track Tonopah & Goldfield RR was hopelessly delayed

---

* A footnote to the great exodus from Tonopah to Goldfield, which was much of the pattern of the by then almost forgotten exodus from Aurora to Bodie, was the dramatic removal of Harry Ramsey's Saloon. There was already a stage line maintained by Wells Fargo between the two towns and returning voyagers to Tonopah reported to incredulous auditors that there was as yet no single barroom in Goldfield. Alarmed by this dire intelligence and correctly figuring that there was more than one sort of gold in them hills, Ramsey put skids under his premises, hitched four span of oxen to the sills and started south, dispensing cheer and encouragement along the way as his tavern bumped across the desert. At no time were his doors closed to customers and it was only necessary for stage drivers to slow their horses to a walk for passengers to be refreshed while still in motion.

by the immense volume of business, and it might take weeks to get a carload of essential machinery into town with great consequent loss. Loftus placed an order with a supply house in Denver for a gasoline ore hoist and a variety of other ponderous and heavy items, specifying that it was to be ready for shipment by Wells Fargo Express upon receipt of a telegram at any hour of the day or night.

The lease fell into his hands late one night and before dawn the machinery was rolling westward by Wells Fargo over the iron of the Rio Grande Western RR, predecessor of today's D&RGW. By paying the express rate, many times over the cost of ordinary freight shipment, he was able to have his hoist in operation five days later instead of several months and realized a handsome profit on the operation. Wells Fargo could function as a humble beast of burden as well as the proud and swift courser of the plains.

Not all freight for the bonanza towns got through as expeditiously. Gilbert Kneiss, historian of Western railroading, in his *Bonanza Railroads* tells of the Goldfield saloon proprietor to whom a shipment of fine new roulette wheels and bird cages had been consigned but which was caught in the bottleneck of the Virginia and Truckee's yards at Carson. The V & T was riding high at the time with more business than it could handle and no inducement was sufficient to get the car containing the implements of chance across the desert out of its turn. The anguished shipper foresaw ruin or at least the daily loss of huge potential profits when suddenly inspiration came to him. Cars carrying livestock had a priority rating over all the others, and in no time flat the saloonkeeper had engineered the purchase of an aging cow and installed her among the green baize tables, bronze cuspidors and other de luxe equipment for his gaming and guzzling palace. The car moved out in the next train.

The year 1906 was to witness a gala event which, even more than all its other extracurricular activities combined, was to put Goldfield on the map of public consciousness and at the same time start Tex Rickard on his career as the greatest sports promoter of all time. This was the Gans-Nelson fight and the idea sprang, practically full blown, from the imagination of Rickard and a couple of ex-newspapermen currently occupied writing market letters and other forms of promotion for local mining brokers.

It should be noted that this was Rickard's first venture into the fight promotion and that he was probably motivated by a combination of patriotic fervor for Goldfield and the consideration that the arrival of a large contingent of the sporting fraternity would inevitably mean a huge rush of business to his Northern Saloon and its already fabulously profitable games of chance. The notion had merit all the way round. A committee of nabobs at the Montezuma Club made up a $30,000 purse to which Rickard magnificently donated a third of its total, and the money in splendid minted double eagles was placed on display, between a couple of Wells Fargo messengers armed with Winchester carbines, in the window of George Wingfield's Bank.

The committee was able without too much difficulty to locate Nelson's manager at Salt Lake, but in the absence of any idea of the whereabouts of

## THE CONCORD ROLLS INTO HISTORY

Before the coming of the Stevens Duryeas, Wells Fargo rode the Concords in their fading years between the booming mining towns and camps of the Nevada desert. Above, a pair of stages traveling together for protection pass down a rocky canyon on the Goldfield-Tonopah run. In the lower picture the afternoon stage for Mina sets out from in front of the Wells Fargo office in Goldfield. A lady passenger, veiled, bonneted and gloved against the elements, is about to start on a shopping trip to San Francisco. The year is 1904.

## GOLDFIELD IN ITS GOLDEN HOUR

In boom times at Goldfield the Montezuma Club and B.P.O.E. together shared this elegant stone structure festooned in Mazda lamps for the Fourth of July. A news vendor did flourishing trade in mining journals and the wagon of the National Ice Company (extreme left) was busy delivering ice for the bar. Today but a cellerage filled with rubble marks the once-proud Montezuma Club where millions were played at faro and roulette. Below, in a less pretentious resort, the Goldfield miners have a banquet with beer, whisky and Rhine wine bottles in plentiful evidence.

Gans, they wired Otto Floto, sports editor of the *Denver Post,* in the belief that this august personage knew who was in what saloon the length and breadth of the Union at any hour of the day or night. Floto, a former billboard poster man and saloonkeeper, had few pretensions to literary fame, but Harry Tammen, one of the proprietors of the *Post,* freely admitted that he was in love with the name — Otto Floto — and must have him on the staff at any cost. Since the sports editor of the *Post* had recently died and the bicycle editor, who was normally in line for the position, was temporarily bedded as a result of attempting to ride a bicycle through the swinging doors of a Larimer Street tavern, Floto got the job. He was later made nominal partner in another Tammen-Bonfils property, the Sells-Floto Circus, simply on the hypnotic authority of his name over Tammen. In any event, Rickard's faith in his powers was justified, and Gans was located and signed for the fight.

The nation was flatteringly interested and Nevada itself was in a paroxysm of excitement. The window full of gold and its Wells Fargo guards was an attraction day and night and although the year 1900 had been achieved but six years previous with a resultant ninety-four to go, *The Goldfield Sun* was busy hailing the approaching event as "the battle of the century." Sports writers were pouring in on every train over the Tonopah and Goldfield RR and Goldfield date lines were appearing on stories filed to home offices all over the nation. Charlie Clark, son of Montana's acquisitive senator, arrived on a private car splendidly stocked with rare bourbon and cigars. Nat Goodwin drew up grandly to the doors of the Northern in a fireman-red Oldsmobile with brass headlamps, and Death Valley Scotty, never one to hide his light under a bushel and a demon performer when the reporters were around, got a hundred dollars in silver from Ole Elliott at the Northern's cash desk and tossed the change into the crowd of loafers outside for the fun of seeing them scramble.

Even the Corbett-Fitzsimmons fight at Carson City on St. Patrick's Day back in 1897 when the first of all newsreels had filmed the affray and the San Francisco *Examiner* had run a special train over the Sierra in record time to get photographs of the fight to the Golden Gate the morning after they were taken, didn't compare for tumult and excitement.

Special trains rolled in over the desert so close on each other's rear markers that it looked like one continuous string of varnish, Pullmans, private cars, diners and club cars all the way from Hazen to Tonopah and the last special got in at five o'clock the morning of the great event. To a man its passengers headed for the Northern.

There were the traditional rock-drilling contests, won by a Tonopah Cornishman who drilled thirty-seven inches in fifteen minutes, burro races and an old men's pony race. The crowd around the entrances to the Northern, the Palace, the Mohawk and the Hermitage was so great that vehicular traffic became impossible in Crook Avenue and Main Street. The crash of cash registers and other sounds of solvent revelry were wafted far out upon the desert to alarm the coyotes and stampede the fuzztails. Rickard was observed shaking hands with himself at frequent intervals, and the Northern set an all-time record with the sale in a single day of twenty barrels of whisky.

The gate was the largest ever taken in by a prizefight until that time: $68,715, and the fight itself was such as sports addicts usually envision only when smoking opium. It ran to the heroic count of no fewer than forty-two rounds. No complete film of the fight is available because the motion picture company engaged in its recording ran out of film during the thirty-eighth round, but is was one of the most hotly contested of all time and only terminated in the forty-second when Nelson fouled Gans and at the same time gave him the lightweight championship of the world. Goldfield wouldn't have traded the attendant uproar and publicity to have become the scene of the Olympic Games.

The crescent proportions of the boom in Nevada mining camps which was inaugurated by Tonopah and spread rapidly to the south and east to Manhattan, Rawhide, Rhyolite and Bullfrog naturally required an increase in the number of Wells Fargo agencies and enormously multiplied the revenue received from the shipment of bullion and currency as well as from the less colorful traffic in mine supplies and ordinary commodities. Between 1903, when only Tonopah of all the twentieth-century camps had achieved the status of a Wells Fargo town, and 1906 the number of Wells Fargo agencies in Nevada rose from twenty-five to twenty-nine and included in this expansion Bullfrog, Goldfield and Rhyolite. During the three-year period, however, Candelaria, where once the Northern Belle and the Home Ticket had produced $55,000,000 worth of precious metals and the Roaring Gimlet and McKissick's Saloon in Pickhandle Gulch had responded with Homeric whoopee on a twenty-four-hour basis, had quietly been dropped from the tally of Wells Fargo agencies. No mining camp needed any other death certificate.

But time was running out for Wells Fargo so far as the old-time flavor of the express business was concerned. Its agencies were to remain in the Tonopah and Goldfield districts until 1911 when every bonanza in southern Nevada either collapsed with a mighty collapsing or had already done so; but, except for Manhattan, Rawhide and a handful of scattered camps, staging had been supplanted by the railroad or the automobile and even in these removed and improbable locales the Lozier and the Thomas touring cars, supplemented by Hayneses and Ramblers and Reos, were eventually to take over.

Four years after the sensational single shipment out of Tonopah which yielded more than half a million dollars on a fifty-ton carload, and two years after the proving of the Jumbo, the Combination and the Sandstorm, the Tonopah and Goldfield RR was a reality into Goldfield. A dozen Goldfield mines had already produced more than $7,000,000 and were just getting into their stride and reduction mills of substantial capacity were treating ore which a few years before had been broken up in hand mortars and shipped out in the treasure chests behind the last of the six horses.

Wells Fargo was now riding "up in the baggage car ahead" on the T & G just as it had already made itself at home in the wooden combines of the Virginia and Truckee, the Eureka and Palisade and the little Carson and Colorado which by now had become the Cinderella of the narrow gages and had paid off its purchase price to the triumphant Southern Pacific in a single year. Until the Southern Pacific was to build its standard-gage cutoff to Hazen and thus obviate the necessity for transshipment with the narrow-gage cars of the C & C, Darius Ogden Mills' once sad little pike was awash with the sort of traffic that had been dreamed for it by William Sharon, now long dead.

Space on its coaches and combines was at a premium among the capitalists, madams, theatrical troupes, gamblers, high-graders, feature writers, stockbrokers and other followers in the wake of mining excitements of magnitude. At one time there were in service to Tonopah, until the line from Sodaville south was broad-gaged, a number of elaborately upholstered little narrowgage sleeping cars of the sort which General William Jackson Palmer had forseen as universal, at least in the Far West, when he built the Rio Grande RR in Colorado. Not only was the construction and operation of three-foot-gage railroads more economical, but its sleepers with their single-width berths made it unnecessary, as the general pointed out, for strangers to occupy the same bed.

It was in such a microcosm of rolling luxury on the northbound sleeper out of Tonopah that two strangers once attempted the assassination of Tasker Oddie, later a first citizen of Nevada, but were discouraged by a fellow traveler who overheard their plans in the smoking compartment at the end of the car.

No such excitements are in the record as having disturbed the midnight watches of Wells Fargo's messengers in the baggage cars of the Tonopah and Goldfield. The long-distance telephone, the sheriff's automobile posse and other modernities were making train robbery too much of a hazard in regions where such vast distances must be traversed for escape. Furthermore the oldtime gun-bearing bandit of the West was being nudged out of the picture by another variety of crook, the high-pressure stock promoter, the high-grader and the labor racketeer.

What Artemus Ward and an earlier Virginia City had mutually discovered in each other, the comedian Nat Goodwin and Goldfield were to discover in themselves. The parallel between the roles the two men were to play in the two booming communities was so close and dramatic as to make remark upon their similarity impossible. Both were comedians, wits, raconteurs and happy extroverts. Both were of notable rank in their professional fields of endeavor; both were tosspots of legendary proportions, gay dogs and merchants of hurrah, and both were captivated by the bonanza times in which Nevada was flourishing in their separate eras. Goodwin, to be sure, became more closely associated with the social and public economy of Goldfield than Ward had done with Virginia City, but both left their imprint imperishably upon the diggings they knew and will be part of the chronicle forever.

Before making the golden journey to the Samarkand of the West, Goodwin, a Yankee brought up on dry New England wit and Lawrence's overproof

Merford rum, had been for three decades a stage favorite of New York and London and the principal ornament of Tony Pastor's in a Manhattan whose stage was enriched by a generation which embraced Clyde Fitch, Maxine Elliott, Wilton Lackaye, the elder Barrymore and a young Otis Skinner. He was fond of a cold bottle, or several, and a hot bird. A *viveur* of standing with waiter captains at Rector's and Delmonico's, he took to the high, wide and handsome style of Goldfield even as Nevada took to him.

He was fond of remarking that he would rather be Nat in Golfield's Northern than Sir Nathaniel in London's Savoy. In 1906, the Hippodrome, the first of Goldfield's two legitimate playhouses, was built and no bill was too good for the occasion, so Nat Goodwin and Edna Goodrich, the ranking Broadway comedy team of the time, were engaged. They arrived in a private car over the dusty rails of the Tonopah and Goldfield RR and all the town was down to marvel at the appointments of the brass-railed green and gold masterpiece from the Pullman shops in far-off Chicago. Its rosewood panels, luxurious carpets, solid-silver cruet stands and crystal epergnes for the service of dinner were gratifyingly complemented by a wealth of cloisonné and ormolu.

The *bon ton* of Goldfield, when it dined out, dined in state at the Palm Grill across the street and down half a block from the somewhat rougher precincts of the Northern. The Palm Grill had everything on the menu, almost, that could be had at the Palace in San Francisco or George Rector's in New York. Local nabobs who had made the grand tour to Chicago said the Palmer House was no better at sluicing and gentling the patrons with White Seal champagne and lobster Thermidor. The house specialty at the Palm Grill, where evening dress was taken for granted and the maître d'hôtel had been trained at Delmonico's, was desert quail, gamey from a diet of sage, split and broiled and served on a rich bed of truffled foie gras from Strasborg. There were twenty champagnes on the wine card, Cape oysters from Buzzards Bay, and by courtesy of Wells Fargo, which once again found itself in the role of de luxe fish forwarder, antelope steak, and sand-dabs from Fisherman's Wharf. In a little balcony above the diners there was Julius Goldsmith's orchestra with Julius Goldsmith himself fiddling the latest Strauss waltzes and taking $100 an evening in gold in tips.

Stanley Ketchel, the promising boxfighter, could be seen at a corner table with Barney Baruch or Sam Vermilyea with fresh-cut flowers on the table and a silver wine bucket at his elbow. Like the oysters, the flowers were by courtesy of Wells Fargo. The nabobs dined in style and paid in gold.

Goldfield was not without its melodrama which moved in the rarefied atmosphere of high society. One of the most exclamatory public assassinations in the Nevada record was accomplished by a gentleman adventurer from San Francisco named Jackson Hines upon the Polish Count Constantin Podorsky who had, in an ill-advised moment, run away with Hines' wife. Hines trailed him to Nome at the height of the Alaska gold rush and caught up with him some months later at Goldfield in the noontide of its brightest bonanzas.

## THE ROAD TO REMEMBRANCE

Third Street in Goldfield was once thronged with miners and their families bound for the Mint Theater or the taproom of the Esmeralda Hotel. Traffic was becoming a problem and runaways a menace to life and limb. Below is Third Street, today without even a trace of Barney Baruch's Oldsmobile or Nat Goodwin's stylish Peerless.

"I guess I was impetuous," Hines said some forty years afterward, "but I was cross by this time at having to follow the fellow into a number of places where the liquor was bad and the company worse. I was seasick on the way to Alaska, too."

Provoked by such a variety of harms, Hines walked into the Palm Grill one evening at the dinner hour while Julius Goldsmith was playing a Viennese waltz and shot the Count Podorsky four times in the head. A few days later a jury acquitted him amidst general rejoicing and Hines was looked upon thereafter as something of a crusader for the sanctity of the home. The record is in the dusty files of Goldfield's county courthouse for anyone to read.

DERRINGER AVENGER

Jackson C. Hines, "monocled sourdough of the Yukon," who, in a moment of vexation, abolished the pusillanimous Count Podorsky in Goldfield's most stylish restaurant and was promptly acquitted as a defender of the sanctity of the American home.

Hines, who later became a fashionable singer in great demand at Newport, Palm Beach and in the Palm Court of the Palace in San Francisco, was once at a lawn party on the fabulous estate of Mrs. Edward T. Stotesbury at Palm Beach when his hostess asked if the story of the shooting were indeed true.

"My gentle lady," said the Sweet Singer of the Yukon and Goldfield's Crook Avenue, adjusting a single glass in his eye, "I blew the fellow's waxed mustaches all the hell and gone over that dreary pothouse. I doubt if they've got Esmeralda County entirely cleaned up from it yet!"

It may be assumed that Hines was striving for picturesque effect, since nobody else ever reported anything but good of the Palm Grill.

When the Goldfield Hotel, still visible to this day, threw wide its doors revealing enough solid furniture of fumed oak to have stocked a department store and an impressive rank of solid-steel private safes for the individual guests behind its reception desk, it was reported that so much champagne was opened and spilled on the barroom parquet that a river of vintage Rheims and Epernay flowed down the front steps to be absorbed by the dusty street outside. Champagne was the favored wine of El Dorado even if the ice to chill it cost five cents a pound and the treatment it received in transit from San Francisco managed to explode or smash three or four bottles out of every case.

But while the fashionable world of Goldfield drank, dined and indulged in target practice among the wine coolers at the Palm Grill and the Goldfield Hotel, there was ample opportunity elsewhere for the prospector, the miner and the stock promoter to absorb nourishment without the formality of evening attire. The conjunction of Crook Avenue and Main Street, a block down the slope from the hotel, was for several years probably the most celebrated guzzling and gaming four corners in the world. There, facing each other and offering to the undecided a perfect bewilderment of choices, were the Northern Saloon, the Palace, the Mohawk and the Hermitage, and most Goldfielders found it convenient to circulate in rotation, some clockwise of habit, some counterclockwise, thus distributing their patronage impartially and enjoying new scenes and faces with each libation. If one wearied of these pleasant premises there were others: the Phoenix, the Oriental, the Mint, the Combination and the inevitable Silver Dollar and Last Chance. Some clue to the patronage enjoyed by the taverners of Goldfield may derive from the circumstance that in a two-year period more than $7,000,000 was grossed by Rickard's Northern alone. Part of this impressive sum, of course, was income from the blackjack, roulette and poker tables, bird cages and other games of chance. The slot machine, now so universal in Nevada as to be found in bus stations and doctors' offices, had not yet established its profitable supremacy.

Today there is scarcely a trace to remind the sight-seer or philosopher that these same four corners once were the scene of such revelry that barkeeps worked in twenty-four hour shifts and the doors of the temples of Bacchus never ceased to swing for a moment of the twenty-four hour day. Two of them are vacant lots and the other two are filling stations, one of which tips a hat to history by preserving the name Mohawk. At its rival's across the street there was also a faint souvenir of the past discernible. Its proprietor does a desultory trade in small golden pellets which he says he unearths in old safes and cellarages of local buildings destroyed by the great conflagration which engulfed Goldfield in the twenties.

Coincidental with the soaring of Goldfield and, in a large measure, as a result of such proven bonanzas as Tonopah, Goldfield, Rhyolite and a few other early comers, there was a rash of strikes in other Nevada communities, all of them dramatic and colorful but not considerable in this chronicle because they did not achieve the status of Wells Fargo agencies.

Yerington, alias Pizen Switch, became a Wells Fargo town between the years of 1903 and 1906. It had been part of the Crazy Louse Mining District back in 1865 and later was reported to have been for a time owned almost in its entirety by that ubiquitous but singularly unsuccessful prospector, Mark Twain, but the record doesn't support this claim. Renamed for the magnificently whiskered chief engineer of the Virginia and Truckee RR and subsequently of the Carson and Colorado, Yerington was more of a mining center than a mining community and today is more an agricultural community than either. Even the Nevada Copper Belt RR, which a few years ago ran through Yerington on its way to Wabuska, has disappeared from the *Official Guide*.

More important and, for a time, very much of a Wells Fargo town, was Manhattan, fifty miles off to the north and east of Tonopah on the way to Austin and adjacent to the also booming camp of Round Mountain. In 1905, at Manhattan, there came into the usual overnight being a false-front township seven blocks long with a post office, auto stages, branches of three Tonopah banks, a wooden one-story hotel and Wells Fargo. *The Manhattan Mail* foresaw a great future and the place assumed all the accustomed features of civilization. Manhattan was largely dependent upon San Francisco capital and its mines: Original Manhattan, Mustang Expension, Manhattan Consolidated, Annie Laurie were promoted to the point of actually shipping ore, but the San Francisco fire of 1906 put an end to Manhattan as effectively as though the conflagration had been on the spot instead of in the brokerage houses of Montgomery Street. Manhattan never recovered its first fine flowering, although two years later it was still showing enough animation to retain its status as a Wells Fargo agency. It provided the last example of holdup of a Wells Fargo horse-drawn stage which could be discovered by the authors and an account of which is elsewhere available in this book. The stage was bound to Manhattan from Rawhide.

Seven Troughs, Wonder, Milletts, Fairview and others contributed briefly to the turmoil that was Nevada until 1910, but they do not figure in this story.

The freely spent money which gave Goldfield its world renown as a spender's town and gave Wells Fargo a not inconsiderable business in remittances and the transportation of jewelry ore was the importation to the mines from Colorado, where the practice was already widespread and had achieved a degree of perfection, of "high-grading." High-grading, which could be practiced only in mines where ores of the greatest concentration and richness were being uncovered, was the simple theft of valuable specimens by miners coming off duty and their sale to illigitimate dealers in such stolen metal. In the early days of Goldfield's bonanzas mine owners and lessors were not too concerned for this share-the-wealth program. They themselves were taking out fantastic profits, the tolerance of regular and organized theft served in place of high wages and the money so brought into immediate and determined circulation served to advertise the resources of their properties.

As the industry became better organized, however, and the number of miners engaged in smuggling out high-grade began to make serious inroads on profits, the big producers were determined to put a stop to the practice and instituted change rooms where miners coming off duty must leave their working clothes. This excited such a degree of indignation among the miners, who had come to regard high-grading as a legitimate occupational bonus, that a series of serious disorders and strikes was inaugurated which culminated in the sending of armed troops into the district. It was at this turbulent period that George Wingfield, by now the richest man in Nevada and to this day a nabob of formidable proportions, gained a reputation for fearlessness which

GOLDFIELD MAIDENS AT A *FETE CHAMPETRE*

is still a legend and which was recalled in some detail by Bernard Baruch forty years after the excitements took place.

"I remember," Baruch told an interviewer in 1948, "a man named Wing-field, George Wingfield. He was a man with a gun. He started out as a jockey. Then he was a gambler in Western mining camps, and a prospector. One day, he stopped in at the bank in Winnemucca, Nevada, and asked George Nixon, the fellow who ran the bank, for a stake of a few hundred dollars. Well, Nixon and Wingfield got to be partners, and Nixon became a senator. On the afternoon of the twenty-eighth of December, 1906 (I believe it was), William Crocker, of San Francisco — he had a pointed beard; he was a great believer in the West, a great optimist — came into my office in New York with Senator Nixon and said Nixon needed two million five hundred and seventy-eight thousand dollars for a gold mine he and Wingfield were developing. Goldfield Consolidated, it was called. Nixon made a noise like a dividend, so I put up a million and got involved in the enterprise myself. The first time I saw Wingfield was when I went out to Goldfield quite a bit later to look the property over. He was carrying five revolvers — two here, two here, and one here. He also had four Pinkerton detectives with him. Wingfield told me he'd been having labor trouble with some of the I. W. W. boys in his mine. One reason was a company rule he had, to the effect that the men working in the high-grade mines had to strip as they started home, and then they had to jump over a bar, so that any nuggets of gold they might have hidden under their arms or between their legs would fall on the floor. The I. W. W. had beaten up

Wingfield's superintendent and some of his foremen and left them out in the desert. Wingfield had ridden out himself and brought the men in and walked right through a mob of the strikers in front of the bank. He was afraid of nothing. When the strikers tried to knock out a newspaper he published by frightening the newsboys and distributors off the streets, Wingfield went out and peddled his papers himself. One of the strikers waylaid him, but Wingfield knocked the man out with the butt of one of his guns. As I say, Wingfield was the best shot I ever saw. Out at one of the mines, someone would throw a bottle up, end over end, behind him, and he'd wheel around and get one of his guns up in a single motion and break the bottle. Now, that's shooting. . . ."

When a stop was finally put to high-grading Wells Fargo experienced a not inconsiderable decline in shipments via its treasure services. The express company had, in the palmy days of the practice, naturally made no inquiry into the nature of parcels it received from even the shadiest shippers, but when the time came for jewelry ore to be retained by the mine operators instead of the fences, it was processed in reducing mills on the spot and sent out in wholesale shipments of bullion on which the rates were substantially less than they had been on individual parcels.

As late as 1946 the Tonopah and Goldfield RR was still in operation, its double-headed freights visible for miles as they smoked over the incredible desert vistas between Mina and Tonopah Junction, between Tonopah Junction and Tonopah, but the insigne of Wells Fargo had, of course, long since disappeared from its baggage coaches and what merchandise was consigned to the American Railway Express traveled in the caboose.

During the second World War there was a brief reminder of old times when solid trains of Pullmans rolled in from San Francisco and the brass-railed private cars of Market Street bankers were parked on the house track a few blocks down the hill from the Mizpah Hotel. An army air field was established at Tonopah and, amidst the oil tankers and other merchandise cars, a sleeper from the Southern Pacific main line at Hazen was dragged over the desert every night to accomodate army personnel. These were the last Pullmans ever to roll over a right of way once populous with diners and drawing-room cars and the private saloon cars of opera stars with the looped and fringed curtains, ormolu and rosewood panelings.

Two years later, however, the last of Nevada's bonanza railroads, save only the Virginia and Truckee, had been abandoned, its tracks torn up from Goldfield to Sodaville and its three or four coaches and four rusting Mikado-type locomotives with their Vanderbilt tenders awaiting the junkman on a siding at Mina. Its ghost had gone to join the Nevada Copper Belt, the Pioche and Pacific, the Las Vegas and Tonopah, the Tonopah and Tidewater, the Carson and Colorado, the Nevada Central and the Eureka and Palisade. The only other remaining short line, the Nevada Northern, owned and operated by the copper interests of Ely, can hardly be classified as a bonanza railroad.

Goldfield, forty years after its great hour, is an astonishment even to those who have experienced the other major astonishments of the Nevada desert.

## WHERE IT ALL CAME FROM

The Navada mines which poured golden wealth into the pockets of George Wingfield, Charles M. Schwab, Bernard Baruch and scores of other venturesome investors sometimes produced ore like that in the fabulous Mohawk, at Goldfield
(above). It was weighed, sacked and stored under armed guard at the Cook
County Bank (below) where more than $1,000,000 in high-grade ore is shown
in this picture.

## THE END OF THE HIGHROAD

Wells Fargo traveled to the end of the road aboard the Goldfield stages just after the turn of the century in southern Nevada. A few years later it still rode behind six horses out of Rawhide, but this was of short duration. When the Tonopah and Goldfield R.R. was finished the last armed messenger descended from the last Concord and an era ended. This was that stage. Below are a couple of Wells Fargo messengers of a somewhat earlier period armed against almost any highway contingency.

## THREE AGES OF GOLDFIELD

In November, 1903, the number of immigrants who had crossed the thirty miles of desert from Tonopah to Grandpa, as Gold-field was first known, came to a grand total of twenty who lived through the Nevada winter, secure in their faith in fortune, in the tent town with the single board shack shown here. Three years later this identical spot, as will be seen from the conformation of the sky line in the background, was the conjunction of Crook Avenue and Main Street, both literally and figuratively the crossroads of the West. Here Tex Rickard's immortal Northern Saloon faced the Mohawk, the Palace and the Hermitage. Here high-livers swaggered, stock promoters flourished and the street crowds were composed of paper millionaires and a surprising number of real ones. The middle scene was taken from a vantage point on the roof of the Northern, sometime in 1906. Below, with the still-unchanging hills for background, is the same scene taken from the drive of the gasoline station which now stands where once the champagne flowed in rivers.

The windows of the Goldfield Hotel, a structure built with an eye to Judgment Day duration, stare sightlessly across the distances toward Tonopah. Two or three beer saloons and a curio store and the Malpais Restaurant are almost its only life. The gloomy Esmeralda County Courthouse, a veritable treasure-trove for the patient researcher, is the community's only excuse for being, and brush and rubbish fill the open cellars which which once were part of the wealthy Montezuma Club, the Elks Building and the stock brokerages which kept open all night so frenzied was the trading in local securities at the height of the boom in 1910. More than fifty city blocks were destroyed by a fire which swept the town one night back in 1923 and since then there has never been any trace of comeback in the mines. The tracks of the Tonopah and Goldfield have been torn up; the depot of the Las Vegas and Tonopah has been moved away from its yards to serve elsewhere as a curio shop. Only a flaking stone step or two show where once the patrons in evening dress ascended to the Palm Grill and the music of Julius Goldsmith's little orchestra floated out into the Nevada night. The glory has forever departed from Goldfield but the splendor of its glittering legend remains in the memories of many men who knew it in its champagne days when thousand-dollar bills were on the faro tables at the Northern in thick packets and Jackson Hines was making ready to do deadly hurt to Constantin, the pusillanimous Count Podorsky.

## III: RHYOLITE

The turn of the twentieth century brought a new architecture to even the most sudden and short-lived mining camps. The wooden false front of early times, the sidewalks covered with wooden awning and the overhead verandas of stores and residences, and the solid red-brick construction with white stone trim were still in evidence. But rich resources or the desire to suggest them brought to the desert the twentieth-century façade of solid stone and concrete masonry as it is known in a thousand American cities today, and of this style of construction, startling beyond description when encountered against the sagebrush and the Plutonian background of the Nevada hills, Rhyolite is the classic archetype.

Rhyolite stood, and in some measure still stands, at the northern extremity of a valley formed by an alluvial wash so vast and comprehensive in its loneliness as be possessed of an almost physical impact upon the human emotions. As far to the southward as the eye can see, the Amargosa Desert reaches in a seemingly illimitable waste, arid and alkaline beneath the noontide, as vast and placid as the implications of eternity under the Nevada moon. Even the nightmare shapes and cosmic shadow play of Death Valley itself are dwarfed by the serene, implacable sterility of the Amargosa.

The remains of Rhyolite are the remains of a modern city in every sense of the word. They are the bare quintessence of desolation, lacking, even on close inspection, the details of ruin encountered in the atomized cities of Europe. The desert's reclamation is too overpowering for detail; its obliteration of trace too complete, and where the desert was not sufficient, man put the final touch. For Rhyolite has been methodically and systematically pillaged of every stick of woodwork accessible to wrecking bar or even more formidable engines of attack. Its beams and joists are part of the economy of scores of homes in Beatty and desert shanties; its most minute splinters have long since been fed to stoves and campfires.

What remains of Rhyolite, except for the Bottle House and the incredible railroad station, is monolithic: stone façades, cement foundations and bank vaults impregnable to all but time, the great and universal burglar. Its main street has long since rejoined the elemental desert; its sidewalks are collapsed into a treacherous labyrinth of vaults and cesspools and cisterns, its cellarages themselves are repositories for an unbelievable and mountainous kitchen midden of tin cans and bottles, representing an all-inclusive grocer's catalogue, a definitive selection of the potations of the earth.

Wells Fargo maintained two offices in Rhyolite in 1906, two years after the camp had come into being: one a few doors up Golden Street from the John T. Overbury block and one in the depot of the Las Vegas and Tonopah RR. The first of these is now a cavernous cellar populated with the tin containers of forgotten table delicacies favored by long-departed housewives, while the depot still stands as a public tavern and beerhall. When it was first built in mission-style architecture and of massive concrete design, the local papers spoke of the Rhyolite depot as the finest railroad structure in Nevada, although this might have been disputed by anyone familiar with the amazing shops of the Virginia and Truckee at Carson City where municipal balls and communal merrymaking had been in order back in the seventies. There is no denying the enduring qualities of Rhyolite's station, however, and Judgment Day will doubtless find it still in a state of tolerable preservation.

The quartz outcroppings that were to become Rhyolite in the Bullfrog Hills were discovered in the summer of 1904 by that Magellan of the Nevada desert, Shorty Harris, later discoverer of Harrisburg, a legendary prospector in the Death Valley region and, even in a society where the consumption of whisky was phenomenal, a notable technician when it came to the absorption of what he was pleased to call "O, Be Joyful." Shorty never managed to retain much of the wealth netted by his discoveries and he died a poor man, like most prospectors, but he lived a full life and was highly esteemed by the pioneers who knew him.

His discovery of the Bullfrog he described in a newspaper interview of the period:

> I didn't get in early enough at Tonopah and Goldfield [said Shorty, in telling of the early days] so I wandered south and followed the Keane Wonder excitement in the Funeral range. I got there about as late as I did elsewhere, so I didn't get any close-in ground. Long before the Keane Wonder was struck I

## THE FOUNDING FATHERS

The first business enterprise in Bullfrog was, of course, devoted to the pioneers' most urgent need and was conducted in a tent.

had traveled across the country from Grapevine to Buck Springs, and had seen the big blowout of quartz and quartzite on the ground that later I located as the Bullfrog claim. When I found that I couldn't get anything good at the Keane Wonder, I remembered the blowout and decided to go back to it. E. L. Cross was at the Keane Wonder; he was there afoot. "Shorty, I'd like to go with you," said Cross. "Your chance is good," said I; "come along." We packed the four burros and struck out, together with some other prospectors who had joined in the Keane Wonder rush. Some of the boys went to Thorps and some to Tokop, but when we came to Daylight Springs I told Cross that I knew of a country that I wanted to take him to; that I had passed up a country some time before, and as it looked good to me, we would go back to it. He was willing, and we came on to Buck Springs, which is only a mile or so east of the objective point.

The quartz was just full of free gold, and it was the original genuine green bullfrog rock. Talk about rich rock! Why, gee whiz, it was great! We took the stuff back to the spring and panned it, and we certainly went straight up. The very first boulder was as rich in gold as anything I had ever seen. No, we didn't locate the claim until the next day. We were safe, as there wasn't another live one in the country, except "Old Man" Beatty. Everybody else had left and gone north; so we didn't build a monument until the next day, and then we located only one claim, together with a millsite and water right.

I went over to the ranch and showed the rich rock to "Old Man" Beatty, and he went right over and located the Mammoth claim, later a part of the Big Bullfrog. George Davis heard of the strike and located the ground on the east. Meanwhile Cross and I went to Goldfield and told M.M. Detch, Len McGarry, Bob Montgomery and others of the boys whom we knew, and right then the rush was on.

Yes [continued Shorty, reverting to his travels] I had been in this country before. Why, I paid old Panamint Joe $50 to take me over to Gold Belt or Tin Mountain as much as fifteen years ago. I went back to the Panamint range for the same reason that I came back here — because I had seen a quartz blowout there similar to that of the Bullfrog. That's how I happened to locate the Harrisburg mine. That mine, too, is close to an old trail, leading from Ballarat to Furnace Creek, via Blackwater. Many had gone that way, close to the blowout, and so had I. I remembered it and went back, and you know that the Harrisburg is one of the best things in the country today.

And let me tell you [said Shorty, brushing back his slouch hat and getting himself into a familiar pose] the Bullfrog district is going to be the banner camp of Nevada after all. I have said so from the beginning, and I still say it. I'm no tenderfoot at the prospecting business. I've been at it since 1878, and I've followed the excitements from the time I packed my blankets into Leadville, down through the Coeur d'Alenes, Tombstone, Butte, British Columbia, Utah and other points. The Bullfrog is a crackerjack, I say. If they will put money into the ground here — sink on these mineral showings — like Rube Bryan has in the Pioneer, there will be all kinds of mines in the Bullfrog district. There are too many holes here that remind me of a prairie dog town. If they will prospect here like they do at Goldfield, where men are willing to sink thousands of dollars before raising a color, then we will have more mines. The day is coming when we will have one of the best camps in the state.

No; I have never made a big stake [said Shorty]. The biggest haul I ever made was $10,000. I let the Bullfrog get away from me because I had too much O, Be Joyful, on board, but I couldn't recover the property. I got only $1000 for the strike. But, don't worry; the short man will never again sign anything when he is under the influence of — well, of — I say — it's about time to be hitting out. I got to see a friend.

Shorty Harris is "short for his size;" is 50 years of age and unmarried. Has blue eyes and golden hair, slightly tinged with gray. Is a confirmed bachelor, and expects to die with his boots on.

Within a fortnight the word of Rhyolite had perceptibly cut into the patronage of the saloons and gambling premises of Tonopah and Goldfield off to the north. From Goldfield to Beatty, along the route of what was shortly to become the Las Vegas and Tonopah RR, the desert choked and seethed and racketed with Wintons and Pope-Hartfords whose radiators boiled and whose primitive fan belts gave way under the least thermal provocation, leaving the frustrated owners to bargain for succor or for continued passage with the scornful mule skinners who followed in their dusty wake. Fortunate indeed was the goggled and helmeted motorist whose seagoing Peerless touring car achieved the shade trees of Springdale on the outskirts of Beatty

## INTERNAL COMBUSTION COMES TO THE AMARGOSA

The first arrivals at Bullfrog in the Amargosa Wash, after the gold discovery there of Shorty Harris, arrived by burro and set up a tent town complete with women-folk in domestic capacities. A few months later, when all of Bullfrog had moved a few miles north and taken up residence in Rhyolite where there was water, motorcars were the merest commonplace outside the Southern Hotel. The lower photograph, taken in 1907, shows the motorcade which brought Charles M. Schwab and his party down from Tonopah where he had spotted his celebrated private car *Loretto*. Later Rhyolite had three railroads of its own.

where the elusive Amargosa River flows briefly on the surface. Beatty, later billed as "The Chicago of the West," was to make possible with its water the overnight civilization of Rhyolite, and Beatty still is a pleasant crossroads oasis in the desert with shade trees over its two hotels, six saloons and four filling stations.

Rhyolite was discovered, came into florid and granolithic being and died in the five years between 1904 and 1909. It hardly had time to get started on a cemetery and there are but a hundred or so desert graves on the arid hillside below the town to mark its mortalities. But during those five years before its ores were found to be of an only superficial order, it acquired a population of seven thousand with saloons, billiard parlors and dance halls in proportion, three railroads, a skyscraper and a hotel of widely acclaimed magnificence. To be sure, one of the railroads never was completed, the skyscraper rose only three breathless floors above the street level and the Southern Hotel's resources included no more than two well-advertised baths, but Rhyolite was a metropolis and its grim skeleton stands to this day above the Amargosa Desert to prove it.

Rhyolite saw the last considerable confluence of the prospectors and investors, speculative stock riggers, rich men and high-graders ever to forgather in the name of an assayer's report in a West already feeling more than a touch of the twentieth century in its bones. It was the last important discovery to be made by Shorty Harris, although several years later he was credited with the unrewarding strike at Harrisberry. E. A. Montgomery was soon to load a forty-ton shipment of $500 ore from his Montgomery Shoshone Mine. Key Pittman, later Nevada's most famous United States Senator of modern times, was early on the scene. Samuel Newhouse, James Farrell and Senator Thomas Kearns were all present.

As had been the case in the mines further north, Rhyolite early rejoiced in the presence of the great and the assistant great. Tasker L. Oddie of Tonopah wealth and fame appeared as organizer of the Bullfrog Mining Company; Malcolm Macdonald registered at the Southern, presumably rating one of the celebrated baths, and the omnipresent Senator Clark of Montana, by now an almost legendary figure wherever mines were being developed and promoted, was ready to get in on a good thing. Perhaps the Senator's notable penchant for traveling in style in his ornate private car was responsible for the boom of Rhyolite as a railroad center with the Tonopah and Tidewater, the Las Vegas and Tonopah and the Tonopah and Bullfrog sharing the imperishable depot a half mile up the wash from the imposing Overbury Building.

The emergence of the Bullfrog district with its three townships and promises of becoming a metropolitan district with three railroads is one of the most amazing dreams ever to parallel the outlines of the other mirages for which the Nevada desert is famous. Beatty had, as it still has today, water, not in Niagaras but in quantities to support a more considerable civilization than ever materialized, and pipelines were laid to Rhyolite.

## BUILT FOR THE AGES

The substantial depot at Rhyolite was being built when this picture was taken. Today it is a desert beer parlor and, excepting the "Bottle House," the only structure standing in the once populous city.

Induced by the attraction of water, of which it had none and insufficient justification for piping it in, Bullfrog removed itself bodily up the wash and joined Rhyolite in the delights of urban existence.

The projection of any railroad into this remote and hitherto almost uninhabited region would have been daring; three was the quintessence of optimism and yet for several years Beatty and Rhyolite gloried in the daily arrival and departure of scheduled passenger trains (toward the end, mixed consists) over the Tonopah and Tidewater and the Las Vegas and Tonopah, and as recently as the middle thirties the Tonopah and Tidewater's gas-electric combines in the winter months showed up with overnight Pullmans out of Los Angeles filled with eager passengers enlisted on tourist agency prowls through Death Valley.

To this day, too, the cuts and fills of the Las Vegas and Tonopah are visible paralleling the road down to Beatty from Goldfield, occasionally crossing it and serving as a reminder that the ghost cities of the north were linked to the ghost cities of the Bullfrog by what is now a ghostly railroad with once large traffickings. The Las Vegas and Tonopah lived a short life and sold its rails during the first World War at what was commonly reported to be a handsome profit over their original cost.

The annals of Wells Fargo, which had arrived in Rhyolite in 1905, were short and comparatively simple. Most of the Bullfrog treasure, which never amounted to more than a trifling $3,000,000 during the five brief years of the boom, was shipped out over the little mixed trains of the Tonopah and

Tidewater to Ludlow on the Santa Fe and it went under the way-bills and was underwritten by the untarnishable guarantee of Wells Fargo. But there was scant need of the guard's Winchesters aboard the little combines of the T & T and the Wells Fargo agents who made the eight-mile trip down the desert to Bullfrog for an occasional consignment of high-grade in an auto stage were more concerned for blowouts and carburetor trouble than for road agents. The *Rhyolite Bulletin* was hard put to it to chronicle anything more hair-raising than the conventional Saturday night breaches of the peace common to any mining community.

Rhyolite was almost as celebrated for its possession and distribution of ice as it was for the Montgomery-Shoshone or the mines of Bonanza Mountain. Before the completion of either the Las Vegas and Tonopah or the Tonopah and Tidewater railroads, Wells Fargo was in the ice-express business as it had elsewhere been in the business of hauling oysters, fresh fish and cut flowers. At first the ice came down by four- and six-horse stage, enjoying a priority over everything but the mails, and it cost ten cents a pound — at Goldfield. It started out in big cakes wrapped in burlap and insulated with sawdust and usually it had diminished to a quarter or a fifth of its original proportions by the time it reached the bins of the Rhyolite Bottling Works, the Bonanza Hotel or the Imperial Grill. Iced drinks, in consequence, were two bits a copy when the universal price of whisky slings without ice was two for a quarter.

As was inevitable, Charlie Schwab arrived in person at Rhyolite and put up at the Southern Hotel, taking one of the bathrooms. The news photographs show him departing from the Southern in the bucket seat of a high-busted Reo touring car crowded with Western characters in Mormons and Eastern capitalists in wonderfully incongruous bowler hats.

Schwab arrived in Nevada aboard his fabulous private car, the *Loretto*, but left this paradigm of rolling palaces in the yards of the Tonopah and Goldfield at Goldfield while making the trip down to the Bullfrog in an automobile. The *Loretto* excited the natives of Goldfield even more than Senator Clark's car had done at the time of the big fight. It had a marble bathtub, gold-plated beds and chandeliers, gold-plated plumbing fixtures and transom windows in its clerestory of Flemish stained glass. The woodwork was solid Cuban mahogany, triple ply, with inlaid marquetry and intricate carvings of cupids around the edges of the upper berths. There were also painted cupids pursuing each other in endless procession around the hand-painted ceilings, like cops in a Keystone comedy. Goldfield was both outraged and gratified by the cupids. They provoked strange, episcene jests.

In the observation compartment of the *Loretto* were huge, overupholstered leather bankers' thrones with fringed tassels around the bottoms. The upholstery on the banquets in the dining salon was tufted like the lining of an expensive coffin and of rose-point tapestry. Electroliers blossomed madly with Mazda bulbs from the ceilings like fireworks sprays against a night sky. There was enough marquetry, ormolu and Morocco leather aboard the *Loretto* to outfit a branch store for W & J Sloane of New York's Fifth Avenue and Mr. Schwab offered all visitors Vega del Rey cigars which cost a dollar apiece from a gold-fitted mahogany humidor specially designed for him by the chief curator of cigars at Park and Tilford. There was nothing cheap about Mr. Schwab. You can still see the *Loretto* if you are in South Carolina, where it is the business car of the president of the Lancaster and Chester RR, the celebrated Elliott White Springs. Mr. Springs, who owns the largest cotton mills in the South and is a tycoon of bounce and imagination, bought the car from the Schwab estate in 1939 for $2,500. The cherubs that excited Goldfield back in 1906 are still visible. *Ars longa, vita brevis!*

The presence of Schwab, who had already invested heavily in paying properties in Tonopah and Goldfield, like the presence of Baruch, Senator Clark and other national names, was a windfall to Bullfrog publicists who reported the great man's least remark as if it were inspired by a combination of the Holy Ghost and J. P. Morgan. Schwab, taking time off from his pipe-organ meditations to journey West, bought out all of Bob Montgomery's holdings in the Montgomery-Shoshone and picked up the water rights on the Amargosa River which were to have their justification in an eight-mile pipe line through the desert to Rhyolite. "With such a man at the head of affairs, Beatty will become the camp of the Bullfrog district," remarked the *Bullfrog Miner* complacently. "His influence will bring railroads, smelters and capital."

Rhyolite lasted for five good years of burro racing, Fourth of July parades and beer-hall carousing. Indeed its fame and fortune rested almost as securely, which was in fact somewhat precariously in its later years, on the circumstance that it possessed an ice plant and sold beer chilled to freeze the sinuses at the gratifying price of a nickel a gelid bottle. In the Amargosa Desert this was an asset on a par with $500 ore. When the bottom fell out of its ledges in 1909, the resulting exodus of Rhyolite's 7,000 citizens left behind it more beer bottles than it did mining machinery.

Towering above its own debris-filled vaults and the adjacent cellarage of Wells Fargo, the façade of the Overbury Building is still an astonishment to the desert and a reproach to its promise. In a grave below the town, in full sight of this classic ruin, and from whose mound, piled in 1907, the rain has washed no appreciable gravel, lies John Overbury himself.

Despite its existence, as a melancholy monument to human aspirations, within full view from the highway that leads over Sunrise Pass into Death Valley, Rhyolite gets few visitors. Bullfrog, further down in the desert and lacking even a signpost on the highway, gets none at all. A grizzled veteran, who now owns the lease on what is left of the mines at Bullfrog, discourages visitors with a barbed-wire fence and a double-barreled, twelve-gage shotgun. Now and then he takes a little jewelry ore out of the property and sells it in Los Angeles as his modest needs require, and it is his claim, maintained either on a basis of truth or simply to cover a distaste for visitors, that the

## GOLDEN STREET IN YEARS OF PROMISE

Looking north in Golden Street, Rhyolite on the Fourth of July, 1907, the spectator found the Miner's Union in patriotic parade, but as yet no cement sidewalks, no Cook Bank Building. During its boom years more than $80,000,000 were invested in properties in Rhyolite and Bullfrog, but only $3,000,000 in gold was ever produced by its much-touted mines. Old-timers recall that Rhyolite, with its modern improvements, was almost as celebrated for its ice-cold beer, a novelty in the midst of the Amargosa Desert, as it was for its true fissures. Golden Street never was paved save with golden promises and today (below) is a desert highway to ruin and futility.

ore is so commonly encountered exposed on the surface that he cannot afford to entertain persons who might turn out to be souvenir hunters.

Beatty, a filling-station pause for motorists en route to Las Vegas, possesses slightly more animation. A handful of professional veterans of the boom are on hand in its dusty saloons to beguile the solvent and willing traveler with tales of the old days. Beatty has what it has always possessed, shade, water, tranquillity and for one or two days each week, ice. It also has as hitching posts, porch supports and other architectural incidentals where wood is required, most of the staircases, window frames and floor timbers of Rhyolite. These are tangible and even credible souvenirs. Beatty itself doesn't believe the rumors that it circulates slyly in its six saloons: that Eastern capital is even at this moment being poured into the abandoned drifts and shafts of Rhyolite. This talk is too common currency in every mining camp of the West to be negotiable on any terms at all.

Every now and then the interested searcher or antiquarian who knows that the Nevada of the last bonanza is, in actual fact, as remote as the civilizations of the Euphrates valley and often far more fascinating, will encounter in the bookstalls of San Francisco or Los Angeles a well-preserved copy of one of the mining-camp papers. The pictorial edition of the *Rhyolite Herald* for March, 1909, is liberally awash with the oval-framed halftones, stylish at the time in periodical make-up, of heavily mustached capitalists in dress evening linen and double-truck layouts of the more solvent aspects of Rhyolite's civic properties and existence.

Only in the face of such evidence of the mutability of human devisings can one apprehend the true grandeur and pathos of the legends of the Nevada desert. Here, in vivid example of the engraver's technique, is the Montgomery Shoshone, a half-mile panorama of hoists, ore dumps, railroad spurs, tramways, terraced reducing mills and enginehouses with smoke pouring from their tall chimneys. In the realm of such factual realities, at least, the camera doesn't lie. Here is the graduating class of the Rhyolite High School with flowered rosettes at its proud bosoms and diploma in hand, on commencement day; here is Miss Dorothy Hubbard and her posy garden, even by comparison to the Overbury Building, a miracle in the Amargosa;

### "WHEN I WAS A KING AND A MASON, A BUILDER PROVEN AND SKILLED . . ."

A year or two after Shorty Harris first prospected the Bullfrog District in southern Nevada, the flourishing town of Rhyolite was served by no fewer than three railroads, had its own telephone exchange, paved sidewalks, metropolitan hotels and office buildings of modern steel and concrete construction. Conspicuous among them was the banking establishment of John S. Cook & Co., in Golden Street. Forty years later Rhyolite was inhabited by two people and the Cook Bank looked out through ghostly windows upon the implacable reaches of the Amargosa Desert, a monument to the lost cause of precious metals and bonanza times.

here the staff of the Imperial Grill in dinner jackets and chef's hats gathered in Golden Street for their photograph; here the proud interior of James A. Moffat & Co., licensed brokers with mahogany desks and stock tickers connected by direct wire to San Francisco; here the façade of the Stock Exchange Cigar Stand, distributors of Cuesta Reys, Fastidios, La Correctas and Van Dyke Coronas.

In Kipling's *Recessional* there is mention of the almost unremembered pomps of Nineveh and Tyre. Surely a later and more comprehensive "Recessional" will have, in its Doomsday stanzas of awe and abnegation, some mention of Panamint or Hamilton, Greenwater, Aurora or Rhyolite.

## IV: RAWHIDE

THE town of Rawhide was the classic and the climax of all the promotional technique, the ballyhoo, high pressure, high grading and high binding of the last bonanza. In its almost wholly spurious precincts the last vestigial traces of the Old West — the covered wagon, the grizzled prospector and the frontier gambler — went into their act abetted by such modern properties as the Stanley Steamer, the long-distance telephone and the expert technological swindler and promoter. The dynamite-laden burro, the bearded ancient with his samples of high-grade and the Colt's Frontier single-action equalizer were nothing more than atmosphere with which to lend the verisimilitude of authenticity to a single mine whose ore ran as high as $1,000 a ton and which was used by Nat Goodwin, Riley Grannan and Tex Rickard to substantiate the belief that here was a second Comstock, a Golconda to make even Goldfield look to its bay leaves.

At Rawhide the biography of every one of the twentieth-century gold camps was reproduced in perfect microcosm. The Nevada scene generally was going through a period of stagnation in 1907. The insurance payments to speculative-minded San Franciscans following the fire of April, 1906, had been exhausted. Eastern capital was consolidating its holdings in Tonopah and Goldfield; something new and dazzling was needed on the mining horizon and that something was supplied with a minimum of reality and an absolute maximum of colorful fakements by Goodwin, Grannan and Rickard with the assistance of H. W. Knickerbocker and George Graham Rice. They pulled all the stops and the resulting organ music swelled across the Nevada desert into every bourse and mining exchange of the world, sonorous, magniloquent, seductive and bogus.

Rawhide was premeditated, commercial, speculative and almost wholly phoney, but Rickard and his friends had fun with it and the tumults of its promotion and the rocketlike ascent of its property values and their almost immediate and resounding return to earth make its name remembered to this day in Nevada where other mining centers of greater promise and authenticity have been forgotten.

## A RAWHIDE ALBUM

By the time Rawhide came into being the Nevada desert smoked and steamed with Locomobiles, Moons, Templars, Apperson Jack Rabbits, Oldsmobiles and Thomas Flyers. Here is an old chain-drive model in Nevada Street about to take off with the Wells Fargo treasure box for Manhattan. Below is an old-time prospector who still favored the burro although the gasoline age was already at hand when this photograph was taken as is evidenced by the tire tracks in the sand. At the bottom is Tex Rickard's Northern Saloon at Rawhide, the third of its name in the Rickard saga. Predecessors were in Nome and Goldfield.

The first intelligence of Rawhide exploded across the general consciousness when the inimitable Rickard's hand made itself subtly felt in foot-high letters across the façade of a Goldfield Methodist church with the legend: "This Church is Closed: God has Gone to Rawhide." Inquiry by immediately interested parties disclosed that the Rawhide strike was located approximately a hundred miles north of Tonopah, and a few days later, also inspired by Rickard, *The Goldfield Review* printed a Rawhide extra booming the property in fabulous superlatives. Rickard himself lent prestige to the bonanza by selling out his interest in the Northern at Goldfield, climbing behind the wheel of a Lozier touring car and driving across the desert 150 miles in a single day, no mean feat in itself in the motorcars of 1908, to open a new Northern at Rawhide with a bar a hundred feet long and every known game of chance located handily adjacent.

Rawhide was already crawling with crooks, confidence men and bogus-stock salesmen, and the one factually operating mine, the Rawhide Coalition, was stacking high-grade in gunny sacks in the public streets where it would do the most good while awaiting shipment. A boulder in the middle of the main street where it constituted a traffic obstruction was dynamited by the highway department and its fragments assayed at upward of $300 a ton. A badly calculated blast of giant powder in a ledge above the town smashed most of the windows in the community and the shards, when recovered from the soft-pine façades and anatomies of the passersby, were found to be equally promising. Rawhide was literally blasted into fame.

Rawhide went through the ecstasies and anguish of boom and bust in terms of the superlative never known before or since to any Western camp. It flowered into instant and good gracious existence overnight and within a fortnight of its inception was going great guns with its own newspaper and a publicity machine such as had never before undertaken the exploitation of any mining community. *The Rawhide Rustler*, a paper "different from other papers and we thank the Gods of prose and verse that it is different," was pitched to a continuous and piercing scream of editorial triumph as "the pioneer in the Greatest Gold Camp in the World."

All roads led to Rawhide. Rawhide was surprising the mining world. Hello girls would soon be located in Rawhide. The richness of the latest Rawhide strike amazed experts. Rawhide was without comparison in the civilized world. Montana's greatest banker, E. W. King, was stricken with amazement at Rawhide's wonder. Rawhide realty was leaping upward. *Collier's Weekly* was to boost Rawhide. A $100,000 hotel was to be built immediately in Rawhide. Experts announced that Rawhide drinking water had beneficial qualities. Rawhide was startling the mining world. Charles G. ("Betch-a-Million") Gates was interesting himself in Rawhide property. Rawhide was a modern Monte Carlo. Nearly solid gold was uncovered in the world's greatest gold camp. Tex Rickard invited the United States Navy to visit Rawhide. Lack of time prevented the United States Fleet from visiting Rawhide. Dynamite shots disclosed glittering gold in Rawhide. All hell was breaking day and night in Rawhide.

These and other modest claims were the headline material of which the *Rawhide Rustler* was built. The camp seethed and roared and performed wild sarabands among the grammatical resources of an editorial staff which operated, like many a better and worse newspaper before and since, from editorial offices handily located in the Balloon Bar or around the corner at The High Grade Saloon. Wells Fargo operated out of Rawhide to Luning from The Butler Saloon and Auto Office in Main Street which was, after all, no more than the 1908 parallel of the stage lines which in a thousand Western communities before it had operated from tavern-terminal to terminal-tavern. Only the bullion chest was hoisted into the tonneau of a Pope-Apperson instead of an Abbot-Downing Concord. If the chug-buggy got out of town without pausing at the Chickencock, The Belmont or the Yellowstone it was sure to stop on the Luning road at the Midway Station to strain fuel gasoline through chamois to exclude alien substances and perform a more or less similar office for the passengers. Sometimes the box went out in six-cylinder Chadwick Racers or "commodious" Thomas touring cars.

What was perhaps the last armed robbery of Wells Fargo in the classic stage holdup style occurred in Rawhide when a coach bound from the mines was waylaid and the Wells Fargo strongbox stolen by masked miscreants.

"One of the most daring robberies in the history of Nevada took place this afternoon six miles from Rawhide," declaimed the *Rustler*, "when two masked men held up the stage bound for the camp and got away with the Wells Fargo express box. It is reported that the box contained $12,000 for the mine payroll. The largest individual loser is the Consolidation Company which is reputed to have lost $7,000. The robbery took place at one o'clock. It was two hours later before the information reached Rawhide, when a posse under the direction of Captain Cox of the State Police rushed to the scene of the holdup in automobiles. The six-horse stage was swinging around the curve at the upper end of the Regent district when the cry of halt came from behind an outcropping. Before the passengers could look out one of the robbers had a grip on the leaders with one hand while the other held a 44-caliber revolver pointed at Tony Cano, the driver. The other robber had a revolver pointed in the direction of the stage. Both came forward leisurely, the taller one ordering the driver to throw out the Wells Fargo treasure box. No attempt was made to molest the passengers and the men were last seen attempting to pry the lid off the treasure box with a chisel."

The saga of Rawhide would be justified in the annals of the West in transition if for nothing more than the classic episode of the fashionably daring English novelist, Mrs. Elinor Glyn. Mrs. Glyn, a three days' sensation on the strength of her torrid bestseller, *Three Weeks*, was promoted into investigating Stingaree Gulch by Nat Goodwin, who had formed a bowing acquaintance with the lady while touring in England, and the reporters and

## MANHATTAN, LAST OF THE STAGING STATIONS

On the Nevada highroad between Manhattan and Rawhide Wells Fargo was for
the last time held up aboard the horse-drawn stage of the great tradition. After
that it traveled by the auto stages of the Nevada Rapid Transit Co., one of whose
Pope-Toledo Flyers with a bowler-hatted stager at the wheel is shown at the
bottom of the page. Manhattan's main street boasted no paving, but free lunch
was available, as the sign says, day and night in its better saloons and its Merchant's Hotel pointed with pride to a bathroom on each of its two floors.

photographers were on hand, liberally sluiced with free booze and with pencils and Folmer Graflex cameras poised for every word or gesture of literary cheescake. The affair was the quintessence of corn.

During her tour of the bagnios and boozing kennels of the Gulch, some deserted shacks were fired and she was able to witness the Rawhide fire brigade in action. Later, at the Northern, while she was being entertained with frontier anecdotes and jargon directly rehearsed from Bret Harte, masked gunmen staged a holdup, flourishing firearms and swearing oaths that would have astounded the invading armies of Flanders. Upon learning the identity of their fair victim, the bandits retired in pretty confusion, confessing that she was too hot an article for them to handle. The bandits had been recruited from the town's more substantial citizens and during this frontier interlude real gunmen held up the business premises of one of them and escaped with a substantial sum.

Photographers' flares created a plausible facsimile of the burning of San Francisco as the reception committee presented Mrs. Glyn with a token of its esteem: a pearl-handled or lady's model six gun which she was later able to display in the drawing rooms of England and the Continent as a souvenir of her experiences in the howling wilderness of America. The resultant publicity was very gratifying.

A few weeks later Mrs. Glyn, by this time having recovered her composure and studied the accounts of her adventures as recorded in the press of the world from the seclusion of her suite at the Riverside Hotel in Reno, saw fit to protest strenuously against the manner in which her seeing the elephant had been played up. "The wagers we laid were nothing," she announced in an attempt to abate the tumults in the Hearst press in an age when no respectable woman had yet smoked a cigarette in public in America. "Women do that sort of thing all the time without attracting comment in Monte Carlo."

Rawhide at once seized upon this implied association with the aristocracy of the Old World, and for some Saturdays thereafter the *Rustler* missed no opportunity to allude grandly to the many points of similarity enjoyed by Rawhide and the Riviera.

Seven months after God had gone to Rawhide at the personal invitation of Tex Rickard and Nat Goodwin, its false-front economy boasted the possession of forty-eight mine hoists either in operation or on order, a population just under 10,000, four stage lines and thirty-four auto stages, an electric light and water plant, a steam laundry, telephones and a telegraph station. There were also one school, forty-one saloons, four churches, obvious evidence that God had safely arrived at Rawhide, one theater, twenty-eight restaurants, six reducing mills with a capacity of 1,000 tons daily and twelve hotels.

This was in July, 1908. On September 5th of the same year fire started in Banfield's Drug Store, spread in the twinkling of an eye to the Ross Hotel in Nevada Street and an hour later all that remained of Rawhide was a cloud of smoke drifting gently across the Nevada sagebrush in the general direction of the Reese. For a brief interlude after that the Poor Boy, Hooligan

## "DUST INTO DUST, AND UNDER DUST, TO LIE

The Apperson Jackrabbit with its right-hand drive and without a windshield gives a date to this piece. It is Nevada Street, Rawhide, Nevada, 1908. Rawhide came into being as a promotion scheme of Tex Rickard and his swaggering associates and it was in its celebrated "Stingaree Gulch" that Elinor Glyn, the lady novelist, was presented with a pearl-handled derringer. In the foreground a newsboy may be seen peddling the latest edition of *The Rawhide Rustler*, while under the window of Evans the lawyer a hokey-pokey man does a brisk business in lemonade and popcorn. Wells Fargo last rode behind six horses out of Rawhide.

288

SANS WINE, SANS SONG, SANS SINGER, AND — SANS END!"

As late as 1949 the Rawhide Queen, once a great bonanza property, was still in operation, but gone was Rickard's second Northern Saloon, and "Stingaree Gulch" was only a memory in the files of *The Rawhide Rustler*. None of the mining towns of Nevada, not even Candelaria or Hamilton, have disappeared from the face of the earth as completely as Rawhide and these two pictures, taken forty-odd years apart from the identical site, bear witness that the contrivings of man are but an allegory of futility. Wells Fargo will not go back there again.

Hill, Rawhide-King, the Mascott-Bullion and a few other mines continued to produce, but the end was already in sight.

As late as the turn of 1909 Mass was still being said in Riley Grannan's Saloon where, after the Saturday night dance, the barroom nudes and flagons of spirits were shrouded with tarpauline and the Host was elevated before a packing case turned into an altar. But Wells Fargo had long since packed up its gold scales and removed itself from Rawhide, pausing only briefly at the Midway Station on the Luning road for its gasoline through chamois and a quick noggin through the handle-bar mustaches of K. J. Watterson, who would return to his agency at Mina wiser but not necessarily sadder for a few months spent among the superlatives of Rawhide. By now the doors of Grannan's Saloon were squeaking on their hinges, and a few months later the site of these palatial parlors, purchased at a reputed price of $40,000 for the lot alone, might have been claimed by any desert squatter who took a fancy to its location.

A final period was put to the Old West, to Rawhide and to Riley Grannan by the death of the last of these, and the funeral oration which was to become one of the folk legends of the last bonanza. Before the sands had run out on Rawhide, Grannan, the foremost product of the gambling fever of the times, caught pneumonia and died. His funeral was paid for by Nat Goodwin and his body, in accordance with his wishes, sent back to be buried under the blue grass of his native Kentucky, but the eulogy pronounced over him by H. W. Knickerbocker, a former minister and mining-camp orator, has passed into the literature of the region and will forever stand as a paradigm of the florid and melancholy style in which it was cast. It has since been reprinted too widely to occupy that space here. It has appeared in pamphlet form and in innumerable chronicles of the age as well as in magazines devoted to Western adventure and annals, and it was but a few months after the delivery of its sonorous clichés that, like Riley Grannan, Rawhide too was ashes and dust upon the face of the earth. The last of the bonanzas had run its course.

# CHAPTER XI

## The Last Roundup

THE last big-time armed robbery attempted against a Wells Fargo treasure shipment carried by train took place in 1912 aboard the Southern Pacific's then *Sunset Express,* now known as the *Sunset Limited, Train No. 1,* westbound at Dryden, approximately 325 miles east of El Paso. A slow enough run even on today's carding, the haul through the Texas desert in 1912 was unbelievably wearisome, and the Espee's big Pacifics, used in tandem on the smoky end of long, heavy trains of head-end revenue cars and Pullmans on this run, paused whenever one of them was low in fuel water, which was frequently. The late Joseph Dyer, general superintendent of the Southern Pacific for many years, once said that even if *No. 1* hadn't stopped for water at Dryden it would have been no accomplishment for two misguided thugs to have boarded the train while it was rolling at its greatest acceleration on that particular stretch of iron.

When Wells Fargo's Messenger David A. Troutsdale was confronted in his compartment with a fellow unknown to him personally but obviously contriving harm against the company in terms of a Winchester rifle of outmoded but nonetheless powerful 40-82 caliber, he was as meek as a lamb. The armed stranger wanted to know where the currency consignment was carried, a question which at once proved him the rankest sort of amateur, and Troutsdale picked up a wooden mallet, more conventionally used for smashing ice for the water cooler, and smote him on the back of the head with such lively smiting that the man fell down completely and satisfactorily dead.

The resourceful Troutsdale, now in possession of a fine shooting rifle, prudently ascertained that there was a heavy, black powder-charged slug in the chamber and more in the magazine in case they were needed, stepped to the door of his car, took careful aim at a confederate who was waiting outside, and blew what brains the man possessed all over the desert.

It is pleasant to remark that Wells Fargo remembered their trusty messenger with a fine gold watch, the traditional Wells Fargo accolade since earliest shooting times, and that the passengers of the *Sunset Express* bought him a gold-mounted fob to go with it. Although there is no record that Troutsdale wasn't satisfied, as much could not be said for the pastor of his home-town church in Columbia, Tennessee, who thought that saving $65,000 for his employer was worth something negotiable to back up the sentiment. Nearly a quarter of a century later he prevailed upon the Congress of the United

### BAD END FOR A BRACE OF BAD MEN

When Wells Fargo's redoubtable Agent Troutsdale had finished with his bung-starter and Winchester, the last two bandits to attempt the holdup of Wells Fargo aboard a railroad train were tossed into the baggage cars of the Southern Pacific's westbound varnish and taken to Anderson, Texas. There willing hands propped up their remains for a photographer, and the tradition of robbing Wells Fargo aboard the cars, inaugurated so long ago at Verdi, came to a close.

States to give Troutsdale a cash reward of $1,000 on the grounds that he had saved registered mail.

Thus, first in 1870, and last in 1912, it was demonstrated that attempting to play armed hanky-panky with Wells Fargo aboard the trains could lead to neither health nor wealth, although it might be conducive of a certain sort of ex post facto wisdom.

For many years, ending with the conclusion of the first decade of the twentieth century, the express companies of the nation had maintained a complete monopoly of the shipment and delivery of small packages and merchandise of less than freight proportions. By the terms of the favorable corporation laws of the era, nobody, save their directors, knew exactly what were their profits, but almost every interested person was aware that earnings were far above anything which was being passed on to the public shareholders. The great dividend melon cut by Wells Fargo in 1910, when there was a stock payment to stockholders of 200 per cent and a cash disbursement of 100 per cent, was sufficient evidence of that. Stockholders in the Southern Express Co., who had not been permitted to hold a meeting since the year 1862, were understandably interested in the Wells Fargo bonus. Interested, hell! They were as fascinated as clergymen at a leg show!

What was more, the practices of the express companies were becoming increasingly arrogant and the customers were complaining that the manners of clerks at railroad depots in Cairo, Illinois, and Trinidad, Colorado, were indistinguishable from those of an untipped maître d'hôtel at Delmonico's. Express charges were self-determined and subject to only the most ginger inspection by the then far from self-assured I. C. C., an organization which was later to become a fuss-budget and nuisance on an almost cosmic scale. Often full payment of charges was required upon acceptance of express matter and, if the recipient at the other end bore any faintest resemblance to Caspar Milquetoast, he was blandly charged full payment again upon delivery. Such practices tended to occasion public comment, and here and there desperately aggrieved individuals who had suffered some peculiarly hideous outrage were heard to mutter that maybe the Federal Government should start a parcels post.

When, in 1913, the government parcels post was in actual fact inaugurated, it was received with glad acclaim and resounding huzzahs by all but the express companies. When, shortly afterward, the I. C. C. took its foot in its hand, as the darkies used to say, and ordered a reduction of rates, a number of express companies expressed their corporate indignation by closing up shop then and there. Wells Fargo, scorning such measures, and still in possession of franchises over 99,000 express miles over land and water, cut their operating expenses and continued to make money, but on a less inflammatory scale. Actually, Wells Fargo was at peace with its stockholders and had for so long been an American household word that to abuse it more than with tolerant affection was the equivalent of defaming mother, the flag or Father John's Cough Medicine.

When, in 1917, the United States entered the war in Europe, the military, sometimes with justification and always with a fine fury of patriotism, clapped hands on a great deal of railway equipment for government business including freight, baggage and express cars. Shipments of freight were delayed for unconscionable periods; foodstuffs which, to any but the military mind, would seem essential to a nation at war, perished by the hundreds of train-loads, and the claims that piled up against the express companies became astronomical. For the first time in decades, Wells Fargo was operating at a loss, and the deficit of all American express companies combined was running to $1,500,000 a month. Then, on May 28, 1918, Woodrow Wilson's son-in-law, William Gibbs McAdoo, announced the merger of the four leading express companies, Wells Fargo, Adams, the American and the Southern, into the American Railway Express Co., to be operated by the United States Railroad Administration by lease over the nation's railroads.

The Southern and a large number of minor expresses went out of existence forever. Three, however, maintained their corporate identities. One was Adams, which became an investment trust company. Another was the American (not to be confused with the American Railway Express of which its former express services were now a part), which to this day maintains head-quarters in New York and is engaged in the business of traveler's checks, remittances and travel agencies in all parts of the world. Wells Fargo's express department, long separated from the banking department of Wells Fargo & Co., in the great merger of 1918 still contrived to retain a hold on its agencies in Mexico and Cuba and eventually became a subsidiary of the American Express Co.

Wells Fargo's banking department is, of course, and as elsewhere detailed, still in continuous and uninterrupted operation in San Francisco in the form of the Wells Fargo Bank & Union Trust Co.

As a subsidiary of the American Express, the name Wells Fargo is now associated with an armored-car service in metropolitan New York, a car-loading service, customs brokerage and commercial representation in Cuba, the importation of Mexican fruit and vegetables to the United States and Canada, and the commercial representation of American firms, travel service and express in Mexico.

Wells Fargo has always, in one capacity or another, been identified with Mexico, and a highly agreeable evidence of its versatility south of the Rio Grande is familiar to thousands of tourists today in the form of the Rancho Telva in the exotic city of Taxco, for centuries the classic overnight stopping place on the road from Mexico City to Acapulco. Rancho Telva is named for opera singer Marian Telva whose husband, Elmer Jones, is president of Wells Fargo of Mexico and a man who has long been identified with the destinies of the expresses in that unpredictable and often tumultuous republic. Jones's company is not only in the hotel and express business but also has been the agent and courier for thousands of American tourists and almost wholly responsible for the vast popularity in recent years of Acapulco as a resort of uncommon attractions and facilities for pleasure.

Back in the middle years of the nineteenth century Wells Fargo maintained an important agency in Acapulco where in 1872 it started to do business with the courtly dons of Mexican finance, although it didn't acquire quarters in Mexico City until the middle eighties. Acapulco with its great shipping in those years and its access to the Orient was more important to Wells Fargo than the national capital, and its affairs were transacted by a long succession of agents in a spacious old office still remembered for its stout vaults, cool patios and incessantly moving punkahs which, in an age innocent of air conditioning and in a civilization where electric fans would have been an anachronism, kept the tropical air in motion with an intricate system of belts, cordage and machinery in the high ceilings of the establishment. Wells Fargo and a drugstore across the street were, until the turn of the century, almost the only American enterprises in old, sleepy Acapulco, and the conduct of its affairs assumed a quality of Castilian leisure and elegance which would have been notably out of place in Wells Fargo's premises in San Francisco or, say, Virginia City. For decades at a time the gold fifty-peso pieces flowed in an undisturbed stream over its counters and across its scales and thence down to the shimmering Pacific in proud sailing vessels with hardly a hitch in the ordered and tranquil routine of their going.

Wells Fargo came into the Mexican capital when British engineers and British investors built the spectacular narrow-gage railway, only changed to broad gage in 1948, between Vera Cruz and Mexico City. Until that year its picturesque little overnight trains with their diminutive sleepers, diners and coaches, many of them originally built for the narrow gages of Colorado in the seventies and eighties, were a celebrated institution south of the Rio Grande and much admired by amateurs of the antiquities of railroading. In 1948, however, and in conformance with a reorganization of the government-owned railroads on a national scale, the entire trackage was broad-gaged, almost in the twinkling of an eye, a feat of engineering which compared favorably in its execution with the original laying of the three-foot iron through the incredible forests and over the mountain grades between Puebla, Oriental and Jalapa.

But although it subscribed to the drowsy atmosphere of Acapulco and came in on the narrow-gage railroad, Wells Fargo in Mexico was a strictly broad-gage business up till the time the government seized a major portion of the nation's railroads and the Wells Fargo contract between Mexico City and the Gulf ports was abrogated. Wells Fargo's last rail contract south of the border was the Sud Pacific de Mexico, with whose great parent company the destinies of the express company have always been so closely identified. Since 1908 the formal title of the firm in Mexico has been Wells Fargo & Company, Express, Mexico, S. A., with a capitalization of $1,000,000.

Elmer Jones has been a Wells Fargo executive and later its president in Mexico since the closing years of the golden regime of Porfirio Diaz, the old dictator, and as Wells Fargo began losing its hold on the hitherto rich monopoly it had enjoyed in the express business in the series of tumults and revolutions since 1910, Jones looked around for new fields of endeavor and profit for the firm. American enterprise generally was effectively looted by the long series of military adventurers who followed one another as quickly as they could murder their rivals, but Wells Fargo maintained itself by the evolution of a vast and lucrative tourist business, most of which came into being through the agency of Elmer Jones. In 1925, it chartered the White Star Liner *Calgaric* for a series of voyages down the Atlantic coast to Vera Cruz where Wells Fargo took its tourists in charge for tours of the inland sights and wonders of the republic and eventually shipped them north to California out of Acapulco on a group of liners also specially chartered for this purpose.

The tourist business in Mexico proved to be another Wells Fargo bonanza and it came to Jones's mind that what his charges needed was a first-rate hotel on the long, old China Road built centuries ago between Mexico City and Acapulco. There were plenty of good stopping places along the ascent from the Gulf on the Atlantic side: at Orizaba, at Jalapa, even in the largely industrial city of Puebla, but none on the western descent to the Pacific. To remedy this hiatus Wells Fargo built the Rancho Telva, which is one of the flossiest, dressiest and most opulent caravansaries in a country noted for the excellence of its hotels and tourist accommodations. Its terraces, verandas and multiplicity of public apartments look down upon the incredibly picturesque and romantic town of Taxco with its silversmiths, saddleries, its tiny public park with comfortable benches in the shade of ageless trees, its bandstand, open-air restaurants and other pleasances, all dominated by the richly baroque cathedral which has been painted, photographed and appraised by tourists more than any other single structure in Old Mexico.

Taxco, in its life and tangible properties, its atmosphere and legend, is about as close as any place in the modern world can come to resemble the century in which Wells Fargo came into being. There isn't much in Taxco that wasn't there in 1852 when Wells Fargo moved into San Francisco, and what there is is discreetly hidden behind an old-world facade of ordered antiquity. Wells Fargo likes being in the hotel business and intends to stay there. It is still, of course, in the express business to a limited extent south of the Rio Grande and in the armed messenger service in New York and intends to stay there too.

But the heart of Wells Fargo's being is still, a century minus three years after it first came into existence, in Montgomery Street. The Wells Fargo Bank and Union Trust Company is no longer in the express business but it is still very much in the banking business, and a vital and active factor in the lives and imaginations of all Californians.

After the world-shaking collapse of the Bank of California back in 1875 and the death of Ralston in such equivocal circumstances that its mystery has never yet been solved, William S. O'Brien, most liberal and least publicized of the Bonanza Kings, together with James Flood, John Mackay and James G. Fair organized the Nevada Bank, named for the source of the

## WELLS FARGO IN OLD MEXICO

In the above photograph Wells Fargo rides the mail stage leaving Quito for Mazatlan about 1910. Below is a picturesque vignette of the Ranch Telva at Taxco on the old China road from Mexico City to Acapulco.

## WELLS FARGO
## ON WHEELS

In 1910, Wells Fargo's insigne was painted on the baggage compartments of these motors of the Central California Traction Co., near Sacramento. Below is the so-called "coin wagon" delivering currency to the firm's customers and making collections in Oakland about 1912. At the bottom of the page is an authentic "express wagon" in San Francisco during the nineties. The horsepower in San Francisco seems in better condition than that across the Bay.

incredible riches and capitalized for the then unheard-of sum of ten millions of dollars. It was later reduced to the entirely ample but more moderate sum of $3,000,000, but the legend of its resources is still part of the saga of the old, wealthy West.

Its magnificent offices at the corner of Pine and Montgomery were, until that fiery day in 1906, legendary. Its overmantels and fireplaces were carved from the richest sort of Comstock ores that were available to the stone-worker's genius and there is a tale still current, when the old days are in conversation, of how a shrewd but not entirely honest broker hired an office for his firm in the Nevada Bank Building for $100 a month. At the expiration of his first thirty days' tenancy it was discovered that the tenant had disappeared. So had a Comstock-ore fireplace, chipped out, removed a fragment at a time and sold to the unsuspecting firm of Shreve & Co. across the street for sums totaling in excess of $5,000.

In 1905, a merger was effected between the Nevada National Bank and Wells Fargo Bank and the emergent firm became known as the Wells Fargo Nevada National Bank under the presidency of Isaias W. Hellman, a pioneer banker of Southern California of sagacity and wide repute. Wells Fargo sold out its banking branches in Salt Lake and in Portland, Oregon, and in 1923 it absorbed the thirty-year-old Union Trust Company and there emerged, still in Montgomery Street, the Wells Fargo Bank and Union Trust Co. and its fifty different banking departments of today.

Throughout the Far West souvenirs of Wells Fargo's great days survive in tangible form and almost at every hand. In Virginia City, Nevada, no fewer than three flourishing saloons claim to possess original Wells Fargo bank vaults as tourist attractions on their premises. All of them are correct and justified, the vaults having derived from the multiplicity of the company's banking and express offices in the Comstock over the years.

In the Western museum maintained by a private *aficionado* at Santa Anita, California, there is a profusion of Wells Fargo properties, messenger's shotguns, wooden, ironbound treasure chests, storm lanterns from coaches, even a complete narrow-gage train salvaged from the Eureka and Palisade complete with Wells Fargo's insigne on the combination car and the messenger's compartment with working props inside. In a hundred saloons and hotel lounges from Tough Nut Street to Deadwood and from Tipton, Missouri, to Mount Shasta are framed yellowing bank drafts drawn against Wells Fargo branches by departed local notables and founders of the community fortunes. Here and there an original coach from Abbot, Downing & Co. still survives intact in public park or private collection.

There may be found in Virginia City, Montana, where Wells Fargo maintained a branch with weekly coaches to Salt Lake as early as 1866, a complete restoration of a stage office with an abundance of Wells Fargo trappings and those of its predecessor, the Virginia City and Red Bluff Stage Line. In the Wells Fargo Coffee House there, the menu as a regular thing in season lists buffalo, elk, venison and bear steak dinners and there is an all-over restoration program for the entire community in the style and manner of the swash-buckling sixties.

And in Montgomery Street, as is fitting and proper, the Wells Fargo Bank and Union Trust Co. maintain in their museum the most comprehensive collection of Wells Fargo and allied Americana in existence anywhere. Here are the massive bullet-scarred iron doors from Chinese Camp, the gold scales from Columbia, still so perfectly balanced as to weigh the mark of a lead pencil upon a sheet of foolscap, the great silver bullion watch engraved with the immortal exploit of Jim Miller, the scrapbooks of Chief of Detectives Hume, characteristic samples of gold from every Mother Lode diggings, one of the finest collections of frontier firearms in existence, a comprehensive Wells Fargo reference library and the world's most precious collection of letter franks, cancellations and the stamped paper of the early express companies.

The hallmark and imprimatur of Wells Fargo upon the West will vanish only when history itself disappears in the gathering mists of the millenniums.

Long gone from the dusty highroads of the Old West now are the glittering yellow Concords and the men who drove them. James Warner Bellah, in *Stage from Elkhorn,* has described the last of them in the grand manner of the magnificent stager:

> He set the brake and clambered down ponderously, and stood for a moment dusting himself. Then he took off his broad brimmed felt, tossed it on the seat, reached to his seat locker for his battered stovepipe silk and clapped it on his head. He took a long tug from a bottle in the skirts of his coat, wiped his mouth with a soiled handkerchief and walked magnificently toward the railroad platform. The last of the drivers, the Dandy, in his long-tailed coat of threadbare broadcloth and dirty silk shirt underneath and a clawed gold pin in his tie from which the Santa Fe turquoise had long since disappeared. His yellow gloves were tattered and his hat looked as if it had been kicked from Elko to Sudro's Fort. He had started driving for Barnum, Veil and Vickeroy and he'd forgotten how many times he'd driven the long route from Fort Larned, Kansas, to Fort Lyon, Colorado. The best damned driver west of K. C. drunk or sober. *

Gone, too, is the proud insigne "Wells Fargo & Co. Express" from the head-end revenue cars of a score of railroads which once transported the armed guards and the iron treasure boxes of the most valiant of carriers.

A hundred years after the first news of the California gold rush set in motion the machinery which was to establish Wells Fargo in San Francisco and as the greatest name in the history of expressing the world has ever known, the public may have its choice as to which of the two surviving services bearing that name is the true heir. Elmer Jones's company of New York and Mexico is in the express business, the Wells Fargo Bank and Union Trust Co. of San Francisco are in the banking business. Both of them were

---

* Reprinted by permission of *The Saturday Evening Post.*

WELLS FARGO BANK

## THE ADDRESS IS STILL MONTGOMERY STREET

Here at the corner of Market and after almost a full century, the Wells Fargo
Bank and Union Trust Co., conducts its multiplicity of affairs in an ornate structure embracing a variety of styles of architecture which is one of the landmarks of
the capital of the Western world.

comprised by the original West Coast firm of Wells Fargo & Co. and both
are in the true and legitimate line of descent.

But Wells Fargo & Co., for all that it ultimately extended its services the
entire distance across the American continent and became national and international in its scope, was first and essentially an integral, vital and dramatic
part of the American West. San Francisco was the ancient seat of its being
and authority, the source and fountainhead of its ever-widening enterprise.
And in addition to this geographic and sentimental heritage, the Wells Fargo
Bank and Union Trust Co. holds and possesses most of the still-available
tangible souvenirs of the old times.

Here, to the enlightened fancy, is a reprise of many pageantries: the past
is as valid as the immediate now. Here is Black Bart to the life in a double-
barreled ten-gage with a battered walnut stock. Here are Shiloh and the
Wilderness in the courant scrawl of a telegrapher's fist. Here the allegory, at
once golden and dusty, of human destinies in a C Street Fourth of July
taken with what pains by what long-forgotten photographer on a summer
afternoon now but a date in yesterday's calendar. Amidst these properties
of the reprise it is no task for the imagining to venture into Bodie during its
tumultuous midnights, to descend the perilous shaft of Con Virginia with
a youthful John Mackay, to pass the hospitable doors of Barry and Patten's in
Montgomery Street for "a smile" at the bar with the Emperor Norton. There
are lingering fragrances of sagebrush, powder smoke and Pisco Punches.

Where the treasure is, there is the heart also, and Wells Fargo's treasure
is in Montgomery Street where its massing and creation began so many
splendid years ago in the hot youth of the old, ineffable West. And there,
most people will be content to believe, is the true heart, *cor cordium,* of the
Old Bearded Banker and the Dangerous Shotgun Messenger who rode the
Coaches.

The continuity, not only corporate and economic, but also of feeling, sentiment and position in the public imagination which has existed over all the
decades between the Wells Fargo & Co. of the Argonaut fifties and the Wells
Fargo Bank and Union Trust Co. of the mid-twentieth century has been so
firmly established and generally recognized by Californians as to be taken,
in a way, for granted like the four or five different climates available at one
time to San Franciscans or the sounds of the cables of the cable cars late
at night when all other city sounds are hushed. Wells Fargo is at once immemorial and immutable, the archetypal creation of the splendid, acquisitive
and uninhibited Lords of Creation of the Old West.

One anecdote will suffice.

In the fifties and sixties, when remittances from the pioneer miners to
their families in the East were sent via Wells Fargo, the draft was made out
in triplicate and, in a time of insecure mails, was forwarded by three different
posts. The original might have been sent overland by Pony Express, for
instance, the "second" and "third of exchange" sent on by Overland Stage
and the Panama steamer service, respectively. Either the first, second or third

of exchange would be cashed, depending on which was presented first. The others were thenceforth valueless.

Every now and then, until the recent enactment of the so-called "Abandoned Property Law" of California, under which all such funds revert to the State, some of these drafts, yellowed by time and mildewed with the years, would turn up in New York bank vaults or among family papers in New England, and be presented for payment.

Against this eventual contingency, the old bearded banker of Montgomery Street was prepared. In the tails of his broadcloth frock coat there was a secret pocket from which, when these bills of exchange were checked in Wells Fargo's ancient ledgers against the serial numbers and amounts of the drafts, he paid their value dollar for dollar on the barrelhead. The years made no difference. Wells Fargo contracted the obligation; Wells Fargo acknowledged the obligation and Wells Fargo discharged the obligation.

Wells Fargo's only regret was that it was not able to redeem this paper in the currency for which it was originally exchanged: the fine gold in dust of the Mother Lode diggings, the fifty-dollar slugs that were privately circulated in California before there was a United States Mint in San Francisco, or the wonderful gold double eagles of another day, proud symbol and undebased coinage of the West when Wells Fargo and all the world were young.

**1830**  In South Carolina, "Best Friend of Charleston" on the South Carolina RR was first steam locomotive in U. S. in regular service. In the north the Baltimore & Ohio RR became first common-carrier RR.

**1831**  Mail carried for first time by railroad in U. S.

**1834**  Boston & Providence RR opened-B.D. and L.B. Earle express messengers on it. Boston & Worster RR opened for a few miles and Wm. F. Harnden was passenger clerk and conductor on first train which was also first train in New England to carry passengers. Harnden held this position for five years. Great numbers of railroads chartered and some built in spite of public opposition.

**1836**  Henry Wells forwarding freight and passengers over Erie Canal. The first two women traveled overland to West Coast.

**1839**  In February, Boston *Transcript* carried announcement of Harnden's Express to commence operation between New York and Boston.

**1840**  Harnden lost $40,000 when the *Lexington* sank with his brother and express shipment aboard. Shortly, Harnden used the new Cunard Line between Boston and New York. Business prospered and expanded to serve Philadelphia. By November he established a transatlantic express business on the Cunard Line including the care of emigrants. Harnden's success encouraged Alvin Adams to enter business with P. B. Burke. They started the New York & Boston Express Co. in direct competition to Harnden.

**1841**  Harnden expanded his business to Albany. Henry Wells became Harnden's agent there for several months. Then Wells left Harnden to become a messenger and partner of Pomeroy & Co., operating between Albany and Buffalo. During this time Wells carried first live oysters into Buffalo as a promotional stunt. Meanwhile Adams business prospered, the name changed to Adams & Co., was worth ten million dollars ten years later.

**1842**  Wm. Fargo became a messenger for Pomeroy & Co., still expanding, purchased part of Harnden's interests. Wells and Fargo together for the first time.

**1843**  Wm. Fargo became agent for Pomeroy at Buffalo. Pomeroy extended business from Albany to New York by Hudson River Steamboat.

**1844**  Wells and Crawford Livingston associated with George Pomeroy, who shortly withdrew; Thaddeus Pomeroy became junior partner; firm became Livingston, Wells & Co., business expanded westward, operating between Cleveland and Buffalo.

**1845**  In January, Wm. Harnden died and business was later absorbed by Adams. On April 1st, Fargo and Wells (with Dan Dunning) organized Wells & Co.'s Western Express to operate between Buffalo, Cincinnati, Chicago and St. Louis. U. S. Govt. wanted Wells to go out of mail business. Government, however, after three years' war with express companies, lowered its rates and expresses had to temporarily vacate mail business.

**1846**  Wells and Fargo split up. Wells sold his interest in Western Express to Wm. Livingston (the firm became Livingston & Fargo) and Wells went to New York to assist Crawford Livingston of Livingston, Wells & Co.

**1847**  Crawford Livingston died. His wife inherited his interest in Livingston, Wells & Co. His brother, Johnston Livingston, and Edward T. Winslow became partners in the firm and the new title became Wells & Co. Thus both Wells and Fargo were in separate businesses with the remaining Livingston.

**1848** January 24th, James Marshall discovered gold at Sutter's Mill near Coloma. December 5th, President Polk announced discovery of gold in California to Congress. Despite the fact that Cincinnati was Western terminus for railroads and stagecoaches went no further West than Independence, Missouri, next several months saw over 10,000 people headed overland and by ship for the gold fields which produced $250,000 that year.

**1849** John Butterfield organized Butterfield, Wasson & Co., to compete with Wells & Co. on New York-Albany run: also organized transportation line across the Isthmus of Panama. Each company paid New York Central RR $100 per day for express privileges aboard the cars. Steamer *California* arrived in San Francisco with regular govt. mail aboard. With arrival of many immigrants numerous small staging companies began operation. Alexander Todd began mail-express-banking business between San Francisco and the gold hills. He returned from his first trip with $150,000 in gold dust packed in a butter keg. Haskell, of Adams & Co., arrived and personally constructed his own office building and opened for business. During the year over 700 ships arrived bringing over 40,000 passengers to the wild and lawless Bay City. On arrival nearly 4,000 sailors deserted their ships to look for gold. Mother Lode produced $10,000,000 this year and San Francisco burned down Christmas Eve.

**1850** The firms of Wells & Co., Livingston & Fargo, and Butterfield, Wasson were merged to form the firms of Wells, Butterfield & Co., and Livingston Fargo & Co. which two organizations became in turn co-owners of a joint-stock association known as the American Express Co. with Henry Wells its president and William Fargo as secretary. In this complicated setup Livingston, Fargo & Co. were to receive the profits of all transactions west of Buffalo while those east of that point were credited to Wells, Butterfield & Co. When, in the next two years, Wells Fargo & Co. was organized its directorate was dominated by members of the directorate of the American Express. California was admitted to the Union and its mines produced $41,000,000. Adams & Co. was by now the biggest business firm on the Pacific coast.

**1851** Despite competition, Adams & Co. continued to expand with offices in many towns including San Francisco, Nevada City, Mokelumne Hill, Marysville and Sacramento. Overland mail took two months and Jefferson Davis suggested camels for desert routes. Cornelius Vanderbilt inaugurated trans-Nicaraguan route. California mines produced $60,000,000 in year and San Francisco burned for sixth time. This winter in New York ,Wells and Fargo and other directors of American Express Co. were planning organization of company to be known as Wells Fargo to operate in California.

**1852** Wells Fargo & Co., organized, March 18th, as joint-stock company in New York. Opened San Francisco office for general banking and express business in July. R. W. Washburn brought first Wells Fargo express shipment West in steamer *Tennessee*. First gold shipment East on *Oregon* worth $21,712 with Adams & Co. sending $600,000 on same ship. Wells Fargo took over Gregory's Express, and by October were issuing their own mailing franks. Firmly established in California by end of year.

**1853** With over $65 million mined this year great rivalry appeared between express companies, especially Adams and Wells Fargo, for the profitable dealings in gold. Both Alvin Adams and Henry Wells arrived in San Francisco to inspect their businesses. Wells Fargo opened offices in Oregon, Hawaiian Islands and Australia. Wells Fargo's shipments from New York included fruit trees and type and machinery to establish the *San Francisco Herald*.

**1854** On Jan. 1st, the California Stage Co. emerged, a near monopoly consolidation of existing California stage lines, with headquarters in the Orleans Hotel, Sacramento. It agreed to handle Wells Fargo's business. Wells Fargo moved to larger San Francisco offices.

**1855** In January, Adams & Co.'s name failed to appear on gold shipper's list. In February, steamer *Oregon* arrived in San Francisco with news of failure of Page, Bacon & Co., of St. Louis with resulting run on Page, Bacon branch and other banks in San Francisco. Wells Fargo and Adams both closed their banking departments, Adams never again to open in the West. Wells Fargo reopened almost immediately in sound financial constitution and took over Adams building. Former Adams employees organized short-lived Pacific Express Co., but Wells Fargo was now supreme on Pacific coast.

**1856** Sacramento Valley RR completed and Wells Fargo rode the steamcars for the first time. Wells Fargo now had over 80 offices, mostly in California, and by June was engaged in a rate war with the Pacific Express Co. Wells Fargo loaned City of Sacramento $65,000; loaned State of California $83,000. Louis McLane became general agent for California.

**1857** Rowe, president of the Pacific Express, committed to prison after embezzlement of $124,000 State Funds. Pacific Express Co. went out of business. Butterfield Overland Mail Co. was formed by representatives of Adams & Co., American Express, and Wells Fargo, and was awarded the Government overland mail contract. Wells Fargo carried nearly sixty million dollars in gold this year.

**1858** Gold rush to Fraser River districts nearly depopulated California. The California Stage Co. now operated over 1,900 miles of staging lines with Wells Fargo aboard; was second largest in the country. Wells Fargo now had 98 offices, mostly in California and was an express monopoly in Sacramento and southern mining districts. On Sept. 15th, the first overland mail and express service started on Butterfield's Southern, or oxbow, route. In the East, work was completed laying the Atlantic telegraph cable and George Pullman's first sleeping car went into operation.

**1859** Wells Fargo the biggest business in the American West as the rush to the Comstock began. Wells Fargo among the first to arrive in Virginia City where it established what was to be its richest of all agencies and one of its major banking offices. The great wealth of the Nevada mines was almost a Wells Fargo freight monopoly as it poured into California. In Washington the freighting firm of Russell, Majors & Waddell conferred with Senator Gwin and the Post Office in the matter of Pony Express. George Hearst, who became first Comstock millionaire, started his fortune in Virginia City this year. Horace Greeley decided to "go West." Pikes Peak Express Co. began operation.

**1860** More mail traveled via Butterfield's Overland stages than by boats. Pony Express service started from St. Joseph to San Francisco with Buffalo Bill as one of its riders. Frazer River excitements were abating but sensational boom was in the Comstock. Virginia City built churches, theaters, hotels and offices on a grand scale and Wells Fargo moved into a fine brick building there. Wells Fargo bought out Butterfield's interest in the Overland stage line and Louis McLane acquired in his own name Jared Crandall's Pioneer Stage Line between California and the Comstock, the next year transferring ownership to Wells Fargo. This marked first time Wells Fargo had owned its own stages rather than renting space aboard other lines. The first International Hotel was built at Virginia City and the Comstock was becoming one of Wells Fargo's greatest sources of revenue. Russell, Majors & Waddell chartered the Central Overland California and Pikes Peak Express Co.; absorbed the Pikes Peak Express Co.; service began following year.

1861   In March, seven states having seceded from the Union, the Postmaster General was directed to discontinue Butterfield Southern Overland mail route. Butterfield equipment was salvaged and moved to form a central overland route. Service was resumed July 1st between Placerville and Salt Lake City eastward. On April 15th, Wells Fargo took over the Pony Express. That fall the transcontinental telegraph line was completed and Pony Express came to an end. C. O. C. & P. P. Ex. Co. lost $200,000 operating the Pony Express. Ben Holladay loaned them money taking first mortgage on the company.

1862   In March, Ben Holladay got control of C. O. C. & P. P. Ex. Co., reorganized and restocked the line, changed the name to the Overland Stage Co. Wells Fargo employee discovered gold in Reese River Valley; the rush was on. Austin, Nevada developing. President signed an act which opened the way for construction of transcontinental railroad.

1863   Wells Fargo extended operations to Mexico; carried over $20 million out of Virginia City; escorted Sandy Bowers and his new Comstock wealth to the Coast on trip to see England's Victoria. Railroad track shipped round the Horn; work began on transcontinental railroad. Wells Fargo, with over 175 offices in the West, did a tremendous mail business in direct competition to the U. S. Post Office. Indians plundered Wells Fargo's connection, Holladay's Overland Stage Co.

1864   San Francisco & San Jose RR completed. Camels in freight service between Walker Lake, Virginia City and Austin. Silver was discovered in Eureka and new Nevada rush was on. Virginia City mines in distress from rising waters. Construction started on Sutro Tunnel and on Oct. 31st, Nevada was admitted to Union with but one sixth the required population.

1865   End of Civil War and death of President Lincoln. Butterfield, with Eastern backers, launched his Overland Dispatch, operating east out of Denver with intent of operating east out of Salt Lake, to compete with Holladay's Overland Stage Co. Butterfield elected Mayor of Utica, New York.

1866   In February, Holladay bought out competing Butterfield Overland Dispatch; consolidated it with his Overland Stage Co. to form the Holladay Overland Mail & Express Co. In San Francisco, the Wells Fargo office was shattered by nitroglycerin blast which killed many persons. Holladay now controlled 2,670 miles of stage lines west of the Missouri River; was now largest staging concern in the U. S. In November, Wells Fargo purchased entire Holladay stage holdings, controlled all staging and nearly all expressing west of Missouri River. Henry Wells broke ground for college in his name at Aurora, New York.

1867   Louis McLane became president of Wells Fargo replacing D. N. Barney. Central Pacific RR kings organizing Pacific Union Express as Wells Fargo opposition.

1868   In February, D. N. Barney became president of Wells Fargo. By May the Central Pacific RR reached east to Reno. The railroad-owned Pacific Union express began operation in June and within a month was running pony races competing with Wells Fargo into Virginia City. Wells Fargo ordered a trainload of 30 new Concord coaches. Henry Wells dedicated Wells College, a girls' school, at Aurora, New York.

**1869** With the completion of the transcontinental railroad in May, Wells Fargo ceased staging operations except as a railroad feeder and concentrated on banking and expressing. Henry Wells retired from business. John Butterfield died. In Nevada, Wells Fargo built an office in the new boom town of Hamilton; Virginia City encountered mine fires and general depression; construction commenced on the Virginia and Truckee RR. In October, Wells Fargo was forced to buy out the Pacific Union Express at an exorbitant figure paid in watered stock in order to operate over the rails.

**1870** The population of Nevada was 42,491, a 600 per cent increase in ten years; state capitol was being erected in Carson City. Wm. Fargo became president of Wells Fargo. Virginia and Truckee RR in operation in Comstock with Wells Fargo aboard.

**1871** Fabulous Nevada bonanzas provided background for "Great Diamond Hoax," State capitol completed at Carson City. Wm. Fargo defeated for senator from New York.

**1872** In February, Lloyd Tevis replaced Wm. Fargo as president of Wells Fargo. He secured express privileges for Wells Fargo on both the Southern Pacific RR, building southeastward from San Francisco, and on the new Santa Fe RR. Virginia and Truckee RR was now in operation from Virginia City to Reno via Carson.

**1873** The "Big Bonanza" discovered in Comstock, largest body of silver ore ever known. U. S. adopted gold standard and silver dropped. Wells Fargo opened agency in Eureka, Nevada, and construction was started on Eureka and Palisade RR to Central's main line in north.

**1875** Expressing now second to railroads in importance in U. S. In Nevada, both Virginia City and Eureka were nearly destroyed by fire. In San Francisco, the Bank of California failed with resultant mining-stock panic; Ralston died. The Palace Hotel opened August 20th. Nevada Bank (of San Francisco) established by Bonanza Kings Flood, Fair, Mackay and O'Brien.

**1876** Wells Fargo separated banking and expressing departments in San Francisco: banking moved to California and Sansome Streets; freight and expressing moved to Sansome near Halleck.

**1877** Alvin Adams died. Depression in San Francisco.

**1878** The Bland-Allison Act was passed insuring annual government silver purchase of $2 million. Nevada hit peak of gold and silver production. Henry Wells died December 10th.

**1879** In fall the Government conducted an investigation of Wells Fargo's letter-carrying practices. In spite of scandal uncovered, no corrective or punitive steps were taken.

**1880** Emperor Norton, old Wells Fargo friend and San Francisco character, died. President Hayes and General Sherman visited Yreka by stage.

**1881** William Fargo died; Wells Fargo entered Kansas City over connections of Southern Pacific and Santa Fe RRs; franchise acquired on Denver and Rio Grande RR.

CHRONOLOGY

**1882** Sutro Tunnel completed to Comstock Lode; Wells Fargo entered Mexico City over Mexican Central RR from El Paso. Jesse James killed by Bob Ford.

**1883** Wells Fargo entered New Orleans over Southern Pacific RR; Hank Monk, old-time stager, died; Black Bart captured by Wells Fargo's Detective Hume and sent to penitentiary.

**1885** Carson City Mint suspended operations; Comstock mines in serious decline.

**1887** Wells Fargo entered Chicago over Santa Fe RR. Flood and Mackay tried unsuccessfully to corner the world wheat market; nearly bankrupted the Nevada National Bank; Fair became president of the bank after coming to its rescue.

**1888** Wells Fargo absorbed Erie Express and entered New York (via Jersey City) over Erie RR., thus becoming first transcontinental express via rail. Black Bart released from prison and disappeared from California forever.

**1889** Carson City Mint reopened. Control of Nevada Bank passed from Bonanza Kings to I. W. Hellman and associates.

**1891** Mining depression in Virginia City; Wells Fargo's manager there found $200,000 short in his accounts. Branch was closed and sold to the Nevada Bank. The Carson City branch also closed. Accounts were found short at the Salt Lake City branch.

**1892** John J. Valentine, former express superintendent, replaced Lloyd Tevis as President of Wells Fargo.

**1893** Silver Purchase Act was repealed and Nevada's population started to decline. *Territorial Enterprise* suspended. Wells Fargo purchased the Commercial National Bank of Portland; eventually lost everything put into it.

**1894** First large railroad strike in U. S.

**1895** Wells Fargo ceased to carry franked mail everywhere except in Old Mexico.

**1898** Carson City Mint finally abandoned for purposes of coinage and became assay office.

**1900** Jim Butler discovered gold at Tonopah, Nevada, inaugurating last great bonanza; all-time low was achieved by production of precious metals in Nevada.

**1901** In Tonopah, Jim Butler inaugurated a whole new system of financing his mining properties. Locations were leased out by their owners, for strictly limited periods, to firms and individuals with sufficient resources to finance necessary work. Wells Fargo was still carrying bullion in Nevada by horse stages. John J. Valentine, Wells Fargo President, died. Control of Wells Fargo passed from California pioneers to easterners and its offices were located in New York.

**1902** John Mackay, last of the Bonanza Kings, died in London. A stock exchange was opened in Tonopah and Tom Kendall and Jim Butler grubstaked Marsh and Stimler who were to make the great Goldfield strike.

**1903** Rush to Goldfield, thirty miles south of Tonopah in Nevada desert, was on. First saloon came to Goldfield from Tonopah, being hauled on rollers without ever closing shop. Wells Fargo still rode the coaches as the long-distance telephone wires were being strung.

**1904** The railroad came to Goldfield and Wells Fargo's bullion shipments rode its cars. Charles M. Schwab visited southern Nevada mines and found Goldfield a real bonanza. Shorty Harris, old time prospector, struck gold in the Bullfrog district.

**1905**  Wells Fargo paid only eight percent to stockholders this year although actually earning forty and there was dissatisfaction among stockholders. Tonopah and Goldfield Railroad reached Goldfield and paid twenty-seven percent the first year. As many as fifteen special trains were dispatched out of St. Louis in a single day for the Nevada bonanzas. The Nevada National Bank largely controlled by I. W. Hellman was merged with Wells Fargo, as the Wells Fargo Nevada National Bank. Wells Fargo's Salt Lake City Bank was closed and sold to Walker Bros. The Portland National Bank, a loss to Wells Fargo since they purchased it, was also sold out.

**1906**  San Francisco was destroyed by fire and Wells Fargo in the Nevada Bank Building was burned out. It opened for business the next day in temporary offices in the home of E. S. Heller, a director, out on Jackson Street, in Pacific Heights. Wells Fargo had by now started to ride the auto stages to Nevada mining towns, only using horses to the most inaccessible points.

**1907**  Financial panic marked the year. In Nevada, Wells Fargo moved into Rawhide, a short-lived mining camp started by promoter Tex Rickard.

**1908**  Wells Fargo was told to "throw down the box" from a Concord stage for the last time on the Rawhide-Manhattan run and a posse pursued the miscreants in open touring cars and roadsters.

**1909**  Southern Pacific RR was now the largest single stockholder in Wells Fargo with Harriman, of course, in control of both.

**1910**  Harriman had died and Wells Fargo cut the most spectacular mellon in financial history when it declared a dividend of 200 per cent in stock and 100 per cent in cash. Goldfield reached the peak of its production: $11,000,000.

**1911**  Nevada mines produced a total of $35,000,000 and Wells Fargo had a monopoly of express rights on all Western railroads. It also acquired rights over vast network of Gould Railroads in Midwest.

**1912**  Wells Fargo was held up on a train for the last time and its messenger on the Southern Pacific's baggage car killed two bandits.

**1913**  Parcels Post inaugurated and spelled the doom of most express companies.

**1918**  Due to government war seizures of rail equipment and delays to express shipments with consequent losses and suits, express companies lost $17,000,000 during first six months of the year. Later in spring all important express companies were merged with railroad interests to form the American Railway Express Co. In the great merger some of Wells Fargo's expressing interests became a subsidiary property of American Express with headquarters in New York, continued some expressing operations beyond U. S. borders. Wells Fargo Nevada National Bank continued uninterrupted business in Montgomery Street, San Francisco.

**1923**  Hellman interests in San Francisco consolidate Wells Fargo Nevada National Bank and the Union Trust Co. to form the Wells Fargo Bank & Union Trust Co. of today. Fire destroyed twenty-six city blocks of Goldfield.

**1925**  John Parrott's fabled granite building, erected for Adams and later occupied by Wells Fargo for so many years in Sansome Street, was torn down.

**1938**  Last train ran over Virginia City division of the Virginia and Truckee RR. Eureka and Palisade RR abandoned. Nevada Central RR suspended service.

**1949**  Wheel comes full circle in the epic of Western wealth with Wells Fargo still in business as the Wells Fargo Bank & Union Trust Co. after three years short of a century in Montgomery Street where it first started in 1852.

# Bibliography

ADAMS, EDGAR H. *Private Gold Coinage in California 1849-1855*
(Brooklyn, 1913)

BANCROFT, H. H. *Chronicles of the Builders of the Commonwealth*
(The History Co., 1891)

BANNING, WM. and GEORGE H. *Six Horses*
(The Century Co., 1930)

BENNETT, WM. P. *The First Baby in Camp*
(Salt Lake City, 1893)

BERTHOLD, DR. VICTOR M. *Handbook of Wells Fargo & Co.'s Handstamps and Franks*
(Paul Bluss, 1944)

BOGGS, MAE HELENE BACON. *My Playhouse Was a Concord Coach*
(Oakland, 1942)

BRADLEY, GLEN D. *The Story of the Pony Express*
(Chicago, 1913)

CARNS, PAUL. *Our Postal Service*
(Open Court Pub. Co., 1904)

CHALFANT, WILLIE A. *Gold, Guns & Ghost Towns*
(Stanford University Press, 1947)

————. *Death Valley*
(Stanford University Press)

————. *Tales of the Pioneers*
(Stanford University Press, 1942)

————. *Outposts of Civilization*
(Christopher Publishing House, 1928)

CHAPMAN, ARTHUR. *The Pony Express*
(G. P. Putnam's Sons, 1932)

CLAMPITT, JOHN M. *Echoes from the Rocky Mountains*
(Belford, Clarke & Co., 1889)

CLEMENS, SAMUEL L. *Roughing It*
(Harper, 1913)

COBLENTZ, STANTON A. *Villains and Vigilantes*
(Wilson-Erickson, 1936)

COOLIDGE, DANE. *Death Valley Prospectors*
(E. P. Dutton, 1937)

CORLE, EDWIN. *Desert Country*
(Duell, Sloan & Pearce, 1941)

COUCH, BERTRAND and CARPENTER, JAY A. *Nevada's Metal and Mineral Production 1859-1940* (Nevada State Bureau of Mines and Mackay School of Mines, 1943)

CUSHING, MARSHALL H. *Story of Our Post Office*
(Boston, 1893)

DANE, G. EZRA. *Ghost Town*
(Knopf, 1941)

DELANO, ALONZO. *Across the Plains and Among the Diggings*
(Ashburn and Buffalo, 1854; Wilson Erickson, 1936)

————. *Life on the Plains*
(Saxton, New York, 1859)

DEQUILLE, DAN. *The Big Bonanza*
(Knopf, 1947)

DEVOTO, BERNARD. *The Year of Decision 1846*
(Little Brown, 1943)

DOBIE, CHARLES C. *San Francisco, A Pageant*
(D. Appleton-Century, 1933, 1939)

DRIGGS, H. R. *The Pony Express Goes Through*
(New York, 1935)

DRURY, WELLS. *An Editor on the Comstock Lode*
(Farrar & Rinehart, 1936)

EARLE, ALICE MORSE. *Stage Coach and Tavern Days*
(Macmillan, 1901)

EDWORDS, CLARENCE E. *Bohemian San Francisco*
(Paul Elder, 1914)

FREDERICK, J. V. *Ben Holladay; The Stagecoach King*
(Arthur Clark Co., 1940)

GLASSOCK, C. B. *Here's Death Valley*
(Bobbs-Merrill, 1940)

————. *Bandits and the Southern Pacific*
(Fred A. Stokes Co., 1929)

————. *A Golden Highway; Scenes of History's Greatest Goldrushes*
(Bobbs-Merrill, 1934)

————. *Gold in Them Hills*
(Grosset & Dunlap, 1932)

————. *Man-Hunt Bandits and the Southern Pacific*
(Grosset & Dunlap, 1929)

GREELEY, HORACE. *An Overland Journey*
(New York, 1860)

HAFEN, LEROY. *Western America and its Settlement*
(Prentice-Hall, 1941)

————. *Colorado Gold Rush*
(A. H. Clark Co., 1941)

————. *The Overland Mail 1849–1869*
(A. H. Clark Co., 1926)

HARLOW, ALVIN F. *Old Waybills*
(D. Appleton-Century, 1937)

HARPENDING, ASBURY. *The Great Diamond Hoax*
(James H. Barry Co., San Francisco, 1913)

HELPER, HINTON R. *The Land of Gold*
(Baltimore, 1855)

HOOVER, MILDRED B. *Historic Spots in California*
(Stanford University Press)

HUNT, ROCKWELL D., and AMENT, WM. S.
*Oxcart to Airplane*
(Powell Pub. Co., 1929)

JACKSON, JOSEPH HENRY. *Tintypes in Gold:*
*Four Studies in Robbery*
(Macmillan, New York, 1939)

————. *Anybody's Gold*
(D. Appleton-Century, 1941)

JACOBSON, PAULINE. *City of the Golden 'Fifties*
(University of California Press, 1941)

KAHN, EDGAR M. *Cable Car Days in*
*San Francisco*
(Stanford University Press, 1940)

KARSNER, DAVID. *Silver Dollar: The Story of*
*the Tabors*
(Crown Publishers, 1932)

KELLEY, WILLIAM. *An Excursion to California*
(London, 1851)

KNAPP, EDWARD S. *Pony Express*
(Scott Stamp & Coin Co., 1936)

KNEISS, GILBERT H. *Bonanza Railroads*
(Stanford University Press, 1941-1946)

LAKE, STUART N. *Wyatt Earp; Frontier Marshal*
(Houghton Mifflin, 1931)

LANE, ALLEN STANLEY, *Emperor Norton*
(Caxton Printers, Caldwell, Idaho, 1939)

LANG, WALTER BURNES. *The First Overland*
*Mail: The Butterfield Trail*
(Washington, D. C., 1940 and 1945)

LAVENDER, DAVID. *The Big Divide*
(Doubleday, 1948)

LEE, BOURKE. *Death Valley*
(Macmillan, 1930)

————. *Death Valley Men*
(Macmillan, 1932)

LEETE, HARLEY M., JR. *Sketches Of The*
*Gold Country*
(Nevada City Nugget Press, 1938)

LEWIS, OSCAR. *Silver Kings*
(Knopf, 1947)

————. *The Big Four*
(Knopf, 1938)

LEWIS, OSCAR and HALL, CARROLL D.
*Bonanza Inn*
(Knopf, 1940)

LILLARD, RICHARD G. *Desert Challenge, An*
*Interpretation of Nevada*
(Knopf, 1942)

LYMAN, GEORGE D. *The Saga of the*
*Comstock Lode*
(Scribner's Sons, 1947)

————. *Ralston's Ring*
(Scribner's Sons, 1947)

MAJORS, ALEXANDER. *Seventy Years*
*on the Frontier*
(Rand McNally, 1893)

MANUSCRIPTS in possession of the Wells Fargo
Bank & Union Trust Co.

MARRAYAT, FRANK. *Mountains and Molehills*
*or Recollections of a Burnt Journal*
(New York and London, 1855)

McCLURE, JAMES. *California Landmarks*
(Stanford University Press)

MORGAN, DALE I. *The Humboldt*
(Farrar & Rinehart, 1943)

NEEDHAM, HENRY C. *Handstamped Franks*
(Collectors Club Philatelist, 1927)

PAINE, SWIFT. *Eilley Orrum, Queen of*
*the Comstock*
(Bobbs-Merrill, 1929)

QUIETT, GLEN C. *They Built The West*
(D. Appleton-Century, 1934)

RICHARDSON, ALBERT D. *Beyond the*
*Mississippi*
(American Publ. Co., 1867)

RICKARD, T. A. *The Romance of Mining*
(Macmillan, 1945)

ROBERSON, JOSEPH S. *Pony Express*
(MS thesis, Stanford University Library)

ROOT AND CONNELLY. *The Overland Stage*
*to California*
(Crane & Co., Topeka, 1901)

RYAN, WM. R. *Personal Adventures in Upper*
*and Lower California*
(London, 1850)

RYDER, DAVID WARREN. *San Francisco's*
*Emperor Norton*
(Dulfer, San Francisco, 1939)

SCHAEFFER, JOHN G. *Early History of the*
*Wells Fargo Express*
(MS thesis, University of California Library)

SETTLE, RAYMOND W. *Empire on Wheels*
(Stanford University Press)

SLOANE, GEORGE B. *William F. Harnden;*
*The Original Expressman*
(Collectors Club Philatelist, 1932)

SONNICHESEN, C. L. *Billy Kings Tombstone*
(Caxton Printers, Caldwell, Idaho, 1946)

STELLMAN, LOUIS J. *Mother Lode*
(San Francisco, 1934)

STIMSON, ALEX L. *History of the Express Co.*
(New York, 1858)

————. *History of the Express Business*
(New York, 1881)

VISSCHER, WM. LIGHTFOOT. *A Thrilling and*
*Truthful History of the Pony Express*
(Rand McNally, 1908)

WELLS, EVELYN. *Champagne Days of*
*San Francisco*
(Doubleday & Co., 1947)

.LS, HENRY. *Truly Yours, Henry Wells*
Vells College Press, 1945)

TON, OTHETO. *Mother Lode Album*
Stanford University Press)

SON, NEILL C. *Silver Stampede*
Macmillan, 1937)

—. *Treasure Express; Epic Days of
'ells Fargo*
Macmillan, 1938)

TSEE, EARNEST A. *The Pioneer Miner &
'ule Pack Express*
Calif. Hist. Society, 1931)

WINTHER, OSCAR O. *Express and Stagecoach
Days in California*
(Stanford University Press, 1936, 1938)
————. *Via Western Express and Stagecoach*
(Stanford University Press, 1945)
WORKS PROGRESS ADMINISTRATION; sponsored
by Dr. Jeanne Elizabeth Wier, Nevada His-
torical Society. *Nevada, a Guide to the Silver
State* (Binfords & Mort, 1940)

ong periodicals consulted were the following:
*ricana Illustrated* (American Historical Co.,
.Y.C.)
*man Magazine, The*
*fornia Historical Society Quarterlies*
San Francisco)
*tury Magazine*
*ress Gazette, The*
1882-1921)
*ressmans Monthly*
1876-1881)
*nk Leslie's Illustrated Newspaper*
*lay's Pacific Magazine*
*per's Monthly Magazine*
*per's Weekly Magazine*
*souri Historical Review*
Columbia, Mo.)
*ional Magazine, The*
*ada Highways & Parks Magazine*
Carson City, Nev.)
*ada Magazine, The*
Minden, Nev.)

Newspaper files in the Nevada State Library of:
Bodie, Virginia City, Aurora, Candelaria,
Hamilton, Austin, Eureka, Tuscarora, Gold
Hill, Rawhide, Tonopah, Goldfield, Carson
City.
*Our Expressman Magazine*
*Out West Magazine*
(Los Angeles)
*Overland Monthly, The*
*Pacific Historical Review*
(Glendale, Calif.)
*Society of California Pioneers Publications*
(San Francisco)
*Sunset Magazine*
(San Francisco)
*Wells Fargo Messenger*
(1912-1918)
*West Texas Historical Association Publications*
(Abilene, Texas)

# Acknowledgments

For assistance and courtesies in the preparation of this book the authors are indebted to a variety of sources both individual and institutional. High in the priority of their thanks must come E. S. Hammack who designed the title page and various other illustrations and decorations with an acute awareness of the subject and the periods involved, and Captain Frederick Shaw, the cartographer, who is himself an authority in many fields of Western Americana. They are also beholden to the Messrs. Gerry Wickland and George Dawson of the Wells Fargo Bank and Union Trust Company of San Francisco and Miss Catharine Haroun of the Wells Fargo Bank Museum, all of whom have made us free of their resources of information, their files and records, photographic dossiers and original manuscript material, and have encouraged us in the progress of this chronicle. Others in whose debt we stand are Miss Helene May Bacon Boggs of San Francisco, Mr. Stanley Todd of the Railway Express Agency, Inc., Mr. Graham Dean of the "Reno Evening Gazette," Mr. Grahame Hardy of Oakland, Major Gordon Sampson of the Virginia & Truckee Railroad, Dr. E. C. D. Marriage, Nevada State Librarian, Mr. Robert Allen, Miss Clara Crisler, Mr. Erle Heath of the Southern Pacific Railroad, Fred Greulich of the Nevada State Bureau of Mines, and lastly only because her function was the final assistance in the preparation of this book, Miss Ruth Teiser of San Francisco who read its manuscript with the eye of a professional in Western Americana.

And to Dr. Jeanne Elizabeth Weir, director of the Nevada State Historical Society at Reno, a tireless servant laboring on shamefully inadequate allowances from a vastly resourceful commonwealth in the vineyard of Nevada history, we are indebted for generous assistance and the contribution of much valued photographic material.